Hatfields & McCoys
REUNION

RON McCOY

Cover design by Shawn P. McClafferty
www.thinkdesignsllc.com

Author photograph by Jessica Lobdell Photography.
www.jessicalobdell.com

Published by Ferguson Creek Publishing
First Edition, June 2015
Second Edition, October 2017

For additional stories, photographs and blogs, visit
www.hatfieldsandmccoys-reunion.com

Contact the author at
hatfieldmccoyreunionbook@gmail.com

Copyright © 2015, 2017 Ron McCoy
All rights reserved.
ISBN: 0692419837
ISBN-13: 978-0-692-41983-0

FOR RANDOLPH

"We remember"

Contents

1	Preface	1
2	Journey	6
3	History	14
4	Discovery	32
5	Beginnings	46
6	Homeland	54
7	Idea	64
8	Momentum	75
9	M2K	83
10	Book	104
11	Reunion	113
12	Festival	131
13	M2K2	147
14	2002	163
15	Court	175
16	Truce	191
17	Sequels	203
18	Hollywood	216
19	Return	228
20	Epilogue	238

Foreword

I first met Ron McCoy during our work on the truce. I was impressed by his dedication to our shared history. When he asked me to write the foreword for his book, I took the opportunity to reflect on our work together over these many years. Of course, for me one of the most important things we did was the truce in 2003. I am often asked why I wanted to write the truce in the first place and why it is so important after more than 100 years of peace. My answer is one of sincere dedication to my country and the freedom we hold so dear.

When the United States was attacked on 9-11, it became clear that evil forces were threatening our freedom. Not only did they attack America, but they also attacked the symbol of a free society for the rest of the world. Ron, his cousin Bo and I wanted to send a strong message to the world: We are one nation, made up of individuals from many countries, who cherish and defend freedom, family, honor and truth.

We wanted all people to know that we are one. We decided to unite our famous families – the Hatfields & McCoys – and to show the world that even feuding families could and would come together to oppose anyone who attacks our ideals and our freedom. We stand together to protect our country and our freedom, and we will fight as one family to defend it.

My son, Reo Bentley Hatfield III, has served the United States in three military conflicts and wars. Ron, Bo and I believe our country is worth fighting for, just as my son has done. We are united as brothers in one family of Hatfields and McCoys and we will not fail to defend America against any evil. Our ancestors may have been on opposite sides of the Tug, but through the truce document and unwavering defense of our country, the Hatfields and McCoys stand together, forever.

Reo B. Hatfield II

Acknowledgements

This book is a special "thank you" to the many people I have met over the course of my personal reunion with history. Of the people written about in the pages of this book, many more are not mentioned. Rest assured that your friendships, kindnesses and efforts of support over the years have never been forgotten.

Like the reunions themselves, this book project would not have been possible without the help of others. I would like to thank Jerry Hatfield, Billy Hatfield, Renee Bradshaw and Clifford Gene New for the use of their pictures. Thanks also to Shawn McClafferty for his work on the book cover and to Jessica Lobdell for the author's photo. I would like to extend a special thanks to Reo Hatfield for his kind foreword, enduring friendship and unwavering support of this project. For this book's second edition, I would like to thank Keith Bartholomew, Betty Howard and Libby Preston for their comments and suggestions. Their welcome insights have served to make this a better book.

Most importantly, I want to thank my wife, Bobbi Harris-McCoy for her tireless work on this project. She listened patiently to my stories over the years and encouraged me to put them into book form for posterity. She has served as my advisor, editor and partner during the twenty-month writing process. This book would not exist without her support.

While for the sake of brevity, I have focused on the paternal side of my family history in this book, I would be remiss if I did not acknowledge other members of my family. I would like to thank my mother, Sally Duffy, my grandparents, K.W. ("Jack") and Evannah Tillman and those on the maternal side of my family. They have had a profound and lasting influence on my life.

The saga of the Hatfields and McCoys continues to fascinate and inspire many people. I am grateful for those family members of the past whose lives have provided a rich heritage of which I am most proud. I hope this book will serve to preserve their legacy – and the accomplishments of the families in the modern era – for generations to come.

Preface

"What is past is prologue."
William Shakespeare

It seemed like a good idea at the time. Seventeen years ago, on the eve of the new millennium, descendants of the infamous feuding Hatfield and McCoy families came together for a joint family reunion in Pikeville, Kentucky and in Williamson and Matewan, West Virginia – the very region in which the feud occurred. More than a century after the historical events of the feud had concluded, it was the first reunion of the two families ever attempted on a national level. The story of the unlikely "Reunion of the Millennium" caught the collective attention of the nation and the world. Beginning in 1999, a series of Associated Press articles that appeared in 500 newspapers in 35 states sparked interest in the story. National Public Radio, the Kentucky News Network and radio stations from WABC in New York to KBCO in Denver broadcast live interviews with organizers and attendees before, during and after the event. Local television outlets from WTVD in Durham, North Carolina to WYMT in Hazard, Kentucky presented news of the reunion from a hometown perspective. Domestic news services such as CBS, NBC, CNN, *People Magazine*, *USA Today*, *Atlanta Journal Constitution*, *Washington Post* and the *Los Angeles Times* were also on hand to cover the event from Pikeville. Reuters, the Canadian Broadcasting Corporation and the British Broadcasting Company carried the story internationally.

At the epicenter of the improbable juggernaut was a pair of McCoy cousins; whose qualifications to host a Hatfield-McCoy reunion were as dubious as the concept. The two McCoys, one a preacher and website designer from Waycross, Georgia, the other a business manager and part-time recording studio engineer from Durham, North Carolina had met just one year prior to the event. With no previous experience or training in event planning, the two set out in late 1998 to organize a reunion in a remote area they had never visited, on a budget that was non-existent, for family members they had not met and from whom there was no guarantee they would attend. Such was the reality for Bo and me on the eve of the now-historic "Reunion of the Millennium," June 9, 2000.

Nearly two decades later, the story of that first reunion has receded into the mists of history. Yet, the legacy of the "Reunion of the Millennium" and the events that followed endures to this day. Annual events such as the "Hatfield McCoy Reunion Festival" and the "Hatfield McCoy Marathon" in Matewan, West Virginia are now in their eighteenth year. New events like the annual "Hatfield McCoy Heritage Days" festival in Pikeville, Kentucky continue to develop. Interest in the feud remains high.

There is no easy way to present a complete and accurate picture of the maelstrom that was the "Reunion of the Millennium." The reunion took on a life of its own, far exceeding our capacity to control it. As the event evolved from a small McCoy family reunion to a joint reunion of both families to a regional festival that encompassed two cities, one town, two counties and two states, it dominated every facet of our lives. While some have suggested that Bo and I were skillful organizational masterminds to have pulled off such an event, the truth is, we never considered ourselves anything more than a couple of novices who counted ourselves lucky enough to have survived it.

Those of us on the inside had no sense of the enormity of the undertaking nor even a true understanding of the historical significance of the event. Willful ignorance insulated us from any thought of giving up on the idea. It was the convergence of providence, sheer luck and the involvement of numerous individuals who believed in us that came together to make-- *and remake*-- history.

The 2000 reunion of the Hatfields and McCoys redefined the concept of a "family reunion." Together, the descendants of the once antagonistic families demonstrated an unprecedented example of grace, forgiveness, hope and peace to the world. The story of the 2000 reunion and those that followed is a tale worth telling, but this is not a book about the Hatfield-McCoy reunions alone.

Nor is this just another book about the feud itself. To date, there have been countless books published on the topic of the Hatfield-McCoy feud. I cannot hope to present any fact, observation or perspective that would offer any new insight or revelation on the subject. I do not shy away from my family's heritage, however. The feud is an integral part of my family's history. My own story, like that of other Hatfield-McCoy descendants, cannot be separated from it.

This book is about something more straightforward. It is the story of my personal exploration of *family*. My earnest desire to learn more about my family set me on an astounding journey of discovery that introduced me to an incredible history of which I was profoundly ignorant.

Reconnecting with my heritage put me on an improbable course that led through a series of events that were unexpected and unprecedented. My personal reunion with history allowed me to take part in events that I never could have imagined. Within two short years of discovering my family lineage, I was sharing the international stage as part of the historic national reconciliation of the Hatfield and McCoy families. In 2003, I found myself in the Pike County courthouse as a plaintiff in a lawsuit to open access to the McCoy Cemetery in Hardy, Kentucky. That same year, I was honored to take part in the Hatfield-McCoy truce signing, broadcast live on national television. In 2014, I had the privilege of participating in an archaeological dig at the site of the McCoy homestead in Hardy, Kentucky that was once home to my great-great-great grandparents, Randolph and Sarah McCoy.

By all rights, I am the person least qualified to write this book. I am neither a writer by trade or training, nor a historian, genealogist or even a savant of feud history. Nor was I the best choice to help orchestrate an event of the magnitude of the "Reunion of the Millennium." I am not an event planner, media spokesperson, marketer, salesman, diplomat or politician, all which were prerequisite skills needed to organize and execute something as dynamic as a national reunion of the Hatfield and McCoy families. It was not even *my* idea.

Although I have been called on to do so numerous times, I can think of many others better suited to tell the families' story. Some have carried the "Hatfield-McCoy" mantle proudly for decades. Through music and art, writings and research, they have worked diligently to preserve the legacy of the families. I was thirty-five years old before I knew that I was related to the clans.

Seventeen years have passed since the "Reunion of the Millennium" in 2000. For almost as long, I have wanted to tell the story of how it – and the events that followed – became history in the making. The Hatfield-McCoy reunions were defining moments in my life. I have been a witness to history. Above all, I have been blessed and enriched by the experience of reconnecting with newfound family – in the past and the present.

In much the same way that M2K grew to exceed its original parameters, this book has evolved into something beyond what I had originally intended. After sifting through reams of email messages, notes and letters, rifling through boxes of newspaper and magazine clippings and watching hours of videotaped interviews and home movies, I expected to present the historic spectacle of the Hatfield-McCoy reunions with all the fervor they rightly deserve. Instead, this book, like my own journey of reunion, has become a far more intimate journey of introspection.

My story is like many I have heard told by those who have attended the reunions over the years. Family members who traveled to Appalachia from around the country for the 2000 reunion, many for the first time, did not do so to make history. Instead, for each of them, it was a deeply personal journey, a chance to make a vital connection to their own history. Through their experiences and that of my own discovery, I learned to appreciate the value of family in a greater sense than I had ever previously considered.

Without question, great progress has been made in the development and preservation of feud history in the last two decades. Feud sites are being recovered and a new generation stands ready to protect them. Yet, much of what the families set out to achieve through the reunions has come full circle and we find ourselves back where we started.

The resurgence of interest in feud tourism has been replaced with lasting questions of how to safeguard its longevity. The integrity of our families' character is being impugned and threatened by old stereotypes. Through social media sites and internet blogs, on cable "reality" shows and in the national media, the specter of old biases and prejudices has reemerged. The example set by the Hatfield and McCoy families beginning in 2000 has become a footnote in history.

After years of consideration and procrastination, the time has come to tell the story of my reunion with history, a discovery that altered the course of my life. Like most great epiphanies, it began as something far simpler. It started with vague recollections of my grandfather's fondness for his Kentucky home and led to the discovery of an old book he once owned. A piece of paper in the back of the book helped me to recover a vital connection to a family history of which I knew nothing. This discovery led me to investigate my history further and to find others who were doing the same. When Bo McCoy, a third cousin I met through an online message board posting, suggested putting together a McCoy family reunion, I made a decision that effectively changed my life. I said "yes."

Journey

> "In every conceivable manner, the family is link to our past, bridge to our future."
> Alex Haley

"Hatfields and McCoys" – the phrase has become part of our popular culture, a staple of our modern lexicon, as uniquely American as Daniel Boone, George Washington and Uncle Sam. The expression implies connotations that are easily recognizable to most people. Heard daily in the arena of the press, sports and politics, the phrase has become media shorthand to describe a tense situation. Though few may know the details of the historic conflict between the families, most understand what the phrase "Hatfields and McCoys" means. In a *Time Magazine* article listing history's "Top 10 Family Feuds," the Hatfield-McCoy feud finished second, edged out only by the original dispute between brothers, Cain and Abel. "The Hatfields and the McCoys practically invented the family feud," said Time.[1]

In the hundred-plus years since the end of the feud, the "Hatfields and McCoys" have come to represent the paradigm of conflict. The story of the two enemy clans, locked in a vendetta fueled by hatred, has become a cautionary parable. As stereotypes, the "Hatfields and McCoys" have become iconic, symbolizing the worst in human nature. When rivals of any sort are lumped together within the context of the "Hatfields and McCoys," the nature of their dispute is understood immediately. They *hate* each other.

In a great paradox of history, the actions taken by the families to rid themselves of the influence of the other have created a symbiotic relationship from which neither can be separated. Hatfields and McCoys are bound together by a common history. It is always "Hatfields *AND* McCoys," not "Hatfields *OR* McCoys" – and never "McCoys and Hatfields." You simply cannot have one without the other.

Indeed, in the years following the feud, the perceived association of the families has resulted in a fusion of the surnames to form the singular "Hatfield-McCoy." In many respects, this hyphenated term is a more accurate depiction of the families in the modern era. "It is a pride on both sides to share this history," wrote Hatfield descendant, Anna Bengel, a graduate student at the Columbia School of Journalism. "In sharing the feud, we share something extraordinary as a clan in a larger sense; now, we're also part of a clan called the "Hatfields/McCoys."[2] For most descendants, the animosity of the past was replaced long ago by an appreciation of the historic link between the families. Overtures of peace between the families occurred long before the M2K Reunion in 2000.

For most in the greater "Hatfield-McCoy" family, there is an acceptance of our mutual history as well as a determination to redefine it. The old stereotypes still linger. As recently as December 26, 2014, the preconception of the Hatfields and McCoys as savages was used on national television to introduce a feature story on terrorism. On the CNN News network program, *The Situation Room with Wolf Blitzer*, Pentagon correspondent Barbara Starr began her story with the following statement: "Just as Al Qaeda and the Islamic State are going after each other (and) threatening the United States, think of it as a sort of Hatfields and McCoys feud."[3] Even for media-hardened family members, the insinuation set a new low.

The lasting stereotype of the ignorant, moonshine-swilling hillbilly perpetually locked in mortal combat with his neighbor, fighting over pigs and fiddles, is a by-product of the tabloid news coverage of the feud in the 1880s. This interpretation of the Appalachian mountaineer is a misconception that has continued into the present day, along with a general misunderstanding of the current relationship between the families. Although I knew nothing about the feud itself or my family's involvement in it, growing up as a "McCoy," I learned to accept that after most introductions, I would be asked about my relationship with the "Hatfields." Likewise, the Hatfields I have met over the years have told me similar stories. To this day, in the court of public opinion, there is an assumption that the "Hatfields and McCoys" are still quarreling in some capacity or, at the very least, have maintained some unresolved grudge between them.

When the descendants of the two feuding families announced that they planned to gather together in Pikeville, Kentucky in June 2000, it piqued the interest of the world. In a frenzy that included local, national and international print, radio and television outlets, the media rushed to cover the unlikely event. It was unthinkable that a reconciliation of the two families was even possible.

The family members who attended the reunion that year did so with a sense of purpose and the world took notice. One editorial in the *Sun Sentinel* in June 2000 summed it up this way: "See? They really are friends now. Just one big happy family and it makes you wonder, doesn't it? Why must peace on this planet always be such an elusive thing? Memo to the Israelis and Palestinians, the Northern Ireland Catholics and Protestants, the North and South Koreans and the Serbs and Albanians in Kosovo: If the Hatfields and the McCoys can do it, why can't you?"[4]

The historic reunion of the descendants of the Hatfield and McCoy families in 2000 was a bit of a misnomer. The notion of a "re-union" implies that at one time there existed a unity with which to reconnect. Historically, the Hatfields and McCoys were prominent and well-established families in the Tug Valley region of eastern Kentucky and West Virginia. They lived on opposite sides of the Tug Fork of the Big Sandy River that divided the region. The extended families were neighbors, associates, friends and relatives. Marriages between the families were common among the close-knit people who made their lives in the rugged Appalachian Mountains. While the relations between the larger, more extended families at the time are thought to have been cordial, there is no doubt of the animosity between the clans headed by Randolph McCoy and William Anderson Hatfield. The feud that erupted between the families of these men was long-lived, bitter, and intensely violent. As the descendants came together in 2000, there was no former "union" of these family branches to be reestablished.

The gathering of the individual families could not be properly classified as a "family reunion" either since most of those in attendance had never met. Members of both families came from locations across the country, genealogies in hand, to discover that total strangers shared mutual ancestries, personal histories and even similar physical characteristics. Most were surprised to discover family they never knew existed. New and lasting relationships were cultivated between Hatfields and McCoys alike.

Perhaps the proper term for what occurred during the reunion of 2000 was "reconciliation." It was a chance collectively to embrace a tragic shared history, to lay aside the sins of the past and to proclaim a lasting peace between the families. It was an opportunity for the families to acknowledge publicly the close relationship between the families that most already knew existed.

If not a "reunion" in the classical sense, then, what was it that compelled thousands of family members to make the pilgrimage to the site of one of the darkest chapter in their family's history? I believe the answer lies in an examination of what inspired Bo and me to consider organizing a reunion in the first place. It was the same motivation that prompted Bo to research his roots and publish one of the earliest websites devoted to the feud: *www.real-mccoys.com*. It was the same reason I made a random phone call to my sister, Renee, to discuss our fractured family tree, only to find that she had in her possession a copy of an old book on the family, once owned by my grandfather.

What prompted me to begin the journey towards reconciliation was an instinctive need to reunite with family. On a spiritual and philosophical level, it is the same odyssey of faith that drives us to seek a connection with a Power greater than ourselves. Family is that which links us to the very origins of Creation itself. Knowing our connection to family reaffirms our value in the present and reinforces the importance of our lives to future generations.

Any exploration of our historical past cannot be conducted outside the constraints of our own personal experiences. Our perception of history is shaped by the profound moments of joy and despair we have experienced in our lives – events that continue to influence us at this very moment. While the importance of our life experiences should not be dismissed, the historic past is more than sum of what we alone have experienced.

The full spectrum of the human experience is on display for us every day, in the news and in our own lives. For every sordid tale of man's inhumanity towards his fellow human being, there are tales of bravery, sacrifice and achievement that inspire us. Our ancestors experienced the same in their lifetimes and their stories continue to enlighten us today.

Their lives are as valid a part of our personal makeup as the limited scope of our own experiences. Likewise, how we determine to overcome difficulties and aspire to greater things forms the fabric of the stories that will inform and instruct our descendants that follow us.

Beyond the limited catalog of my life experiences, I felt a keen desire to know more about my family's heritage. The discovery of my family's story began as a basic need to make a connection with my past, wherever it might lead me. The same is true for those who attended the reunions over the years. For most, the reunions were the culmination of their individual explorations into their own family histories. In this sense, the events were *reunions*, after all.

Our historic past exists, whether we acknowledge it or not. Beyond the summary of our own narrative in the present era, a distinct family history dates backwards through millennia. These stories from our past remain relevant to us today. We are the summary of the decisions, choices, prejudices and preferences of generations of our ancestors. Our place of origin, culture, ethnicity and social status are the result of where our ancestors chose to live, whom they decided to marry and how they chose to work, play and learn.

The future remains unknown, outside of our suppositions of things to come. Therefore, having an appreciation of our past allows us to understand and appreciate more fully the value of our lives in the present. One day, our lives and experiences will become the past to which future generations will look to for guidance, understanding and inspiration.

The invitation to examine the past is not an all-together appealing prospect in our contemporary American culture. Pop-culture mentality encourages us not to limit our future with any consideration of what has come before. While letting go of memories of negative, painful or destructive events can be a healthy and reasonable approach to improving our well-being, we ignore centuries of family history to our own detriment. The historic past is a vast wealth of knowledge that is uniquely ours. There are stories to be discovered, lessons to be learned and a heritage to be passed on to future generations.

Exploring the past is not without peril. Our preconceptions of the past based on our life experiences are bound to be compromised. Nor is the past as romantic or idyllic as we have imagined. Imperfect men and women of history were as capable as we are today of actions and deeds, both magnanimous and shameful. While we may be quick to embrace the heroic and selfless acts of our ancestors, we should be equally willing to accept those that were less virtuous. The exploration of the past is not an exercise for the faint of heart. Rest assured, there are far more sinners than saints in the closets of history.

As we begin to explore our family history, we should not ascribe undue relevance to it. While the past establishes the foundation on which our lives are built, it pales to the relevance of our existence in the present. Our lives today should never be overshadowed or restricted by the past. While we cannot "un-write" or rewrite history, we can add new chapters to it in the present. The past may be examined and the future may be considered, but only in the present can we actively make decisions and take actions that will truly affect our lives.

The relationships we cultivate in the present are simultaneously the most challenging and the most rewarding. The voices of our ancestors may speak to us across the eons of time, but their lives remain consigned to history. The lives of our descendants exist only in our imaginations. We must learn from the lessons derived from our past to improve the well-being of our family in the present and to provide a greater foundation for the welfare of our family in the future.

The advent of the internet and the availability of genealogy resources online has made the invitation to explore the past more enticing than ever before. Once difficult to find court records, transcripts, documents and censuses are now readily available for research. Large numbers of fellow seekers daily make use of the internet and social media to connect the trail of digital breadcrumbs left by other researchers. More individuals are discovering their family histories and their relationship to a greater human family. Our inherent desire to belong to a family provides the impetus to begin the journey of connection. Reuniting with history unlocks a near limitless fount of life experiences that helps us to realize our place in the family line. Past, present and future are linked together through the common bonds of family.

The search for family is a deeply personal endeavor. No matter one's surname or ethnicity, connecting with the past is a journey as exclusive as the individual who sets out on it. It is a voyage of self-discovery that involves a reunion with a past that has always existed, a reconciliation with a history that is distinctly our own and a resolution to share the benefits of our history with others.

The journey of discovery may begin with looking through a family photo album or an old shoebox collection of love letters. Something as innocent as a parent's old high school yearbook may launch an exploration that transcends centuries. Even the smallest of clues, be it an oft-repeated family story or an obituary clipped from a newspaper, may provide the basis for a life-changing encounter with history. In my case, it was reading a tattered copy of a book written by my grandfather's aunt that started it all.

Beyond connecting the genealogical dots, reconciliation involves accepting the history we discover as our own. While the horrific events of the feud cannot be rationalized away, we descendants understand that they form vital chapters of our history. The loss of seven of Randolph and Sarah McCoy's children produced incalculable effects on my family that have lasted generations. I would not be the man I am today, however, had not the events of history transpired as they did. While I mourn the loss of my ancestors, I am a better man because of the lives they lived, the examples they set and the sacrifices they made.

Accepting the past at such an intimate level comes with a price. In the case of the Hatfields and McCoys, such recognition often can stir the flames of deeply held emotions. When preaching at the joint family unity service on Sunday, June 11, 2000, Bo McCoy was keenly aware that such feelings needed to be put to rest. He asked those family members in attendance to forgive the actions taken by our ancestors against one another and to cast any lingering resentment symbolically into the waters of the Tug Fork below.

The conscious determination to make peace with history allows us to appreciate more fully the value of our fellow human beings who share it. The Hatfields and McCoys are now effectively one hyphenated family, grafted together by our mutual history and uniformly resolved to pursue peace. The reconciliation of the Hatfields and McCoys sets an example for anyone looking to discover the commonalities that bind us all together as human beings. Our blended family is merely one small part of the greater human family.

Dr. Otis Rice, a professor of history at West Virginia University Institute of Technology, wrote that the "Hatfield-McCoy troubles were rooted in the everyday (lives) of two families who were essentially no different than thousands of others" living in Appalachia.[5] They were ordinary families caught up in an extraordinary confrontation. As such, the story of the tragic feud between the families of Randolph McCoy and William Anderson Hatfield is one that strikes close to home. It is a modern American fable that continues to resonate with many, more than a century after its conclusion. The Hatfields and McCoys are representative families, not unlike so many others, with all the qualities that make up the full range of human experience.

Likewise, my journey to rediscover my family history is not unlike one that many have taken before me and that some are just beginning. While my path is distinctly my own, it is no more or less important than the new odysseys into the past that are being started every day. I hope that the stories of successes and failures in my own reunion with history will encourage others to consider embarking on journeys of their own. Rediscovering history is a task that can only be undertaken by those of us living in the present who are one day destined to become the past for future generations yet to come.

History

"History is the version of past events that people have decided to agree upon."
Napoleon Bonaparte

No book can be written about the Hatfields and McCoys without first acknowledging that, outside of the realm of modern American folklore, *the feud really happened.* It is not a myth, fable or figment of our collective imagination. Protecting the fidelity of the feud story, however, has remained a challenge for both families. "If you look up the feud in the encyclopedia, the first word is "folklore" and I think that is a travesty," said Bo McCoy.[6] Wayne Hatfield, a reunion attendee from Vassar, Michigan once told a reporter that "his daughter's teacher wouldn't let her do a (school) report on the feud (because) the teacher said the Hatfields and McCoys were merely a myth."[7]

The feud is the true story of two families who lived and loved, fought and died, in the name of family honor. Author Truda W. McCoy says of the conflict, "as literature it has the breadth of a folk epic and as art, it has the cleansing force of a classical tragedy."[8] As descendants, we do not glorify the violence of the feud, but rather pay homage to the memories of those family members who were lost.

Although most people understand the connotations of the phrase "Hatfields and McCoys," few truly know anything about the feud story. It is necessary and proper, then that before the story of my reunion with history can be told, due respect must be paid to those ancestors who came before me. They are, after all, my family.

I do not presume to present the definitive historical account of the feud here. The subject of the feud is one that, more than 120 years after the cessation of hostilities, still enflames the passions of some. The facts of the feud have been researched, analyzed, interpreted and argued by every means imaginable by individuals from all levels of study, from the academic to the amateur. While most known facts are beyond contention, understanding the motivations of the individuals involved in the struggle leaves much open to interpretation. The quest for understanding the actions taken by those involved in the conflict is what makes any study of the feud so compelling.

The search for the "truth" behind the feud is an ongoing and zealous field of study for amateur genealogists and historians alike. Websites, online genealogy forums and social media groups avidly discuss the minutiae of the subject daily. For decades, there has been a steady diet of national media output on the subject including television series, movies, documentaries and books. The latest opus by Dean King was a *New York Times* bestseller in 2013. In Pike and Mingo counties, the publication of feud books by local authors is a cottage industry.

The strong oral traditions of Appalachia have ensured that stories of the feud have been passed down through generations of both families, sometimes with contradictory perspectives. While some remain entrenched in a specific point-of-view, most family members take a more conciliatory approach when examining the feud story. Long-time family troubadour Jimmy Wolford, a McCoy descendant, had this to say at the M2K dinner in 2000 about the divergent accounts he had heard over the years, "I never disagree with any of them, because I didn't live through it."

The following is a brief, condensed timeline of the feud. It is not intended as anything other than a testament to the fact that the Hatfield-McCoy feud actually happened. It is a brief synopsis of a family heritage that many people cherish. Consider it an introduction to the feud story, a summary at best, and an invitation to learn more about it.

The Hatfield-McCoy feud is integral part of the fabric of Americana. The story of two noble strong-willed families locked in the throes of mortal combat is the stuff of legend. It has all the elements of a classic Shakespearean drama or a modern Greek tragedy, played out in the isolated, rugged mountains of eastern Kentucky and lower West Virginia.

The Hatfield-McCoy feud took place in the Tug Valley region in the late 1800s, an area that was squarely in the center of the Civil War conflict. While officially "neutral," Pike County was the home of the Union

Army's 39th Kentucky Mounted Infantry. West Virginia was allied with the Confederacy and remained so even after seceding from the Commonwealth of Virginia in 1861.

Both families were well represented in the area. Ephraim Hatfield, considered the progenitor of all Hatfields in the region, and his counterpart, William McCoy settled on the Virginia side of the Tug Fork of the Big Sandy river nearly 75 years prior to the onset of hostilities between the families. Both families were early immigrants to the United States. The Hatfields hailed from the area of Yorkshire, England, in the northeastern sector of the country. The McCoys, though sometimes said to have mixed with "lowlanders," were a sept of the Mackay clan of the upper region of the Scottish Highlands before moving to Ireland in the early 1700s.

Curiously, linking the families with their respective English and Scottish familial ties has produced a long-standing myth that the antipathy between the families predated the feud itself. This unsubstantiated story has been repeated often in the media, as recently as 2012. "The bad blood between the Hatfields and McCoys may have started during the English Revolution when the McCoys supported King Charles I and the Hatfields took the side of Oliver Cromwell, an English military commander and political leader," said Hatfield descendant Carolyn Riddle.[9] While linking the feud to such ancient conflicts defies credulity, the ancestral ties to Great Britain remain a source of pride for both families.

The feud transpired over the course of twenty-five years, from about 1865 to 1890. Violence was not continuous during this time, however. There were gaps of inactivity during some periods, with an intensification in hostilities between 1882 and 1888.

The official number of lives lost during the feud is 12. The number often has been exaggerated by the media over the years, usually propagated by those seeking to sell more books or newspapers. Some historians and family members have attempted to link other incidences to the feud story, although these have never been substantiated. No matter the actual tally, the loss of a single life was more than one too many.

Feuds were commonplace in Kentucky in the 1800s, for a variety of reasons. Kentucky was a harsh frontier region, inhabited by equally self-reliant individuals, isolated from the reaches of the surrounding developing country. Although law enforcement was effectively in place in areas like Pike County, it was disrupted by the onset of the Civil War. In such a climate, it was the responsibility of individuals and families to band together to safeguard their own interests. Notable Kentucky feuds occurred before and after the Hatfield-McCoy feud. The Baker-Howard Feud of Baker County, the Strong-Amy Feud of Breathitt County, the Martin-Tolliver Feud of Rowan County, the French-Eversole Feud of Perry County and the Turner-Howard Feud of Harlin County, are but a few.[10] The Hatfield-McCoy Feud, however gained national attention when West Virginia and Kentucky took their cases against each other to the Supreme Court in 1888.

William Anderson "Devil Anse" Hatfield

Generally, the Hatfields of Logan (now Mingo) County lived on the West Virginia side of the Tug Fork, while the McCoys of Pike County lived on the Kentucky side. Members of both families could be found in abundance on both sides of the river, however. Many of the children of Daniel McCoy, the son of William, including Randolph McCoy himself, first lived in Virginia before making the move to Pike County. Those members destined to become involved in the "great vendetta" were distinct branches of larger families extended throughout the region. In that regard, the feud was not a conflict between the Hatfield and McCoy at large. It was an engagement of hostilities between the families of two formidable men whose character matched the qualities of the mountains they called home.

William Anderson "Devil Anse" Hatfield and Randolph "Ol' Randall" McCoy were men of similar, yet contrasting natures. Both were heads of large families. Hatfield and his wife, Levisa "Levicy" Chafin, lived in the Mate Creek area of West Virginia and had 13 children. Randolph married Sarah "Sally" McCoy, his first cousin, and moved to Blackberry Creek in Pike County, Kentucky where together they raised a family of 13 (perhaps 16) children. Both families enjoyed a position of prominence in the community.

Both men were hard working, industrious and adept at surviving the harshness of Appalachian mountain life. Both were men with ingrained notions of duty, justice and family honor. "Devil Anse" was purported to be a physically large and imposing man, although his reputation may have exceeded his true stature. Known as a gregarious storyteller and a gracious host, he was an able outdoorsman and excellent marksman. As one version of the story tells it, his penchant for hunting bear earned him his nickname as a young man. After a three-day long encounter with a cantankerous bruin, he declared himself ready to take on the devil himself. Great-granddaughter Heather Vaillancourt of Greenbrier, Arkansas attributes the nickname to Anse's "ability to suddenly disappear after an engagement with Union soldiers who said, "only the devil could get away that fast.""[11] Hatfield was also an affluent entrepreneur with successful ventures in timbering and moonshine. Born in 1839, he was fourteen years younger than his McCoy counterpart.

Randolph, by contrast, was said to be a more introverted, thoughtful and sometimes sullen man. He was said to be tall, perhaps over six foot. He was a man of fascinating contrasts. Despite his reputation as a man possessed by a fiery temperament, he was also a farmer and devoted family man. "His features wore a kindly expression. He was quiet in his talk, and one of the most hospitable citizens of Pike County…he was brave, when necessity demanded it. He had demonstrated it on many occasions. But he was not, and never had been a bully, nor was he bloodthirsty," one author wrote of him.[12] Despite living in a predominantly Union region and later befriending Colonel John Dils, organizer of the Union's 39th Kentucky Mounted Infantry, Randolph nonetheless enlisted to fight in the

Confederate Army. Conversely, his brother, Asa Harmon McCoy, owner of two house slaves, fought for the Union Army. Tradition holds that "Ol' Randall" and "Devil Anse" may even have served for a time in the same unit. Hatfield left his squad and returned home to form his own "home guard", the Logan Wildcats to defend his assets and those of his family. McCoy was captured and served time in the Camp Douglas Union prison camp.

In the post-Civil War period, many journalists turned to escapist stories of sensationalism to placate a public hardened by years of contending with the brutal details of war. These "yellow journalists" were content to whet their reader's appetites with lurid stories of illiterate, hillbilly clans engaged in barbaric conflicts. Kentucky was a hotbed of feud activity and a welcome source for such stories. When visiting urban writers from the North found themselves unwilling or unable to understand the mores and ethics of rural mountain-folk, they created sensational stories of massive gunfights between men overcome with unbridled passions and bloodlust. Given the relative isolation of the Tug Valley region, "details" of such tales went unchecked and further exaggerated by editors keen on selling more newspapers. By the time the feud had escalated to the point that it captured the collective national imagination, the true story of the feud was forever clouded by inaccuracies that have long since become part of its "history."

Randolph "Ol' Randall" McCoy

Though taking place two decades before the height of the conflict, the slaying of Asa Harmon McCoy is usually cited as the opening salvo of the Hatfield-McCoy feud. Asa Harmon, brother of Randolph McCoy, was a man whose own internal struggles mirrored those of the Commonwealth of Kentucky. With the onset of the Civil War, Kentucky was declared a "neutral" state. As such, the region was often at the mercy of the competing forces of the North and South as they marched through the region. Asa Harmon was a keen observer of the times. He defied the general sympathies of the Tug Valley region and enlisted in the Union Army. On furlough from the Army after being felled by a broken leg, McCoy returned home on Christmas Eve, 1864.

The Union solider was threatened by Jim Vance, the uncle of "Devil Anse," who promised him a visit from the Logan Wildcats, a group that was decidedly sympathetic to the Confederate cause. After escaping a series of gunshots that were fired on him, Harmon fled for the relative safety of the hills and found refuge in a cave. For several weeks, he hid there, visited only by his pregnant wife, Martha "Patty" Cline, and his slave, Pete, who brought food and supplies. On the night of Jan. 7, 1865, Pete inadvertently revealed McCoy to his adversaries as he left tracks through the snow. Asa Harmon met his fate at the end of a rifle. His unborn child, Nancy, would blossom into a fiercely independent-minded woman who, in time, would marry Johnse Hatfield and later, Frank Phillips.

The slaying of Asa Harmon was followed by a resounding silence. There were no calls for vengeance and no cries for legal reciprocity from the McCoys. Several factors may have contributed to this indifference. Despite Pike County being home to the 39th Kentucky Infantry, there was a general lack of sympathy for the Union in the Tug Valley. By 1865, there was a prevailing sense of apathy in the region, weary of war. Although the McCoys were confident they knew the identities of those who attacked Asa Harmon, there were inconsistent accounts of the event and no tangible proof linking anyone to the crime. The man most likely to take offense to the slaying of his brother was Randolph McCoy and he was being held in a Union prison camp until the end of the war. Whatever the reason for the lack of response to the attack, the tensions between the Hatfields and

McCoys had yet to cross the bloody line of interpersonal violence that one day would become a staple of the feud.

An infamous argument over the ownership of hogs initiated years of bitter strife between the families. In the mountains, it was common for the owners of livestock to mark their animals by notching distinguishing marks on their ears or hides. The animals would then be allowed to forage freely through the mountainside, grazing on the vegetation that was plentiful during the spring and summer months. In the fall, the animals would be rounded up by their rightful owners for harvesting. Since honesty and integrity were important aspects of mountain values, livestock owners could count on their livestock being recovered.

In 1878, Randolph McCoy happened on the property of his neighbor, Floyd Hatfield, a cousin of "Devil Anse." While there, Randolph noticed a pen full of Floyd's razorback hogs, some of which he believed bore his trademark. In a sudden outburst of anger, McCoy accused his neighbor of stealing his "sow and pigs."[13]

Randolph rode to the home of Rev. Anderson Hatfield, the presiding Justice of the Peace, and placed charges against Floyd Hatfield. "Preacher Anse," with an acute sense of concern over upsetting either of the families, selected a jury comprised equally of Hatfields and McCoys to rule on the disagreement. Bill Staton, a nephew of Randolph's whose sister had married Ellison Hatfield, swore that he had witnessed Floyd marking the hogs as his own. Staton's testimony was an unforgiveable affront to Randolph. The pendulum of justice further swung in favor of the Hatfields when Selkirk McCoy, a cousin of Randolph's but married into the Hatfield family, sided with Staton and voted with the Hatfields. Livid, Randolph left the courtroom, vowing vengeance on the two men who had betrayed him. The men took him at his word. After receiving numerous threats, both Staton and Selkirk McCoy moved to West Virginia.

Sometime later, "Squirrel-Huntin" Sam McCoy and his brother Paris, nephews of Randolph, were hunting in the dense woods. Staton, certain that he was being tracked, panicked and fired on the two. Soon Paris and Staton were locked in a heated, physical struggle. As Staton gained the upper hand, Sam took aim at Staton, and shot and killed him. Sam McCoy stood trial in Logan County for the shooting of Staton, with Valentine Wall Hatfield, brother of "Devil Anse" presiding. The McCoy family was stunned when the decidedly Hatfield jury acquitted Sam based on his contention of self-defense. It is speculated that "Devil Anse" was instrumental in swaying the verdict. Tradition maintains that he wanted the well-respected Sam released in the interest of maintaining the peace.[14]

Election days were festive times for the residents of the Tug Valley. Elections were held in August, before seasonal changes made travel and outdoor activities more difficult. Communities would use the day for socializing, with the more adept candidates providing food and alcohol in hopes of coercing votes. Families separated by the severity of the land would traverse great distances to come together for a time of celebration.

The Hatfields were a prolific family in the region. "River" Hatfields resided on the West Virginia side of the Tug Fork while "Creek" Hatfields made their home in Kentucky. "Devil Anse" was a respected member of the community with social, political and business contacts on both sides of the Tug. As a rising timber entrepreneur, he had a vested interest in the outcome of local elections in Blackberry Creek, Kentucky in 1880.

Eighteen-year-old Johnson ("Johnse") Hatfield, a young man said to have a well-earned reputation with the ladies, traveled with his family to the site of the Election Day polling center. Also on hand that day were Randolph McCoy and his clan including his daughter, Roseanna, a mature 19-year-old, said to be one of the comeliest young women in the valley. When Roseanna and Johnse met for the first time, there was an immediate attraction. As the afternoon worn on, the two ran away together into the woods for privacy, leaving the Election Day festivities far behind. As night fell, the pair returned to the polling center to discover that the families had dispersed and returned home. Fearful of the wrath of her father, Roseanna made the fateful decision to go home with Johnse. Her choice to join in with the Hatfields left her estranged from her father, Randolph. Neither was "Devil Anse" inclined to allow his son to wed any daughter of

Randolph's. It was a decision he is said to have regretted in the years to come.

In the ensuing months, Randolph sent Roseanna's sisters as emissaries to bring her home but to no avail. A disheartened Roseanna, pregnant with Johnse's child, left the Hatfield homestead and went to live in nearby Stringtown, Kentucky with her Aunt Betty and Uncle Uriah McCoy. Uriah, the brother of Sarah McCoy, was a prominent landowner and one of the wealthiest men in Pike County. An infatuated Johnse made regular trips to visit her there.

The eldest son of Randolph, Jim McCoy, acting as a Pike County deputy, decided that Johnse should be brought to Pikeville to face moonshining charges. After the McCoys engineered a successful ambush of Johnse, pregnant Roseanna, fearful that the father of her child was being led away to be killed, performed one of the most daring acts in feud history. Borrowing a horse from neighbor Tom Stafford's farm, she rode bareback through the night over the dangerous mountain terrain to tell the Hatfields about Johnse's capture. "Devil Anse," his son Cap Hatfield, Jim Vance and others mounted up and navigated familiar shortcuts until they found the McCoy forces. The Hatfield party surrounded the McCoys and successfully negotiated the release of Johnse.

Following the incident with the McCoys, Johnse was less inclined to continue his forays into Kentucky. Roseanna now was faced with the greater injustice of raising her child alone. In 1881, Roseanna gave birth to a daughter, Sarah Elizabeth, named after her mother and her aunt. Roseanna's joy was short-lived, however, as the child fell ill to measles and died at eight months of age. She was buried on the hilltop overlooking the home site. Family tradition tells of a grieving Roseanna prostrating herself daily in anguish over the grave of her child.

Johnse soon found solace in the arms of Roseanna's 16-year-old cousin, Nancy, the daughter of Asa Harmon McCoy. The spirited young woman met the tacit approval of "Devil Anse," since she was not the daughter of Randolph McCoy. In time, the two married, resided in West Virginia and had several children until Nancy had her fill of Johnse's ne'erdo-well ways. Nancy left Johnse and returned home to Kentucky to marry the most dreaded of the Hatfield's antagonists, Frank Phillips.

Roseanna's life was not so fortunate. Following the siege on the McCoy cabin in 1888, a broken Roseanna returned to the home of her parents in Pikeville to tend to the recovery of her ailing mother. Lost in in a lingering depression, Roseanna found her health gradually slipping away. Despite repeated assessments by doctors that she bore no illness, Roseanna passed away at the age of 30. She was the first of her family to be laid to rest in Dils Cemetery, overlooking Pikeville. The story of Roseanna's tragic life soon became a staple of Appalachian folklore. It is said among those in Pike County that whenever her name was mentioned, it was spoken of in whispers.

It was another Election Day dispute, on August 7, 1882, that propelled the families into a bloody conflict from which there was no return. Although the cause of the argument is unclear, tradition maintains that Tolbert McCoy, representing the leadership of his family on that day, got into an altercation with Elias Hatfield over money owed him for a fiddle. Ellison Hatfield, brother of "Devil Anse," unwilling to see his family bested by the McCoys, stepped up to confront Tolbert. Realizing he was overpowered by his larger opponent, Tolbert began attacking Ellison with a knife. Soon, Bill McCoy joined in the fray and the elder Hatfield was cut twenty-six times. As Hatfield continued to put up a vigorous fight, another McCoy brother, Pharmer came to his brothers' defense and shot Ellison in the back. Despite the severity of his wounds, Ellison Hatfield lived for another three days.

The three McCoy brothers were rounded up and detained for transfer to the Pike County prison. The Hatfields misidentified Randolph "Bud" McCoy Jr as one of the attackers, and he was taken in Bill's place, despite his brother's protests. Expecting his sons to be delivered to the authorities in Pikeville, Randolph made his way to town to enlist legal and judicial help. Before the prisoners could be taken to jail in Pikeville, however, "Devil Anse" Hatfield arrived with a posse on the morning of August 8, to claim the boys.

The detainees were carried to the security of an abandoned schoolhouse in Logan County to await their fate. Despite a driving rain, Sarah McCoy and Tolbert's wife, Mary, made their way to the schoolhouse one night to plead for the lives of their loved ones. After they had enjoyed a lengthy visit, the women were sent away with the assurance that the fate of their loved ones rested on the outcome of Ellison's fight for life. "Devil Anse" gave his solemn word that the boys would not be slain on West Virginia soil.

Ellison Hatfield died on Wednesday, August 9. The Hatfields led the McCoy boys up to the mouth of Mate Creek, and then crossed over to the Kentucky side. The three young men, Tolbert, Pharmer and Randolph, Jr., were bound to paw-paw bushes and executed in a barrage of more than 50 bullets. On August 10, funerals were held on both sides of the Tug. Ellison Hatfield was laid to rest by family, while friends and neighbors buried the three McCoys in a common grave.

As tragic as the attack on Ellison Hatfield and the execution of the McCoys was, there is another sad caveat to the story. Tradition holds that Bill McCoy was so despondent over the slaying of his brother "Bud" in his place that he went into the woods and grieved himself to death. Bill was buried with his three brothers in the family cemetery overlooking the former McCoy homestead in Hardy, Kentucky.

Once again, the feud settled into a period of tense silence. Acclaimed Pikeville attorney Perry Cline, fueled by his own ulterior motives, took to the pursuit of the Hatfields with a vengeance. As a child, Cline had lost an inherited claim of 5000 acres of timberland in a lawsuit to "Devil Anse," a misdeed he had never forgotten or forgiven. Cline had other ties to the feud as well. He was the brother of Martha "Patty" Cline whose husband, Asa Harmon McCoy had met his fate at the hands of the Logan Wildcats in 1865.

Cline was backed by the considerable financial resources of the eminent Colonel John Dils. Dils was charitable in his service to war orphans and had served as the legal guardian of both Perry Cline and Frank Phillips, providing for their upbringing and education. He was also responsible for the creation of the 39th Kentucky Mounted Infantry, the region's premier Union unit. Colonel Dils became an active supporter of the McCoy cause and was Randolph McCoy's benefactor upon his move to Pikeville. Under Cline and Dils, warrants were sworn out for more than twenty men for the murder of the McCoy boys. The Hatfields remained safely on their side of the Tug Fork, however, and Pike County law enforcement was reluctant to pursue them there.

Some minor skirmishes transpired in these quiet years. The Hatfields suspected that many of their activities were being telegraphed to the McCoys through Johnse's wife Nancy and her reputedly talkative sister, Mary Daniels. Taking matters into their own hands, Cap Hatfield and Tom Wallace assaulted Mary as punishment for her gossiping ways. This attack did not sit well with Mary's brother, Jeff, the son of Asa Harmon McCoy.

In 1886, after being accused of killing postal carrier Fred Wolford in Kentucky, Jeff fled to the relative safety of his sister's home in West Virginia. Now on the soil of his enemy, Jeff plotted revenge against Cap and Wallace. Serving as a special constable, Cap arrested Jeff for the murder of Wolford. Jeff escaped his captor and swam across the Tug in a desperate bid to reach safety. Just as he touched the Kentucky shore of the river, he was felled by a bullet from the rifle of Constable Hatfield.

With the onset of the Kentucky gubernatorial race of 1887, Perry Cline seized the opportunity for political gain. He promised Simon Buckner his support in exchange for his help in bringing the Hatfields to justice. He revived the warrants sworn out in 1882; warrants now accompanied by financial bounties. He appointed Pike County Deputy "Bad" Frank Phillips as his special agent in charge of the effort to capture the Hatfields. Phillips was a man known for his courage, his tenacious resolve and, by some accounts, his ruthlessness. Organizing his initial excursion into West Virginia, Phillips netted his first capture easily. Ironically, the man taken was none other than Selkirk McCoy, the notorious swing-vote of the pig trial. Phillip's effectiveness and tactics warranted the attention of Hatfields on both sides of the Tug. Pike County Sherriff Basil Hatfield soon stripped

Phillips of his badge, but this action left him undeterred as he continued his raids into West Virginia.

With the forays into West Virginia increasing and the threat of arrests continually hanging over them, the Hatfields contrived a daring plan intended to bring about a definitive end to the feud. Cap, Jim Vance and Johnse rounded up a cadre of more than twenty men. The group included Ellison "Cotton Top" Mounts, the illegitimate son of Ellison Hatfield, killed during the Election Day fight. Mounts was said to have been mentally impaired and incapable of the actions for which he would later be executed. Declaring himself too ill to participate, "Devil Anse" dispatched the party in the early hours of January 1, 1888 to put an end to his family's struggle. As the party surrounded the cabin of Randolph McCoy, Jim Vance called out for the McCoys to surrender. Randolph and his son, Calvin took up positions to defend the homestead as Sarah and her daughter, Alifair gathered up the smaller children. Suddenly, the first shot was fired, perhaps by Johnse as a warning intended for his former love, Roseanna, whom he mistakenly believed to be in the cabin.

A massive onslaught of gunfire proved ineffective against the double-logged walls of the cabin. Frustrated by the futility of the attack that lasted hours, Jim Vance ordered the house to be set afire. Cotton gathered from a nearby storage pen was pressed into crevices between the logs at the rear of the house and set ablaze. As the flames reached the upper loft of the cabin, Alifair, knowing that Appalachian social code would never permit the shooting of a woman, grabbed a bucket and ran from the cabin, heading in the direction of the well. She was killed, by most accounts, from a shot fired by Cap Hatfield. Sarah, running out into the darkness after her daughter, encountered Jim Vance. Vance beat her ruthlessly with the butt of his rifle until her skull was smashed.

With the fire collapsing the cabin around them, Calvin offered a plan of escape. He would provide covering fire from a nearby corncrib, allowing time for his father and the children to get away. Reluctantly, Randolph agreed. Snatching up Melvin McCoy, his grandson by Tolbert,

Randolph ran for the woods as Calvin made a dash for the corncrib where he, too met his fate as a bullet pierced his skull.

By the dying embers of the fire, the Hatfields retreated back into West Virginia. At morning's light, the McCoy family returned to the cabin site to find Sarah, miraculously clinging to life. Alifair lay dead beside her, her long hair now frozen to the ground. Friends and neighbors once again performed a familiar duty as they buried two more of Randolph and Sarah's children alongside their brothers in the McCoy Cemetery.

Randolph, along with his sons Jim and Sam and their families, moved from the Tug Valley to the comparative safety of Pikeville, 25 miles to the west. There he bought a home on East Main Street, beside the noted Pikeville attorney, Jim York. He and Roseanna reached a reconciliation of necessity as she moved into the home to care for her mother. Randolph spent the remainder of his years in Pikeville operating a flat-bottom pole boat, perhaps in the service of John Dils, ferrying passengers across the Levisa Branch of the Big Sandy River.

The assault on the McCoy cabin seized the attention of the region and the nation. Public opinion in Kentucky turned against the Hatfields. Rewards were offered for their capture and freelance bounty hunters operating as "detectives" made regular, though unsuccessful, excursions into West Virginia in pursuit of Hatfields. Frank Phillips resolved to narrow his focus and concentrate his efforts on capturing Cap Hatfield and Jim Vance. When Phillips and a posse of men finally caught up with the two, Vance suffered a wound to the leg, possibly fired by Jim McCoy. In what was to have been his last defense of the Hatfields, Vance ordered Cap to run to safety while he remained behind. As Cap escaped, Phillips walked up to the injured Vance and steadfastly put a bullet in his head.

Further excursions into West Virginia resulted in the capture of Wall Hatfield, Cap Hatfield, Tom Chambers and others. They were held in the Pike County jail to await trial. In response, West Virginia swore out warrants for the arrests of 23 men, including Frank Phillips, for the murder of Jim Vance.

The Hatfields organized local defense patrols to combat the intrusions into their territory. These groups elected to remain on the West

Virginia side of the Tug Fork and not risk the possibility of capture and incarceration in Kentucky. In response to the threat of further incursions, West Virginia Governor Willis Wilson and his Kentucky counterpart Governor Simon Buckner ordered their state militias to standby for possible deployment in hopes of securing their borders.

On Jan. 18, 1888, the mounting tension finally erupted in the largest open gunfight of the feud. Frank Phillips and a party of eighteen men met a Hatfield party of thirteen at Grapevine Creek, a West Virginia tributary of the Tug. Young Bill Dempsey, fighting for the Hatfields suffered a gunshot to the leg and crawled away to safety. He too met his fate at the end of a gun held by "Bad Frank" when Phillips answered his cries for help. Later that year, a feud-weary "Devil Anse" moved his family to a location 25 miles further east, near Sarah Ann, West Virginia.

The legal maneuvering by Governor Wilson of West Virginia advanced the story of the feud into the arena of national discourse. Suing the Commonwealth of Kentucky for illegal encroachments into his state and the unlawful seizure of his citizens, Wilson appealed to the United States Supreme Court. In May 1888, in the case of "Mahon v. Justice," the court upheld the legal right of Kentucky to prosecute the Hatfields, now held on Kentucky soil, despite the actions taken by private citizens like Frank Phillips to affect their capture.[15]

In the summer of 1889, the months of legal wrangling and the harsh war of rhetoric between the states finally resulted in the Hatfields being brought to trial for murder in Pike County. In a bid for leniency, Ellison "Cotton Top" Mounts, the son of Ellison Hatfield, pleaded guilty to the murder of Alifair McCoy, a decision that precipitated one of the pivotal events in feud history.

On Aug. 24, 1889, a court made up of nonaligned jurors began the process of passing down sentences of life imprisonment for eight Hatfields including Johnse, Cap and Wall. Wall eventually died in prison. Johnse later received an abbreviated sentence after he saved the life of a prison guard from an attack by a fellow inmate. Cap Hatfield never served time. On Sept.

4, "Cotton Top" received the ultimate sentence for his involvement in the feud: death by hanging.

It has been speculated that Mounts was enticed into his confession, either by the Hatfields, or by the prevailing legal authorizes in Pike County in search of a scapegoat. Given his limited mental faculty, Mounts made an able sacrifice for either side. In the months spent awaiting his execution, "Cotton Top," sincerely though errantly, believed that the Hatfields would break him out of prison.

Public hanging had been declared illegal in Pike County long ago. Prior to Mounts' execution; it had been forty years since the punishment was enforced. As the day of reckoning approached, Pike County officials reached a compromise that satisfied the law as well as the public's desire to see justice served. The gallows, though surrounded by a high fence, were conveniently erected at the base of a tall hill that allowed bystanders an unobstructed view of the execution. On Feb. 18, 1890, more than 5000 bystanders gathered to see Ellison "Cotton Top" Mounts led up to the platform. As the hangman's noose encircled his neck, a distraught Mounts, abandoned by the family he loved, spoke his final words: "the Hatfields made me do it!"

The last hanging in Pike County's history brought the sounds of feuding gunfire to a halt. Perry Cline, whose enmity with "Devil Anse" had fueled much of the antagonism in the feud's latter days, passed away of tuberculous in 1891. John Dils died of natural causes in 1895. Randolph McCoy lived in Pikeville until March 1914. He died after succumbing to injuries he sustained from falling into a cooking fire at the home of his grandson, Melvin. William Anderson Hatfield lived out his days peacefully in Sarah Ann, West Virginia. At the age of 72, he was baptized into the Christian faith in the waters of Island Creek by his friend, Reverend Dyke Garrett. He passed away in January 1921.

More than one hundred years after its conclusion, the story of the Hatfield-McCoy feud continues to captivate those fascinated by even the smallest details of the story. Many look to the examples set by the people of the feud era, industrious, enterprising men and women who steadfastly lived their lives by a strict code of moral conduct. We are drawn to their embodiment of those noble traits of rugged individualism, inseparable devotion to family and unwavering commitment to the pursuit of justice. The feud is an epic story of unimaginable tragedy. Yet even within the context of prevailing violence, we can discover examples of bravery, sacrifice, loyalty and faith. Amidst the moments of violence, there was a profound longing for peace.

Discovery

> "A people without the knowledge of their past history, origin and culture is like a tree without roots."
> Marcus Garvey

The road to discovery of the past is most often made up of a collection of seemingly random events than it is a single grand epiphany. The journey begins with a subtle internal longing to find answers to those basic questions that are common to all of us: why am I here? Where did I come from? What purpose does my life serve? How can I make a lasting difference in this world? As we begin to explore our family history, each clue we uncover encourages us to press forward to locate the next one. With each step along the way, we find ourselves growing closer to the answers that really have been there all along. Sometimes, these answers may reveal themselves in strange and mysterious ways. In my case, the clues came in the form of a book…and a paperclip.

The improbable scenario that Bo and I would be the ones to organize a national reunion of the Hatfields and McCoys was made more remarkable in that I was perhaps the least qualified person to do so. Beyond the obvious dearth of talent and experience necessary to orchestrate such an event, I was lacking in another important aspect. Until two years before the reunion, I did not even know that I was the great-great-great grandson of Randolph McCoy.

How I came to find myself so woefully ignorant of my family's past was the result of a convergence of life experiences and circumstances, some of which were beyond my control. Although growing up as a military dependent traveling the globe served to broaden my world view, I was seriously disconnected from eons of my family's history. My historical perspective was myopic, limited to the sum of my own experiences, along with a cursory knowledge of the lives of my parents and grandparents.

My own story is not especially noteworthy, although it is specific to the person I have become. It is also relevant to any discussion of the Hatfield-McCoy reunions since it helps to underscore the motivations of those of us involved in organizing and attending them. This same need I felt to discover my family heritage is in the heart of those family members who return to Appalachia each year, for the first time or the twentieth, seeking to make that vital connection to their past.

Understanding our past involves coming to terms with our place in a human equation that dates to the Creation of man. Irrespective of our own initiative, will and decision-making, we are the sum product of the actions taken by untold generations of ancestors. We are here in this place and time because of the actions and decisions of our parents, grandparents and their parents before them. We, in turn, represent that same important link to the past for the future generations of family who will follow us.

My own foray into history began in late 1997, following a family camping trip in the mountains of Eastern Tennessee. Raised as a U.S. Air Force military dependent, living in Japan, Holland and Italy, I spent most of my youth as a "flatlander," living in cities around the world. Interestingly, however, I have always held an affinity for the mountains. As a young teenager growing up in Aviano, Italy, our house sat at the base of the Alps, with rolling foothills filled with wild grapes and blackberries located just behind us. My dog, Rusty and I often enjoyed daily hikes in the hills.

On the long drive home from Gatlinburg that night, I was enjoying a period of introspection while the rest of the family slept. With a splendid view of the Great Smoky Mountains in the rear-view mirror, I was overcome by a sense of melancholy. There was something about the mountains that seemed familiar to me, as if there was something I was supposed to remember but could not. My mind began to wander, back to my earliest memories of my grandfather and the stories of his Kentucky home that he used to tell.

Called "Mack" or "Gene" by his friends, my grandfather, Eugene McCoy was an imposing man, despite his unremarkable physical presence. Standing just five feet, eight inches, he was nonetheless a formidable personality. There was something in his demeanor that suggested an indomitable determination, grit and strength of character. His upbringing as the son of a coal miner, coupled with his service as a paratrooper in

World War II, gave my grandfather an air of strength and resolve that was palpable.

My grandfather was born in his parent's home on Ferguson Creek in Pikeville, Kentucky on July 4, 1919. The youngest of four children born to Clyde Floyd and Florence Cox McCoy, Gene had two brothers, Ernest and Clyde and a sister, Zelma. Florence was the widow of Vernon Ferguson. He died in 1908 leaving a 110-acre farm to his only son, Vernon Ferguson Jr, who was born to Florence soon after his death. Clyde Floyd married Florence in 1909. He served as Vernon's legal guardian, even after Vernon married at the age of 15 in 1923.

My Grandfather, Eugene McCoy

The family lived on the Ferguson farm until Vernon's sudden death in 1927, leaving his wife, Vadna as his immediate heir. It was a tough life for the family. Floyd, the son of Samuel and Martha McCoy, worked as a miner and a farmer and struggled to support his family. It was a task further compounded by Florence's death in 1921 when my grandfather was two years old. Floyd married Myrtle Wooten in 1928. With three children of her own, Myrtle and Floyd had one child together, a son named Clarence. Myrtle and Clarence were not well received by Florence's children.

My grandfather never talked about his parents much. By some accounts, Myrtle was not an especially kind woman, nor did she try to befriend Floyd's children by Florence. For his part, Floyd devoted his time to his new wife, creating a lasting rift with his own children. Clarence, alienated from the family, fell out of touch with them. His life remains something of an untold family mystery to this day.

Zelma left Pike County as a young woman, marrying early and settling in San Diego, California. With World War II in full swing, the three

McCoy boys—Ernest, Clyde and Eugene—resolved to escape a future life in the Pike County coal mines and answered the call of their country. My grandfather enlisted in the U.S. Army Air Force on October 14, 1939 and served in the 677th Glider Field Artillery Battalion of the 13th Airborne Division. While stationed at Fort Bragg, North Carolina, he met and married Geraldine Adams, a local girl from the nearby town of Angier. The 677th spent most of the war stationed in England preparing for imminent combat in the Western European Theater. The "Unlucky 13th" was the only airborne division not to see combat on D-day. Although slated for further service in the Pacific, the 677th was demobilized on December 15, 1944.[16] Gene served the remainder of his tour at Fort Bragg until he was discharged on March 30, 1946.

After the war, my grandparents settled in Durham, North Carolina. The pair had a son, Ronald Gene and a daughter, Sue. Gene found gainful employment at the American Tobacco factory in Durham. My grandmother, Geraldine worked at a competing factory, Liggett Myers Tobacco Company, also in Durham. Gene's brother, Clyde settled in Detroit, Michigan while his brother Ernest lived in southern Virginia.

My grandfather died when I was 15 years old, following a prolonged battle with cancer. Except for a brief time in Durham when I was seven years old and one summer visit for my tenth birthday, my family had been abroad for nearly ten straight years due to my father's military service. As my grandfather's condition worsened, we were permitted to return stateside in 1979. The last four months of his life was an especially difficult and painful time for him. He had little time for reflection or recollection. The strong robust man I remembered from my youth was fighting for his life.

I am not Ron McCoy. Until I was an adult, I was usually referred to as "Mack," a nickname that still surfaces occasionally among family members today. Most often, I was "Little Mack" since the title of "Mack" was held by its rightful owner, my grandfather, Eugene. Ron McCoy was my father, and I have spent the better part of fifty plus years living in his considerable shadow.

I was born in Wichita Falls, Texas in August 20, 1963, the first child of Sally Margaret Tillman and Ronald Gene McCoy Sr. Much like his father before him, my Dad was a larger-than-life man who, despite his own share of failings, lived life with vigor. He was a Senior Master Sergeant in the Air Force, a career "lifer" who spent twenty-one years in the service. I grew up as the quintessential Air Force brat.

Born on December 7, 1942, one year to the day after the attack on Pearl Harbor, my Dad was a product of his times. He was a child of the 1950s, a rebel without a cause, hell-bent on getting out of Durham and determined to be somebody. After a tumultuous childhood that included frequent bouts of quarrelling with his father, Dad left home when he was just 17. He lived in the back room of a service station until he was old enough to enlist in the service. He married his childhood sweetheart, Sally, a 15 year old country girl from neighboring Wake County in 1961, the same year he joined the military, and set out to see the world.

While in the Air Force, Dad worked in communications. For most of his career, his work was kept secret to us. As a teenager, I learned that he had been working in cryptography, involving the encryption and transmission of strategically encoded messages. While he was not a spy, as a child, it seemed close enough to it for me. My mother, my little sister Renee and I were fortunate that we could travel with Dad as his work took him throughout the world. We lived two years in Japan, five years in Holland and three years in Italy.

On occasion, the Air Force would send Dad on remote assignments. In 1970, Dad was given a yearlong assignment to Johnston Island, a mile-long island in the Pacific that has since been used by the military for nuclear testing. The Air Force was launching communication satellites into orbit from there and apparently needed Dad worse than we needed him at home. My mother, sister and I spent that year living in Durham while he was away. It was the year I fell off a bicycle and suffered a severe compound fracture, breaking my left arm in multiple places around the elbow. I can still remember my grandfather, Eugene, steady and unflinching as he drove me to the hospital in his pickup truck at speeds far exceeding the posted limits.

My father was a scuba diver, weight lifter, private pilot and a black belt in Karate. His greatest claim to fame, however, was as a musician. Dad was a studio-quality lead guitar player who spent years performing in clubs around the world. During his time in Texas, he met an up and coming songwriter named Hugh "Willie" Nelson and once had the chance to perform for his idol, guitar legend Chet Atkins. While in Japan, Dad was asked by the Air Force to join a band accompanying a then unknown country singer on a USO tour of the island. The tour culminated with a concert broadcast live on Japanese television. Dad was duly impressed with the petite, young woman with a powerful voice who demonstrated an amazing command of the guitar, fiddle, banjo and steel guitar. In the years following the tour, Barbara Mandrell went go on to have a long and successful career in country music.

My Dad, Ronald Gene McCoy, Sr.

No matter where he was stationed, Dad always put together a band. Most weekends, he played Friday and Saturday nights at the local NCO or Officer's club. Sometimes, the Air Force would send him off to play venues elsewhere. In 1978, he spent the better part of a summer touring full time with his band, the "Sounds of Nashville," playing US military bases throughout Europe.

As an Air Force dependent, I lived a remarkable, vagabond childhood. I spent five of my first seven years in Texas and Japan, before our yearlong tenure in Durham in 1970. In 1971, after my family moved to Europe, we lived five years in the Netherlands and three years in Italy. By the time we returned stateside in 1979 when I was nearly 16, I had spent most of my formative years abroad.

My father was the first generation of our branch of the Randolph McCoy line to be born outside of Pike County, Kentucky. Still, my father was a proud McCoy and instilled in me a sense of pride in the family name. The feud was not something we talked about in my immediate family, however.

I have discovered that this was not a situation unique to my branch of the clan. In the decades following the execution of "Cotton Top" Mounts, the story of the feud was not something that was talked about much within the greater McCoy family. Indeed, the McCoys were notoriously close-mouthed about it. "In my generation, if we did not talk about it, we did not have to bring back those sad memories," said Paul McCoy, my grandfather's cousin and fellow great-grandson of Randolph.[17] The reluctance to address the issue created a divide among those in my father's generation of "baby boomers," the children of post-World War II America. They were also the first generation to hear the story of the feud second-hand.

Behind closed doors and within the relative safety of the immediate family, however, those family members of my grandfather's era maintained a strong oral tradition that ensured the sacrifices of the past would never be forgotten. Although his grandfather, Samuel died when he was two years old, my grandfather, Eugene grew up hearing eyewitness accounts of the feud from his grandmother, Martha. While my grandfather and his brothers were some of the first of the family to leave Pike County, Pike County never truly left them.

I do not remember my grandfather ever saying the name "Hatfield." For him, the memories of the feud were still vital; the wounds were still fresh. He grew up listening to feud stories from those who knew all too well what it was like to have lost grandparents, fathers, husbands, uncles and aunts. My cousin, Bo told me once that his grandfather, Clyde, never mentioned the Hatfields without the addition of a derogatory adjective. "Hatfield" was not a name to be spoken of in polite company.

I vaguely remembered the stories of Kentucky my grandfather told me as a young child. At the time, the stories seemed to me to be just great mountain yarns, like the adventurous bedtime tales my Dad would sometimes make up. The stories made an impression, however. My grandfather's deep affection for his Kentucky home was never in question. It is something I recall vividly to this day. Still, growing up, I had no real knowledge of the feud or my family's relationship to it. By the time I was a teenager, having spent most of my years away, the stories my grandfather told had long since faded into forgotten memories.

Smoking cigars was one of my grandfather's favorite past times, a habit that eventually resulted in his developing lung cancer. Doctors had removed his left lung and he bore a substantial scar that wrapped completely around his body. My grandfather was never a man to be deterred from things he enjoyed, however. He lived with one lung for 17 years…and continued smoking cigars.

My grandfather was an expert marksman. At home, he maintained an extensive collection of guns and rifles on the wood-paneled walls of the den that was his personal sanctum. The guns brought back affectionate memories of his days hunting squirrels as a boy in Pike County. The collection was a testament to a fact we all knew to be true. For all the years my grandfather lived in North Carolina, he never considered it his home. He was always *from* Kentucky.

One of his guns I remember most fondly was a silver plated, pearl handled Colt 22 pistol. As a young boy, my grandfather would take me shooting at a nearby creek where a local beauty shop sometimes discarded their used aerosol cans. My grandfather knew they made especially good targets when fired at from the bridge above. I recall that they exploded rather spectacularly when hit by small pistol fire.

As my grandfather's illness slowly progressed, he gradually sold off his extensive gun collection piece by piece, except for the coveted pearl handled Colt 22. It was an heirloom he intended to give to me when I got older. Unfortunately, shortly after my grandfather's death, my father temporarily loaned the revolver to another family member, purportedly to serve as protection on a long road trip home. I never saw the gun again.

The McCoys of Ferguson Creek, circa 1920

An old, fading black and white picture in a heavy wooden oval frame held a place of importance on my grandfather's den wall. It was the only known picture of my grandfather's family. In the picture, Gene's brothers and sister, dressed in their Sunday best, were seated on the steps of an old cabin. My grandfather, nearly two years old, was in his mother's arms. This picture held a special place in my grandfather's heart. It was the last picture taken of his mother, Florence. When my grandfather was diagnosed as terminally ill, he gave the picture to his niece, Ida Gaye Plum in Michigan, a daughter of Ernest's, for safekeeping. I did not see the picture again until 2000. Despite her own ongoing bout with cancer, Ida Gaye attended the 2000 Reunion and presented me with a photocopy of my grandfather's cherished family portrait.

Another picture of importance to my grandfather, an artist's rendering of a wooden cabin on a mountainside, hung in the living room of my grandparent's home. The print of the "McCoy Homeplace" was one-half of a set painted by renowned Kentucky artist Russell May in the 1970s. My grandfather never owned nor had any use for the companion piece, a similar rendering of the "Hatfield Homeplace." Following the reunion in 2000, my Aunt Sue gave my grandfather's Russell May print to me and it remains one of my most cherished possessions.

His den was my grandfather's sanctuary. It was where he would sit, smoke cigars and tell stories. In many respects, the den was his personal connection to his Kentucky home, a place to which he longed to return. He and my grandmother once purchased a mountain property in Kentucky with a small cabin on it that they and my aunt Sue had worked hard to renovate. As an adult, I learned that my grandfather had hoped to pass the cabin down through the generations, a dream that never happened as his health worsened.

With the urgency to attend to my grandfather's declining health, Dad, Renee and I returned home to North Carolina in March 1979. My mother remained behind in Aviano, Italy to wrap things up there. Dad stayed in North Carolina for a time until he deployed to this next assignment in Biloxi, Mississippi. He made regular visits home to visit his father. Renee and I lived with my grandparents until my mother returned and remained there for several months following my grandfather's death. My parents separated that same year, divorced the year following and my Dad remarried soon after that.

While my grandfather's illness left him extremely frail, he never lost the vitality that defined his character. My grandfather was someone you paid attention to and he was not especially happy to repeat himself. On one occasion, my grandfather was sitting up in an easy chair in the living room of his home. My Dad, in full military uniform, had come into the room to speak to him. My grandfather's voice was quite weak as he spoke, and my father struggled to hear him. My Dad made the mistake of asking my grandfather to repeat what he had said. Suddenly, my grandfather reached up, grabbed my father by the hair and pulled his head down to him. "Listen to me when I'm talking to you, boy!" he said. Even in sickness, my grandfather demanded to be heard.

My grandfather celebrated his 60th birthday in 1979, and then lost this long battle with cancer several days later on July 10. In the short six months he and I had to become reacquainted, my grandfather had neither the time nor strength to regale me with the tales from my childhood, stories I could scarcely remember. One of my sincerest regrets is that I never had the opportunity to get to know him better.

Soon after my parent's separation, my Dad learned that an untreated mole on his back had developed into a malignant melanoma. For five years, on a roller coaster ride of metastasis and remission, my father fought his own battle with cancer. He continued his service in the Air

Force, serving in Homestead, Florida and Incirlik, Turkey. He died on March 11, 1983 at the early age of 40. I was 19.

With my father and grandfather's passing, I found myself to be the last remaining McCoy male that I knew. My Aunt Sue had three daughters and my sister, Renee was my only sibling. Ernest and Clyde's branches of the family were unknown to me, outside of having met Uncle Ernest and his wife a few times when I was child. My grandmother, Geraldine remarried but her newfound happiness was short-lived. She died unexpectedly on December 17, 1985 from a brain aneurism.

For many years, I mourned the loss of my father and grandparents and the connection to my McCoy heritage. Having my family stripped away left me a disillusioned and angry young man. Although I married young and had children of my own, I struggled with a sense of familial disconnection. While I discovered a newfound Christian faith that helped guide me through the darkness, I nevertheless wrestled with a nagging sense of loss. I could not help but feel that there were things about myself that I should know and did not.

It was this persistent and familiar sense of doubt I was entertaining while driving home from the mountains of Tennessee in 1997. I thought about the time spent in my grandfather's den, listening to him talk about his Kentucky home. I was then that I slowly began to remember another family treasure my grandfather held dear. There was this…*book*.

My grandfather was an avid reader of pulp adventure stories. Alongside his collection of *Tarzan* novels and Zane Grey paperbacks, he held another precious book, one that his aunt had written about the McCoy family. I seemed to recall that the hardcover book had a paper cover jacket with a collage of old family pictures on it. Beyond that, I remembered little else about it. Following my grandfather's passing, the book's location was unknown, and I presumed it was lost. It was strange that memories of the book had come to mind on the drive home from the mountains that night. I had not thought about it for twenty years.

A few months later, I had a phone conversation with my sister, Renee, and casually mentioned my odd recollection of my grandfather's book. To my great astonishment, Renee said that she had the book in her possession. My grandmother had given her the book to hang on to, along with a collection of family pictures. Surprised by my sudden interest in the McCoy family history, Renee agreed to let me borrow it.

My grandfather's copy of the book, *The McCoys: Their Story* written by his Aunt Truda was well worn, with yellowed, dog-eared pages. The hardback book had a faded red cover. Its photo-gallery dust jacket was in pieces and too fragile to handle. Bound inside the book were two sections of black and white pictures, most labeled as McCoy family members, none of whom I recognized.

An extensive genealogy section in the back of the book detailed the history of the McCoys in Pike County, beginning from the earliest settlement of the family in the region. On page 310, I found a typed erratum paper-clipped to a page listing the fifth generation removed from the McCoy family progenitor, William McCoy. The paper spelled out additional information on Floyd McCoy that had been omitted from the initial printing and listed sixth generation descendants including a name I recognized: Eugene McCoy. I was surprised to find my grandfather's name listed in the book, although I did recall that his father's name was Floyd. I turned back a page to discover a fourth generation listing for Floyd's parents, Samuel and Martha McCoy. Empowered by the unexpected discovery of two generations of my family I had known nothing about, I turned back to page 308 to learn the name of Samuel's father, a third generation descendant whose story would change my life.

A brief perusal of the genealogy listing was my introduction to my great-great-great grandfather, Randolph McCoy. The listing offered a brief synopsis of his life, including his 1849 marriage to Sarah, his injury by fire, his subsequent death in 1914 and his burial in Dils Cemetery in Pikeville, Kentucky. There was little else of note in the listing, with no mention of his role in the feud or his place in American history.

I soon came to the realization that, somehow, my grandfather was related to the names and pictures of the people I saw in the book. Recalling my grandfather's unyielding affection for Kentucky, I began to read the book and learned for the first time of my family's tragic war with the Hatfields. With each successive chapter, I began to share an affinity with the characters involved. They began to come to life in a way that transcended the spectacle of the feud saga. The stories were not fictional, and the people involved were no longer strangers. They were my family. My pulse began to race as I faced an even greater realization; that not only was I related to the feuding clan, I was the great-great-great grandson of the man at the heart of the conflict, Randolph McCoy.

It was a turning point in my life. It was a reconnection with my family's rich heritage; the story my grandfather heard from his grandmother; and the story he wanted me to remember and to tell my children. The feud story introduced me to generations of family members whose choices, decisions and actions, good and bad, had directly affected and shaped the lives of generations to come.

One individual leaped from the pages of history. He, like my grandfather, demanded to be heard. As the patriarch of the family during the feud, Randolph McCoy was a man who suffered unimaginable loss. Before the feud's conclusion, he would lose his home and possessions, his brother, a nephew, seven children and his wife Sarah, who eventually succumbed to the injuries she sustained during the attack on the McCoy cabin. Living out his final years in Pikeville, Kentucky, he earned a reputation for wanting to talk about the feud to anyone who would listen, ensuring that the sacrifices of his family would be remembered. His persistence was not always appreciated. The burgeoning urban center that Pikeville became following the Civil War was eager to consign the events of the war and the feud to history. As I read the feud account, I could hear an urgency in Randolph's voice, speaking to me directly, demanding that the family story be told. I soon realized that it was incumbent upon me to continue his legacy.

This indelible image of Randolph McCoy's last years in Pikeville so impressed me that it became fundamentally part of everything I hoped to achieve with the "McCoys:2000" reunion. My cousin Bo felt the same way. As the great-great-great grandsons of Randolph McCoy, we understood our responsibility to retell the feud story as accurately and as often as possible. The loss of our family members and those on the Hatfield side would not be in vain. "We remember" became our mantra for the 2000 reunion.

Reconnecting with my family history took me back to my earliest days as a small child, listening to stories of Kentucky in my grandfather's den. Yet my journey of discovery might never have happened were it not for a vague recollection of a book my grandfather once owned – a book that somehow ended up in my sister's possession – and the insertion of a single piece of paper with my grandfather's name on it. Incredibly, I owe my reconciliation with my family's history to a *paperclip*.

Beginnings

> "The past is not dead; it is living in us, and will be alive in the future which we are now helping to make."
> William Morris

AJ Jacobs, noted *New York Times* best-selling author, lecturer and editor, encountered his own genealogical epiphany after receiving an email from a fan in Israel. The man whom he had never met claimed to be married to a distant cousin of his whom he did not know. To his surprise, Jacobs discovered that the man was correct. Further, Jacobs found through his research that he was related to some 80,000 other strangers as well. His newfound interest in genealogy resulted in an innovative book project about ancestry and human history. Because of the project, Jacobs found himself hosting the "Global Family Reunion" in New York City in June 2015. AJ's years of research led him to a straightforward realization: all seven million of us on this planet we call home comprise one enormous human family. Whether we approach this idea through a study of genetics or genealogy, the conclusion remains the same. We are all, in some form or fashion, related to one another. We are cousins.[18]

Jacobs' premise is sound on philosophical, theological and mathematical bases. We are a singular species which, at some definitive point in time began with one man and one woman. In tracing our lineage far enough backwards through time, we discover that at some point in time, all of humanity must eventually share a common point of origin.

Most human beings seem to acknowledge this idea of commonality, at least on an intrinsic level. While some strive to find ways to exaggerate our differences of race, creed, religion and culture, we human beings are, in fact, remarkably similar. Each of us has an inherent sense that we are part of something greater than ourselves. Reuniting with our historical past allows us to understand and better appreciate our place in the present day. We rediscover a sense of value that we can apply not only to ourselves but to others with whom we share our lives. We come to understand that we are inextricably connected with the rest of the human family occupying this terrestrial ball. We are indeed cousins, after all.

It was an introduction to a cousin whom I had never met that began a series of events that changed my life and helped make history. Bo McCoy and I are third cousins, the grandsons of Clyde and Eugene McCoy, two of the sons of Clyde Floyd and Florence. Although we did not know of each other's existence until 1998, both of us were on similar quests to learn more about our family history. This journey eventually led to our paths crossing online.

For me, the discovery of fellow McCoys was the most welcome outcome of exploring my family's heritage. With the passing of my father and grandparents and the marriages of my sister and aunt, I found myself in a curious predicament. Except for my children, Rachel and Jacob (and their mother), I did not know anyone else named "McCoy."

The family was not always so fragmented. Following their respective tours of duty in the military services, my grandfather and his brothers remained in close contact, despite their settling in different parts of the country. My great-uncle Ernest and his wife would come down from Virginia to visit my grandparents in North Carolina from time to time.

I do not remember ever meeting my great-uncle Clyde and his wife, Gertrude, although old family pictures bear testament to the fact that they did visit on occasion. Clyde and his family lived in the Detroit, Michigan area, which made long trips to North Carolina prohibitive. Eventually, Clyde's branch of the family relocated to southern Georgia, an area that Bo came to know as home.

Ernest, Eugene and Clyde McCoy

Following the passing of the three brothers and their spouses, the branches of the families drifted apart. Military service kept Bo's family on the move, just as it took mine around the world. Tenuous connections to my extended family were lost. It was not until fifteen years after my grandfather's death that the advent of internet technology enabled my divided family to rediscover one another.

In 1995, I purchased my first home computer, a Tandy unit from the neighborhood Radio Shack. With a 56k modem and a monthly subscription to America Online, I found that I could connect to an online community of fellow computer owners. Social media as we know it today was in its infancy. Online message boards on which users could post digital "notes" were commonplace. These boards became an invaluable tool in searching for other like-minded individuals with similar interests. By 1997, AOL and other services began to offer a new and promising innovation, something called the "world wide web." This service allowed virtually unlimited access to websites, message boards and connections with other computer users on other services around the world.

On May 25, 1998, as I was online searching for information on McCoys, I came across an interesting post on a genealogy message board that was part of a larger "Hatfield and McCoy" discussion thread. "I am looking for the children of Samuel and Martha McCoy...you may view our (family) line at *www.real-mccoys.com*. We have a message board and would love for you to stop by." The short message, while not especially noteworthy in its content, caught my attention. It was posted by "Clyde McCoy," a name that I certainly recognized.

I thought it was unlikely that the person posting on Genforum could be my grandfather's brother, Clyde. I was excited, however, by the prospect that there was someone else out there, like me, searching for more information on my branch of the family tree. It seemed prudent to accept the invitation to visit his website and to learn more about the identity of this mysterious individual.

In those days, the *real-mccoys.com* website was a bare-bones affair. The website presented a brief timeline of feud events as well as a genealogical tree, not unlike the information available in Truda's book. Although the identity of those behind the website was still unclear to me, the authors clearly stated that they were of the lineage of Sam and Martha McCoy, my grandfather's grandparents. It was clear to me that whomever these individuals turned out to be, we were at the very least, related...somehow.

On July 31, 1998, I set aside two months of trepidation and responded to Clyde's posting on Genforum. "Just stumbled across your post as I was web searching..." I began, before outlining my family history for a total stranger and the entire world to see. I finished the posting, held my breath and waited for a response.

For the next few weeks, I checked the message board daily, hoping for a response to my posting but found none. Finally, on August 13, 1998, a reply to my query came in the form of an email. As my message board identity was the same as my email address, Clyde had decided to reply to me directly. The response was more than I could have imagined. "Your Dad was my cousin. Your grandfather Eugene was my Dad's brother. My Dad was Clyde, also born in Pikeville..." I was elated. For the first time in my adult life, I was in contact with my great-uncle Clyde's branch of the family. "I remember your Dad staying with us in Detroit, when he was younger. I am sure it was prior to him going into the service. That was the last time I ever saw him. I remember that I was overseas in Korea....when your Dad died," wrote Clyde McCoy, my grandfather's nephew. It was my first time exchanging memories of a shared history with a stranger who was, in fact, *family*. Clyde extended an invitation for me to stay in touch and then he suggested that I should reach out to two other family members. "My two sons (Bo and Sean) set up the Real-McCoys (web) site..." Like the discovery of a paperclip in the back of an old book, my first-ever posting on an internet message board in response to the appeal of a stranger, had introduced me to a family I had never known. Little did I realize the enormity of the series of events that Clyde's response had set into motion.

I first met Bo through his website in August 1998. I began corresponding with him through email and later by phone calls, only to discover that we had been living parallel lives. It was pleasantly disconcerting to realize that previously unknown family members could have comparable life experiences, possesses similar physical, emotional and psychological traits and share a common history, despite never having met. Both of us would experience this same feeling numerous times over the years as we met extended relations from around the country.

Bo and I shared many common dispositions including similar interests in music and the church. One unusual commonality became a prime motivational factor and an impetus for the reunion in 2000. Neither of us had attended the funerals of our grandfathers.

In 1993, Bo was away at school when he received the news that his grandfather, Clyde had passed away. With little resources at his disposal, Bo heeded the advice of his father and did not make the trip back home. It was a decision that haunted Bo for years to come. "I was in college here in Waycross when my grandfather died. I really didn't have the money or the means to travel back and attend the funeral. Since his wishes were to be cremated instead of being buried, I couldn't even visit a gravesite when I was able to return home. That bothered me so much. I guess I began to feel I hadn't honored his death in a proper way. That's why I made the decision to do something about it," said Bo.[19]

When my grandfather, Eugene died of lung cancer in July 1979, it was my first experience with death. Curiously, like Bo, it was my father's advice that persuaded me not to attend the funeral. My Dad made the case that I should remember my grandfather for the man he was and the life he led, not the shell of a man that he had become. In hindsight, I believe my father had ulterior motives of his own for his counsel – the twenty-year veteran Senior Master Sergeant did not want his son to see him cry.

Missing his grandfather's funeral affected Bo profoundly. He felt that he had somehow disrespected his grandfather. It was a cycle of self-condemnation that plagued him until he confronted a serious health crisis in 1996. Bedridden for nearly six weeks, followed by months of therapy and rehabilitation, Bo emerged with a renewed sense of direction and purpose. He began a passionate foray into studying feud history. As an early internet advocate, he was dismayed to find that search engine inquiries for "Hatfields," "McCoys" and "Real McCoys" returned few results. In June 1998, he launched *www.real-mccoys.com* as both an informational website and as a tribute to his grandfather's memory. Bo intended the site to be a "cyber tavern" where family members or those interested in the feud could visit and carry on virtual conversations with like-minded individuals. At the behest of his brother, Sean, Bo became a prolific and talented website designer. Long before the internet was commonplace, there were few software tools available for website development, so encoding websites from scratch was a rare and valuable skill.

Bo's first "McCoy" website was a labor of love, although by his own assessment, it was "skimpy." When Bo launched his homegrown site, he had no thought of the juggernaut his humble endeavor would inspire. As time went on, his streamlined and upgraded website became an invaluable tool for organizing and promoting the historic reunion to come.

It was Bo who first suggested the idea of a "McCoy reunion," although he credits another family member with emailing him the idea. As the *real-mccoys* website began to gain notice, it became the virtual hub of internet Hatfield-McCoy related activity. Unlike the text-only postings on the popular Genforums, the website presented the chance for greater interaction between both families. It was an ideal platform for offering historical tidbits, swapping opinions and sharing pictures and stories. Visitors to the website joined as "list members" and, by the time of the reunion in 2000, the list had grown to more than 450 members. In a time before modern social media, this was no small number.

List members proved to be an important source of information on Hatfield-McCoy happenings across the nation. One list member mailed Bo a newspaper story in early 1999 on the feud-site preservation work by Pike County Tourism Director Bruce Bennett Brown. Although we had not met him at the time, Mr. Brown would become an invaluable source of help for us as we began making plans for the 2000 reunion. The article's author, Associated Press writer Kimberly Hefling, would become the media catalyst that transformed our concept of a small family reunion into an historical event beyond anything we could have imagined.

Although Bo and I would not meet in person until nearly a year later, I was intrigued when the idea of a McCoy family reunion came up in late 1998. When Bo asked if I would consider working as a co-organizer, I responded with an emphatic "yes." The prospect of meeting new family members was an opportunity I could not pass up. We agreed that the idea of a McCoy family reunion had merit and that it might be possible for the two of us to organize it, although neither of us had any previous event planning experience. Still, we felt that if we made the event a lowkey affair, it would be easily manageable and inexpensive. The "Hatfield McCoy Reunion Festival" of 2000 proved to be none of these things.

Bo christened the prospective reunion as "McCoys 2000" (M2K). In 1999, "Y2K" was a popular buzzword that resonated with the American public. The turn of the twenty-first century was set to arrive as a benchmark that heralded the end of civilization as we knew it. The specter of "Y2K," a catastrophic shut down of global computer systems that would trigger the collapse of governmental and financial systems, loomed over the world. Disaster was imminent because the internal calendars in computer operating systems had no date provisions to account for a new century. It was a contemporary version of the apocalypse story. As with most doomsday scenarios, however, the reality of the threat proved less notable than its potential. New Year's Eve 1999 passed quietly and uneventfully into the new millennium.

Without considering an open invitation to website list members, Bo and I felt that we could invite 50 immediate family members to attend any event we managed to put together. Where to hold such an event was a more problematic. With known family members in Georgia, North Carolina, Virginia and Michigan, selecting a venue site that was centrally accessible was a necessity. We felt that costs and travel time might discourage some from participating. Others had serious health issues that made long distance travel difficult. Bo and I wanted to make certain that family members would have no excuses for not attending.

With the skeleton premise of hosting a McCoy family reunion in a convenient location, for little or no money, with no idea what we would do once we gathered everyone together, Bo and I began to consider the options for where to hold the event. It was during one of our many phone conversations that I offered a possibility that was even more vague than the bare bones plan we were already putting together. Since reconnecting with my past, I had been earnestly wanting to visit eastern Kentucky for the first time. I suggested there might be other family members who felt the same desire to visit there and that a McCoy reunion in Pike County might provide the necessary incentive to come "home."

Bo was captivated by the idea. Pike County, Kentucky was (and is) the home soil of the McCoy clan. It was a good central location and seemed to be reasonably accessible to most family members in the region. As the historical site of the feud, it also provided an added inducement for our family members to attend. Further, hosting a McCoy reunion in feud-country permitted us to broaden our scope of potential attendees beyond immediate family members and to extend an invitation to the list members group on the website as well.

Pikeville, Kentucky seemed a logical choice for the event, despite some potential logistical obstacles. At the time, Pikeville was a small town of about 6,400 people, nestled in the southernmost corner of eastern Kentucky. We learned that the city offered limited infrastructure, hotel spaces and venue options. The nearest airport was three hours away in Frankfort or Lexington and no bus or passenger train lines serviced the area. The best access to Pikeville was by car, but navigating mountain roads would prove challenging to those family members driving in from out of town. Still, Pikeville was the host site of the Shriner's "Hillbilly Days" festival, an event that attracted nearly 100,000 visitors annually. Surely the city could handle the limited number of family members we hoped might attend our event.

There was one other problem with selecting Pikeville as the site for the reunion, however. Neither of us had ever been there. Without the slightest prompting on Bo's part, I offered what I thought was a reasonable solution. One of us needed to make a reconnaissance trip to Pikeville and the logical choice was me. Although it was a six-hour drive from Durham, I had been looking for an excuse to make the trip anyway. Bo, with just the slightest hint of envy, agreed. The McCoys were going home.

Homeland

*"When the past no longer illuminates the future,
the spirit walks in darkness."*
Alexis de Tocqueville

As the concept of a McCoy family reunion inched closer to reality, making an exploratory trip to Pikeville became a practical necessity. It was also a chance for me to take the exploration of my past one-step further. It was one thing to develop a working knowledge of my family's heritage. Having the chance to step back into history and visit the location where it all took place was another thing entirely. In the fall of 1998, I set out alone to make the trek to the land of my ancestors and to walk the soil they once trod, the same ground on which they shed their blood and in which they were now buried.

Long before the innovation of MapQuest, smart phones or global positioning systems, a crumpled-up Rand McNally map was my only guide for travel. I grabbed my trusty map and a small suitcase of clothes, kissed the kids goodbye, hopped in the mini-van and headed deeper into the Appalachian Mountains than I had ever been. From Durham, the road to Pikeville headed due west, then north into Virginia, then west again into Kentucky. Over the years, I have made more than 35 trips to the area. The well-worn path has become second nature to me, but in 1998, it was a precarious venture into the unknown. The serpentine mountain roads were a daring ride for a city-boy on his first trip to Pike County. The journey took a full seven hours; the pace more than a little hindered by my preoccupation with the rugged beauty of the mountains.

Alone in my vehicle, it was quiet except for intermittent AM radio stations playing bluegrass music that would come and go as I crossed over one hill to the next. With each passing mile, I slowly made my way to the land my grandfather considered home. The closer I got to Pikeville, the more it seemed I could sense his presence, as if he were guiding me to a place I had never been, yet in some respects, had never truly left. As I crossed into Kentucky, I glanced up at the rearview mirror of my van. In my mind's eye, I could almost see my grandparents and my Dad in the backseat riding along with me, smiling and proud to be headed home.

The importance of Pikeville to feud history and to the McCoy family cannot be underestimated. While most feud events took place in the Tug Valley some 25 miles east of the city, Pikeville played an important role, nonetheless. The city was the site of the hanging of Ellison "Cotton Top" Mounts for the killing of Alifair McCoy in 1890. The Pike County Courthouse on Main Street was the site of several feud-related trials. Following the burning of the McCoy home in Blackberry Creek, Pikeville became the new home for Randolph McCoy, his sons, Jim and Sam and their respective families. Randolph and Sarah's last home still stands today on the corner of Main Street and Scott Avenue in Pikeville. The city's historic Dils Cemetery is their final resting place.

Pikeville is the ancestral home for generations of my family. It is a place my family holds dear. As Bo and I began putting together plans for the reunion, we were not always successful in communicating this affinity for Pikeville to those who presently called the city home. Some doubted the sincerity of our affection, even going so far as to question the legitimacy of our claim to Pike County roots.

One of the earliest accusations leveled at us was that our assertion of lineage was not legitimate. While it was obvious that we both bore the McCoy surname, some considered it preposterous that a couple of "outsiders" who were neither born nor raised in Pike County could claim to be the progeny of "Ol' Randall" himself. Although Bo and I worked hard to dispel such charges, we were too busy contending with other organizational issues to be overly preoccupied with disproving our roles as "carpetbaggers."

To me, the allegations were a personal offense and I felt that I needed to protect my grandfather's link to the place he called home. The question of legitimacy raised a true concern for me. Although I was certain my grandfather was born in Pikeville, I had no real proof of it. Fortunately, I discovered that I could order a reprint of my grandfather's birth certificate from the state archives in Frankfort, Kentucky. The certificate could be ordered by the individual or, in the event of his death, by a surviving child or spouse. Although no provision was made for grandchildren to acquire a certificate, given that my father and I have the same name, I provided the relevant personal information and hoped that my order would go through.

Several months later, I received in the mail a certified copy of my grandfather's birth certificate, attesting to his birth on July 4, 1919, at the home of his parents, Clyde Floyd and Florence McCoy, on Ferguson Creek, in Pikeville, Kentucky. Although I never had cause to produce the document for examination, the fact that I had gone through the trouble to acquire it both reaffirmed my connection to Pikeville and Pike County and helped quiet the voices of those who opposed us.

With a current population of about 6,900, Pikeville is the largest city in Pike County. It is the home of Pikeville Medical Center, a prestigious regional medical facility, the University of Pikeville campus, part of the Kentucky's public university system, and the 7,000 seat Eastern Kentucky Exposition Center, built in 2005. Established in 1824, the city was built on the Levisa Fork of the Big Sandy River that once circled it like a horseshoe. The river access helped Pikeville to become a valuable trading center, transporting coal and timber products. During the Civil War, the city played an important role as a staging area for the Union army. In 1862, James Garfield was sworn in as brigadier general of the army while stationed there.[20] As the county seat, Pikeville remains the center of all-things political in eastern Kentucky.

Pikeville has been called the "city that moved mountains," for good reason. It was the dream of Dr. William Hambley, mayor for 29 years, to reroute the river that was prone to flooding the city on a near-annual basis. In 1973, in cooperation with the U.S. Army Corps of Engineers, the city undertook the "Pikeville Cut Through" project, a $76 million dollar effort that lasted 14 years. Cutting through Peach Orchard Mountain effectively redirected the river and reclaimed nearly 150 acres of land for use in downtown Pikeville.[21]

I arrived in Pikeville late on a Friday afternoon, with a full heart. Taking exit 23 from US Highway 23, I drove past the Landmark Inn, with its yellow-bricked veneer and distinctive red-tile roof. At the time, I did not realize the important role the hotel would play as the future site of the historic M2K reunion. Just beyond the hotel was a landmark of a different sort, one that I recognized easily. Tired from the long drive, the McDonald's restaurant seemed like a good place to stop, stretch my legs and get my bearings.

The visit to the Pikeville McDonalds proved to be one of the most surreal experiences of my life. As I made my way inside, I discovered that the restaurant was not unlike one that could be found in a small town anywhere in America. The red-haired young woman behind the counter was amiable, though reserved. She took my order with an easy smile, then stepped back towards the kitchen to fulfill it. Suddenly, I noticed that her vibrant hair color easily set her apart from all the others in the restaurant.

Except for the red-haired girl, everyone in the restaurant – kitchen cooks, counter clerks, managers and customers – bore strikingly similar physical characteristics. Their black hair, dark eyes and pale complexions were the hallmarks of the "Black Irish" and Scottish Highland heritage they shared. I had traveled three hundred miles into the mountains of eastern Kentucky to a place I had never been before, to find myself in a local fast food restaurant filled with people that looked remarkably like me.

Heading into town, I found a place to park on a side street, got out of the van and decided I was smart enough to find my way around. I felt a keen sense of wonder as I made my way through the peaceful city streets, knowing that I was walking where my ancestors once trod. The beautiful historic Pike County Courthouse and jail on Main Street stood as a testament to the feud trials that had taken place there.

I was surprised at how little mention there was of the Hatfields and McCoys. I found one "feud" highway marker near the courthouse, one on the college campus denoting the hanging site of Ellison Mounts and another at Dils Cemetery. Around town, however, I saw little mention of the feud or of Pikeville's link to it. In my ignorance on that first visit, I walked past the McCoy home on Main Street without knowing it because there was no sign that denoted its status.

I did find that my family surname was prevalent in town, however. The McCoys were more common than Smiths and Joneses in Pikeville. On one billboard advertising eyeglasses, I was surprised to find my own name prominently on display. Ron McCoy was a well-regarded ophthalmologist in Pikeville, a man I sometimes would be confused with in the coming years.

The lack of Hatfield-McCoy signage on display defied my expectations. How could a city that played such a significant role in a historic event of the magnitude of the feud not have signs promoting that association everywhere? As Bo and I began organizing the 2000 reunion, we learned that the answer to this question would challenge us often.

Hoping there might be somewhere I could find information on the area, I met a passerby who suggested I consider going by the tourism office or the Chamber of Commerce, which was just a few streets over. Given that it was nearing the end of the business day, I decided to visit the Chamber instead and to postpone my visit to Tourism until Saturday. The visit to the Chamber proved to be a pivotal moment in the reunion's history — one that could have stopped it in its tracks had it turned out differently.

The Pike County Chamber of Commerce would become a source of some resistance to our efforts to organize the "Reunion of the Millennium." The Chamber's close association with "Hillbilly Days" meant that much of its resources were taken up in planning, organizing and executing the massive festival. They did not need to be responsible for or to compete with a secondary event.

On my first day in Pikeville, however, it was the involvement of the Chamber of Commerce that made certain our M2K event would become a reality. That afternoon, I found that the office was open and staffed by a young woman with the same dark hair and dark eyes of the people I had seen at McDonalds. She was one of the first people in Pikeville that I spoke to at length and her reception of an out of town stranger with lots of questions has never been forgotten.

I told her that I was a McCoy descendant from out of state and advised her of our plans for a family reunion. In retrospect, proudly announcing myself as a "McCoy" was somewhat foolish, given the generous number of McCoys in Pike County. She listened politely, however, then offered that the Landmark Inn was the facility in town best equipped to host the type of dinner were planning. Owned by Thomas and Deborah Huffman, the Landmark Inn was the largest hotel in town. With 103 hotel rooms, a restaurant to cater the event and several additional outbuildings capable of hosting larger groups, the Landmark could easily accommodate any sized event we put together.

She provided me with a map of town and indicated several nearby feud sites that I should visit. Although I never saw the young woman again, I have often wondered if she knew how much her kindness to me that afternoon meant for the course of history. I left the Chamber office that afternoon reenergized, armed with two bags of maps, business cards, brochures, multiple copies of the Pike County phonebook and a newfound determination. Beyond a doubt, I was certain that Pikeville was the ideal place to host a national reunion of the McCoy family.

On Saturday morning, I set out on another excursion into town. The local tourism office seemed the logical place to gather additional information. Polite strangers helped direct me to a restored train car that stood in the Pikeville City Park. The blue railroad car with a covered porch that extended from the rear of the vehicle was then home to Pikeville-Pike County Tourism. As I made my way up the porch steps to the office door, to my surprise, I found that it was locked. In 1998, the tourism office was not open on weekends. I was profoundly disappointed.

In the coming months and years, I learned to appreciate the hard-working staff of the tourism office. The office toiled on a minimal budget with a limited staff of part-time employees and volunteers. Tourism Director Bruce Brown would become a welcome ally of ours. Later, he would be replaced by Phyllis Hunt, his administrator, a woman who became our point-of-contact in Pikeville and chief collaborator. Lenna Goff was the office manager for Tourism, a position she still holds today. Phyllis and Lenna were invaluable in building the Hatfield-McCoy Reunion Festival from the ground up. They worked long hours managing an inordinate amount of details, juggling event schedules, guiding visitors and managing the media. Without their help, our event never would have happened.

Following my unproductive visit to Tourism, I visited Dils Cemetery for the first time. The cemetery, listed in the National Registry of Historic Places, sits high above the City of Pikeville on Lower Chloe Road across the street from the City Fire Department. Dils Cemetery is believed to be the first integrated cemetery in Kentucky. Of the 500 graves there, more than 130 are those of African-Americans. John Dils, a Colonel in the 39th Infantry of the Union Army and a prominent Pikeville businessman, employed many freed slaves in his tannery business and general store. He provided burial plots for these employees and their descendants on the large tract of land he purchased for the cemetery in 1871.[22]

Colonel Dils was a great benefactor of the McCoy clan and an instrumental player in the legal action taken against the Hatfields during the latter part of the feud. Upon Roseanna McCoy's death in 1889, he offered the family a burial place for her in Dils Cemetery. When Sarah McCoy died a few years later, she was buried near Roseanna, as was Randolph in 1914. Randolph's son, Samuel and his wife Martha, my grandfather's grandparents, were buried there as well.

Ascending the precipitous wooden steps to the cemetery, I stepped into the ancient graveyard that spread over steep hills rising upwards to the left and right. Grey headstones of various sizes of shapes, many of them more than a century old, lay askew in every direction. Disheveled and with grass grown up to my knees, the cemetery was a lonely place, sacred and undisturbed. Except for a historic marker placed in 1996, listing the name of African Americans interred there, the cemetery had no other signs of any kind.

Just a few steps to the right from where the wooden steps opened into the cemetery, I discovered the gravesite of my great-great-great grandparents, Randolph and Sarah. The large, granite headstone bearing the surname "McCoy" stood out above the tall grass. The cemetery was eerily quiet, a fitting place of rest for those who had suffered so much in their lifetimes.

It was somehow fitting that, despite her estrangement from the family during the height of the feud, Roseanna was buried near them. Her grave, identified with a smaller, flat granite marker was just below her parents, to the left. Her marker was eloquent in its simplicity: "Roseanna, daughter of Randolph and Sarah McCoy."

Gravestone of Sarah and Randolph McCoy, Dils Cemetery, Pikeville

As I reached the "McCoy" marker, I knelt and placed my hand on the stone to touch the names of Randolph and Sarah inscribed there. In the stillness of that moment, I could almost hear the voice of my great-great-great grandfather prompting me to tell the family's story and never to forget the lives of those family members that had been lost. I expressed my regrets to him for all the lost years of my life spent not knowing my family's history. I apologized for taking so long to find my way back. I promised him that I would always remember our family's story and I reassured him that Bo and I planned to bring more family members to visit. The family had been away for far too long, but now, we were coming home.

Finding the gravesite of my great-great grandparents, Samuel and Martha proved more challenging. Although I knew that they were buried at Dils, without further information to go on, I was unable to locate their gravesite. I walked the rugged, grassy hills for a long while that day, unaware that Sam and Martha were buried just over a knoll overlooking the city. It was not until a return visit the following year in 1999 that I would be able to find their gravesite with the helpful guidance of Bruce Brown. That same trip would be Bo's first visit to Pikeville and to Dils.

While the historic value of Dils Cemetery is unquestionable, its value as a landmark has evolved substantially in the past few decades. In August 1977, a plan was in place for the City of Pikeville to relocate 262 graves at Dils Cemetery, including those of Randolph, Sarah and Roseanna, to make room for a planned civic center and parking lot. While some city officials "expressed doubt" that Randolph was buried at Dils, family members such as O.R. McCoy of Huntington, West Virginia were quick to testify to the fact that he was interred there. "I remember the funeral as a kid…his grave is marked in that cemetery with a stone with the letter "M" on it," said McCoy.[23] The owners of Dils Cemetery sued the city to prevent the action and prevailed.

Following the settlement of the suit, the McCoy graves at Dils were upgraded with new granite headstones that remain to this day. The monuments are similar in style to the larger monument placed by Joe and Leonard McCoy at the McCoy Cemetery in Hardy, Kentucky in 1975. The similarity has led to a commonly held assumption that they were placed by the McCoy brothers as well. However, the markers at Dils Cemetery were placed by my grandfather's cousin Paul McCoy, the son of author Truda McCoy, in late 1977, to honor his grandparents, Samuel and Martha, great-grandparents, Randolph and Sarah and great-aunt Roseanna.

Before the M2K reunion, the responsibility for the care and maintenance of Dils Cemetery was an unanswered question. The cemetery was privately held property, and, despite its historical value, its upkeep was not mandated by public works. Phyllis Hunt of Tourism was instrumental in negotiating with Pike County officials to secure an agreement to clean up the cemetery in time for the 2000 reunion. Sixteen years later, the county continues to honor its commitment to maintain the upkeep of the cemetery.

Ironically, a similar question of maintenance has befallen the Hatfield Cemetery in Sarah Ann, West Virginia, the burial site of William Anderson Hatfield and his family. The remote cemetery was visited infrequently until the 2012 History Channel mini-series spurred the interests of tourists. Visitors discovered that accessing the historic cemetery was no easy task. The road leading to the cemetery was steep and rocky and weeds and wild grasses had overtaken the cemetery itself.

Reo Hatfield of Waynesboro, Virginia has made it his personal mission to see that the situation is resolved. For years, he has pushed to have the cemetery repaired and made accessible. "They come here with expectations of seeing something special," he said in an interview with the *New York Times*. "But you start up the road, and you can hardly walk up there. And once you get there, the graves are unkempt and the fence that guards the grave site has fallen down in numerous places."[24]

State and local officials, while sympathetic to the situation, have declined to act since the burden of upkeep belongs to the owner of the property. The situation is further complicated by the fact that there has been no clear determination as to the identity of the landowners. While local citizens have taken to cleaning up the cemetery in recent months, the long-term prognosis for its care remains unclear. Reo remains hopeful that the situation may be resolved soon and that the cemetery will be restored to its rightful appearance and maintained for future generations.

My initial trip to Pikeville, Kentucky proved to be fruitful, despite my lack of preparation and unfamiliarity with the area. Without traveling outside the city limits, I had barely scratched the surface of feud sites to be visited. I was convinced, however, that Pikeville was the ideal place for a McCoy family reunion. Heading home that early October evening, I felt a sense of satisfaction that was both the culmination of my reconciliation with my past and the beginning of a new and more profound exploration of it. I was certain that my first trip to Pike County would not be my last.

Idea

"The past speaks to us in a thousand voices, warning and comforting, animating and stirring to action."
Felix Adler

The historic "Reunion of the Millennium" in 2000 was the first national reunion of the Hatfield and McCoy families after 110 years of estrangement. It was a noble and ambitious sentiment that captured the interest of the media and the public. The truth of the matter, however, is that Bo and I never intended to host a Hatfield-McCoy reunion at all. In fact, the idea never occurred to us.

Our original plan was to have a McCoy family reunion in Pikeville, Kentucky, if we could convince any family members beyond ourselves to attend. The McCoys are a stubborn lot, so persuading additional family members to join us was not a given. The prospect of hosting a small family reunion was daunting enough without adding a second family to the event.

Inviting the Hatfields to our event never crossed our minds, but only as a matter of oversight. It was never our intention to exclude them. While our grandfathers actively resented the Hatfields, neither Bo nor I felt any compulsion to do so. Bo had known but one Hatfield in his life, a fellow student, Mark Hatfield, that he bumped into in 1986 as a junior in high school. As for me, I had no one against whom to hold a grudge. Before 1999, I had never met a Hatfield.

The "Reunion of the Millennium" was not the first public reconciliation of the families either. In 1928, Tennyson "Tennis" Hatfield, youngest son of "Devil Anse" came across an elderly Jim McCoy, a son of Randolph's, while visiting in Pikeville. The two men shook hands, made their peace and posed for pictures together.[25] In May 1976, another Jim McCoy, great-grandson of Samuel McCoy, brother of Randolph shook hands with Willis Hatfield, the last surviving son of "Devil Anse" at the dedication ceremony for the placement of the monument in the McCoy Cemetery in Hardy, Kentucky.[26]

Given the close historic association of the families, most family members were used to the concept of "Hatfield-McCoy." With the families' exodus from Appalachia following the conclusion of World War II, several generations of descendants had been born and raised beyond the boundaries of the region and now had families extending across the United States. For most, being a "Hatfield" or "McCoy" was fun and the threat of animosity had faded long ago.

With my positive early scouting report, Pikeville was the one and only site considered for the 2000 reunion. We hoped that the historic relevance of Pike County to the McCoy family would make the idea of attending a reunion appealing to other family members. Early on, we decided to cast a broader net and reach out through the internet to a larger group of potential attendees. As further inducement, we intended to add as many feud-related activities to the schedule as possible, including visits to feud sites in Pikeville and down in the Tug Valley.

In planning the M2K event, we began a concerted effort to establish local connections in Pikeville-Pike County, although we had yet to understand the tenuous nature of the hyphenated relationship between the two. My initial trip to Kentucky in 1998 focused on Pikeville exclusively, due primarily to my lack of knowledge of the area.

With each successive trip, I began to develop a greater appreciation for Pike County, for its historical relevance to the feud and my family. With nearly 800 square miles of territory, Pike County is, geographically, the largest county in Kentucky. It has a population of 69,000. Named after famed explorer General Zebulon Pike, it was founded in 1821, three decades after Kentucky's secession from Virginia in 1792.[27] With 620 mines in operation, it is Kentucky's second largest producer of coal.[28] The economic concerns of the county are challenging, however. The US Census recorded 23.4% of the county living below the poverty level from 2009-2013.[29] In 2013, the unemployment rate for the County was 12.3%.[30]

Including the county in our event offered us a welcome chance to give back to the community that had provided so much to the Hatfields and McCoys. To our surprise, we discovered that bridging the gap between Pikeville and Pike County, was nearly as formidable as crossing the divide between Kentucky and West Virginia. From our vantage point, it was easy for us to envision a partnership between the local factions with a common interest in the success of feud tourism. Achieving that level of cooperation, though meant working to overcome decades of social and economic differences between them.

The primary cause of disassociation among the local organizations, agencies and groups from whom we solicited support was the finite amount of economic resources available. Pikeville-Pike County Tourism was supported by a tax levied on area hotels and motels, most of which were located inside the Pikeville city limits. Although the majority of feud sites were in Pike County, there was little financial support there to maintain them. Likewise, similar economic circumstances existed in West Virginia between the tiny hamlet of Matewan and the larger city of Williamson. Given the dissension between the local parties within Pike County, there was little hope of our garnering the cooperation of those across the river. Enlisting the participation of the various factions for the benefit of the visitors we hoped to bring to the area meant walking a tightrope of political and financial affiliations. We did not always manage this careful balancing act well.

Part of the issue with promoting our idea for a McCoy family reunion is that we did not have more than a general idea of what we hoped to put together. Without events scheduled in Pikeville-Pike County in which visitors could participate, there was no compelling reason for family members from across the country to invest the time and financial resources necessary to make the trip to Pikeville. With the M2K reunion and the others that followed, we always insisted that there be plenty of fun activities scheduled for visiting family members. In hindsight, asking local agencies to commit their limited resources to an unproven event based on the unsubstantiated promises of a couple of men they did not know was a ludicrous proposition. It was no wonder that our pleas were ignored. We desperately needed feud-related events on the schedule to help draw visitors to area and there were none to be found.

The greatest underlying organizational problem with the M2K reunion was that it was being organized inversely, from the outside in. Even before it became the "Hatfield-McCoy Reunion Festival," Bo envisioned M2K as a local event that brought in visitors from outside the area to participate. "For us, it's a labor of love. For the people who live here, it could be an economic boom," said Bo.[31] Try as we might, we were unsuccessful in convincing the local interests in the validity of the idea.

One reason for the lack of interest locally was that on the surface, the premise made little sense. I counted over 400 separate listings of McCoy surnames in the Pike County phonebook. Offering to bring more McCoys into the area for a weekend event was anything but noteworthy. While family reunions are a popular occurrence in Appalachia, to our knowledge, no one in Pike County had ever thought to host a McCoy reunion on the scale that we envisioned. Why two out-of-town cousins from Georgia and North Carolina would want to do such a thing was beyond comprehension.

With little regard for the idea in Pikeville-Pike County, organizing the reunion from afar became an insurmountable obstacle. In the days before social media, smart phones and texting, bridging the gap between Pike County, Georgia and North Carolina was made possible through phone calls, mail and email. Bo and I drafted countless letters and email messages to city and county officials and anyone else we could think of, introducing ourselves and outlining what we hoped to achieve. Bo called upon everyone he could think to reach out to, but to no avail. With email ignored, mail unopened and phone calls not returned, frustration on our end was mounting. The prospect of holding an event in Pikeville was proving more difficult than we had ever imagined.

Desperate for help, Bo and I decided to make a trip to Pikeville together to meet with Tourism Director Bruce Brown in May, 1999. Bo had contacted him and reading an Associated Press article about him that recently had been published. Bo expressed our support for his feud-preservation work, a notion that Mr. Brown found encouraging. He reciprocated the sentiment in earnest. As we moved forward with our plans for 2000, Mr. Brown became our front line of support in Pikeville-Pike County.

Bruce Bennett Brown was an erudite man of means, always well dressed, well read and well spoken. He was also a man of letters and had been active among Pike County's literary academia for years. He and Dr. Leonard Roberts established the Appalachian Studies Center at Pikeville College.[32] A poet in his own right, Mr. Brown served as the editor of *Twigs*, a noted literary magazine published by the school. He was active in local government, serving in a variety of roles over a period of nearly forty years.

Mr. Brown was patient with our inquiries and helpful, even though the reunion was not yet a "public" event. He was instrumental in connecting us with a group of key individuals who proved to be invaluable in organizing the reunion including Pikeville Mayor Frank Morris, City Manager Kenny Blackburn and Tourism Commission Director Walter "Doc" Fletcher. Later, Mr. Brown's successor, Phyllis Hunt would introduce us to additional sources of support including Pike County Judge Executive Karen Gibson, John Gatling and Marilynn Payson, both with the Judge-Executive's office, Dils Cemetery owner and Tourism Board Member Nancy Forsyth, historian and genealogist extraordinaire Betty Howard, local historians Ed and Connie Maddux, and Sherrie Marrs of Pikeville College.

Mr. Brown's successful efforts on our behalf quickly exposed the flaws in our own plans to make inroads in Pikeville. His introductions were a subtle education in the fine art of conducting business properly in Pike County. Pikeville-Pike County was (and is) a place built on relationships. Despite a reluctance on the part of some to welcome "outsiders," we soon discovered that a personal introduction from Mr. Brown validated us to the point that we were immediately embraced as extended members of the "family." Repeatedly, we found that an introduction, a cordial conversation and a handshake was all that was required to get things done.

Bo and I made more than a dozen trips to Pikeville between us, from the period of late 1998 until the reunion in 2000. Sometimes jointly, sometimes separately, we made the journey to eastern Kentucky often, knowing that a brief face-to-face meeting was infinitely more valuable than multiple phone calls and email. With few exceptions, our newfound acquaintances quickly became friends and supporters who worked tirelessly on behalf of the Hatfields-McCoys for years to come, usually without recognition, compensation or accolades.

I met Bo in person for the first time in early 1999. Until this visit, our relationship as cousins and as reunion organizers consisted entirely of email messages and phone calls. Over a period of months, we managed to plan the reunion as effectively as we could remotely. It was becoming increasingly apparent, however, that not only did we need to meet face to face, but we needed to take our reunion cause directly to the powers-that-be in Pike County.

Until shortly before this meeting, I did not even know what Bo looked like, not that it mattered much. Bo had broached the subject from time to time, although tentatively. We had talked on the phone many times and I found that my cousin was intelligent, affable, quick-witted and energetic. I sensed there was something else he wanted to talk about, though he seemed reluctant to do so.

Finally, we exchanged family pictures via email. In the pictures Bo sent of himself, he was dressed in a dark black suit, with a distinguished appearance that befitted his position as a pastor. I was struck by the remarkable physical similarities Bo shared with my Dad. He had the same distinctive McCoy traits of dark hair, dark eyes and large ears which are common to many family members.

Less important to me was the fact that Bo was a physically large man. Despite ongoing health challenges, Bo had lived a remarkable life, seemingly unhindered by any physical limitations. He attended Okefenokee Technical Institute where he studied computer and system administration before leaving school to pursue his higher calling. After graduating from Christ to the World Bible College in December 1989, he served as a missionary in Quebec, Canada, then as a counselor and teacher in Richmond, Indiana. He transferred to Evangel Christian University in Monroe, Louisiana where he received his degree in Theology. After serving as a missionary to Haiti, he returned to Waycross, Georgia where he worked as a Bible college administrator and pastor. In 1997, following six months of recovery from a serious illness, Bo discovered a new avocation for which he had an exceptional talent: website design.

Bo bought a plane ticket and flew to Raleigh-Durham airport, where I met him for the first time. In person, the family resemblance was even more striking. During that visit, Bo stayed at our home in Durham, as he would many times in the future. In the coming years, he and I would spend more time together than I imagine most third cousins ever do, certainly under more duress than either of us ever expected.

Bo and I are imperfect people, each with our fair share of personal fallibilities. For all our similarities, our operational styles are quite different. Bo was one who kicked in the front door, announced his presence, and then proceeded to cajole, entertain and persuade others by the sheer force of his personality. I, on the other hand, preferred to slip in quietly through the side door and mix into the crowd unnoticed. Bo was a "big idea" guy, a master of sales and marketing. I was a "nuts and bolts" man, an accountant, who sweated the details and worried about how to pay for it all. Early on, we recognized these differences and respected each other's strengths. When we performed within the limits of these attributes, we were stronger as a team than we were apart. It was only later, as the M2K event outgrew our capacity to manage it, that we got into trouble, as each of us was called upon to operate well outside the boundaries of our comfort levels.

It was Bo's idea for a small McCoy family reunion that gave birth to the modern resurgence of interest in the feud that has occurred in the past twenty years. However, the germ of the idea for a Hatfield-McCoy reunion came unexpectedly in the form of an off-handed query. It was a question that reset our plans and changed the course of feud history: "are the Hatfields invited?"

It was a simple question, offered at the conclusion of our very first interview on the subject of the reunion, asked by an Associated Press reporter, Kimberly Hefling. Hefling is currently the national education writer for the Associated Press in Washington, DC. When we met Hefling, she was in the second year of her assignment to the regional AP office in Pikeville, following her graduation from Kansas State University in 1997.

As a "not-for-profit cooperative of news organizations," the Associated Press employs "3,700 employees globally in more than 300 locations worldwide."[33] AP reporters are embedded in local offices, providing stories to the network which may be reprinted in newspapers throughout the world. A newsworthy article by the Associated Press can be picked up by any interested network member, be a small rural newspaper or a major urban one. It was the Associated Press media network that would soon carry the news of a Hatfield-McCoy reunion to the world.

Hefling was an adept reporter, whose work had come to our attention indirectly. In early April 1999, Hefling had written an article detailing Pike County's feud-site preservation efforts led by Tourism Director, Bruce Brown. A copy of the newspaper article was mailed to Bo by a website list-member who thought he might be interested in the work being done in Pike County. The feud site project, funded by $25,000 from the county with an additional $100,000 grant from Kentucky included the development of six additional sites in Pike County. The investment of public monies in feud-preservation was not without its detractors. In his response to the cynics, Brown was unapologetic. "It's like coal; it's messy, it's black, it's here. The Hatfield-McCoy feud is part of our history."[34]

As much as Bo was inspired by Mr. Brown's work, he was equally impressed by the balanced and positive tone of Hefling's article. Never one to shy away from an opportunity, Bo suggested that we reach out to Ms. Hefling with our idea for a McCoy reunion. After a word of introduction from Mr. Brown, Bo made a preliminary phone call to Ms. Hefling to thank her for her article on the Pike County preservation efforts and to pitch our idea for a reunion.

Hefling was kind enough not to scoff at our idea. When she agreed to meet with us the next time we were in town, we were delighted. Neither of us had ever given a press interview and it was our first for the reunion. Since we were still earnestly vying for acceptance into the Pike County community, it made sense to sit down with a reporter for what we incorrectly assumed was a local newspaper article.

In April 1999, Bo and I embarked on yet another planning excursion to meet with Tourism and other local parties in hopes of soliciting support for our affair. Kim Hefling met us at the tourism office to discuss our plans. I felt ill-prepared for the interview, although Bo seemed comfortable, relaxed and unfazed by the questioning. Ms. Hefling was patient with my incomplete answers to her well thought out questions. She was genuinely respectful to us and thoughtful enough to overlook our naiveté. After about 30 minutes, Hefling indicated that she had enough to put together an article and began to gather up her notes. As she began to leave, she hesitated for a moment as if to consider one final question, one I now suspect she had always intended to ask. With a gleam in her eyes, she turned to Bo and asked, "*Are the Hatfields invited?*" There was a long silence. Neither of us had ever expected the question. After a moment that seemed frozen in time, Bo responded nonchalantly and with no apparent reservation, "Of course, they're invited." His answer surprised me. It was the sound of history being made.

Ms. Hefling smiled knowingly, as if she understood fully the nature of the genie she had released from the bottle. "A McCoy reunion is great. But if you invite the Hatfields, then you've got something," she added. Bo glanced at me with an incredulous look in his eyes as the reality of his answer settled over him. I smiled back. I had no problem with inviting the Hatfields. I was not sure that either of us honestly expected they would be interested in attending. Almost as an afterthought, Hefling asked as she made her exit, "If the Hatfields do come, what will you do?" For want of an answer, I shrugged and said, "I don't know. Maybe we can play softball or something…"

Following our meeting with Ms. Hefling, Bo and I were decidedly anxious. Nearly six months after my first visit to Pikeville, we continued our struggle to gain traction with our reunion plans. Disappointed by how little interest there seemed to be for our idea, we hoped that Hefling's article might help to generate some much-needed local support.

A few days after returning home to North Carolina, Ms. Hefling called to inform me that her article was ready to go to press and that it was necessary to have a picture to accompany it. Bo had deferred and volunteered me for the photo opportunity. The print deadline was looming, so it was necessary to get the picture done as quickly as possible.

An Associated Press photographer from Raleigh, NC met my family that afternoon at the Woodlawn Memorial Park in Durham, NC. As the final resting place of my grandparents and father, the cemetery was an appropriate choice for the picture. Given that my grandfather was the inspiration for both my personal exploration of the past and my involvement in the reunion itself, staging the picture at his grave marker was my way of paying tribute to him. I could not have predicted the effect the picture would have. With the inclusion of the photograph in Hefling's article, I would soon find myself the "face" of the Hatfield-McCoy reunion around the world.

Graves of my grandparents & father at Woodlawn Memorial

On May 9, 1999, Kim Hefling's Associated Press article broke the news of the upcoming first-ever national reunion of Hatfield and McCoy families to the world. The "local" article we expected appeared in five hundred hometown newspapers across the country including the front page of my own, the *Durham Herald-Sun*. The story was carried by most major domestic newspapers from New York to Atlanta to Los Angeles. It was also picked up by the international wire and appeared in newspapers in Great Britain, Canada and Australia.

The die was cast. Our idea for a modest McCoy family reunion, a conceit that elicited little more than tepid interest even among family members, had been replaced by the far grander concept of a Hatfield-

McCoy reunion. Seemingly overnight, Hefling's article awakened dormant media interest in the families that would inundate us in the months to come. Soon, Bo, I, and others would be called upon to represent the Hatfield-McCoy clans in the modern age, setting the stage for renewed interest in the feud and a new era of unity between the families. It was a challenge for which we were not entirely prepared.

Momentum

"Disregard for the past will never do us any good.
Without it we cannot know truly who we are."
Syd Moore

As the announcement of a Hatfield-McCoy reunion began circulating in the media, Bo and I were faced with a new and sometimes arduous predicament. News of our plans spread quickly, creating and perpetuating the demand for still more information on the subject. The media's appetite for the "Hatfields and McCoys" was all encompassing. We quickly found ourselves overrun by ever-increasing constraints on our time and resources. The *real-mccoys.com* website experienced a seismic shift in the number of visitors to the site; ultimately exceeding 100,000 – no small sum for a non-retail website in 1999. We began fielding email inquiries daily from members of both families wanting to learn more. Community leaders and public officials in Kentucky and West Virginia began calling for us to meet with them. We quickly realized that the decision to invite the Hatfields had transformed our little family reunion into a major event that was gaining notice.

The "Reunion of the Millennium" still lacked two key ingredients necessary to make the event a success, however – funds and manpower. The twenty-three months leading up to the reunion were a frantic search for both. The financial burden for planning the event up to this point had been borne entirely by Bo and me. The costs of multiple trips to Pike County were exacting a toll on the financial stability of both of our households. As the event continued to grow in stature, so did its mounting fiscal requirements. From a purely financial perspective, M2K and the reunions that followed were a losing proposition from which we never fully recovered.

Even before our family reunion had evolved to include the Hatfields, we realized the need for additional help. In an August 28, 1998 GenForum entry, Bo posted an open invitation to anyone interested in "a staff position on our planning committee" for a McCoy family reunion. The man who most selflessly volunteered for anything we needed him to do was Billy Jack McCoy of Florence, Wisconsin. Billy Jack, a descendant of "Squirrel-Huntin" Sam McCoy, became the true unsung hero of the "Reunion of the Millennium." He was the first person to believe in the concept of a national McCoy

Billy Jack at the McCoy house in Pikeville

reunion and the first to respond to the call for help. He was the third-leg of our organizational tripod. A twenty-four year old truck driver whose route ran coast to coast, Billy Jack was one of the most diversely talented men I have ever met. He was an avid ham radio operator who built his own set and installed his own radio tower. Once, he became interested in the process of distillation and constructed his own home still. He built his own fiberglass surfboards and braved the icy waters of Lake Superior in the winter to fresh-water surf when the swells were strongest.

Even as press coverage fanned interest in the reunion, the greatest obstacle we faced with organizing the event was getting the word out. Though we could reach many family members through online postings and the website, we knew this appeal was limited to a younger demographic. After Bo purchased a national database of more than 100,000 household addresses with Hatfield and McCoy surnames, we were certain there were more family members than we could ever hope to reach. We selected names at random from the list and mailed informational postcards to them, primarily targeting areas that were geographically within the vicinity of Kentucky.

Our mailing campaign was futile and ineffective, but the database we purchased proved to be useful in another way. Many of the entries in the database included email addresses which opened the door to a more dubious marketing tactic. Reaching 100,000 households by email was a time-intensive and nearly impossible task. It was just the kind of challenge that piqued Billy Jack's interest. Long before it became a common and illegal practice, email "spam" was an essential part of our M2K advertising plan. We drafted a one-page document about the reunion, complete with an apologetic mea-culpa for the intrusion at the bottom of the page. With a laptop mounted on his truck dashboard, Billy Jack operated a mobile marketing unit that emailed family members across the country. Billy Jack single-handedly reached thousands of Hatfield and McCoy family members, many of whom attended the reunion because of his efforts.

A full year before the M2K reunion, media interest in the event had begun to build up steam. One of the first national outlets to contact us was Court TV (now TruTV), one of the many cable outlets owned by Turner Broadcasting. They were polite but insistent on getting our story. Outside of covering the legal aspects of feud history, I was not sure what interest they might have in the reunion. We agreed to do the story, however, as we did with most requests, because we were not in a position to be discriminating. Ironically, years later, Court TV was one of the few networks not to cover the legal proceedings when we went to court in 2003.

Our first television appearance for the reunion took place on WRAL, a CBS television affiliate in Raleigh, NC. Several stations in North Carolina expressed interest in the story, given my local connection to it. This opportunity was not unique to me, however. As news of the reunion spread across the country, many local media outlets conducted interviews with descendants and potential attendees, culminating in a diverse stream of media coverage that only served to heighten interest in the event.

The reporter for the WRAL piece was a man of some reputation in the central North Carolina market, for his twenty years of reporting assignments as well as for his over-the-top personality and on-air antics. Mark Roberts was a rapid-fire bundle of energy, one of those rare talents whose public persona was the same as his private one. He was excited about the reunion story and eager to be the first reporter to cover it. When I mentioned that Bo and I were headed to Kentucky to meet Billy Jack for a scheduled press conference with Pikeville Mayor Frank Morris, Mark asked to come along.

On the morning of June 17, 1999 Mark and his videographer, Jim Young followed behind us for the drive to Pikeville. Mark called us numerous times along the way, peppering us with endless questions about the feud and the reunion. Over the course of three days, whether meeting for an early hotel breakfast or scampering up a flight of steps to view a cemetery, Mark never yielded in his pace or his enthusiasm for what he dubbed the "fierce family devotion that fueled the feud."[35]

Friday, June 18, 1999 was a day of firsts for those of us on the M2K planning committee. For Billy Jack, Bo and I, it was our first press conference, a joint announcement about the reunion with Mayor Frank Morris, held in the Pikeville City Park. On his first visit to the park in the heart of Pikeville, Bo took a few moments to himself to take it all in. "I just closed my eyes and talked to my grandfather, if you can do that, and just told him, *this one's for you.*"[36]

The three McCoy boys arrived for their meeting with Mayor Morris dressed for the occasion, although Bo and Billy Jack were smart enough not to wear their dress jackets in the sweltering Pike County humidity. Mayor Morris was friendly and accommodating. "Things have changed, and people want to know about (the feud). They are proud to be a Hatfield and proud to be a McCoy and we're proud to be hosting the reunion," he said.[37] Following the brief formal announcement, Mark Roberts conducted his interviews on the spot. As with most media interviews, there was no advance notice given to us about the questions to be asked, nor any opportunity to script a response. All our answers were spontaneous and off-the-cuff, a style that suited Bo well. Mark's causal but energetic approach prompted an atmosphere of good-natured fun. The approach worked so well that we tried to emulate it in all our successive interviews, particularly with reporters who were taking the matter of the Hatfields and McCoys far too seriously.

Bo was the first to lead off. "Even though we're laughing, you can feel an undertone, obviously…there still needs to be a national event to put this to bed and there hasn't been one, so there will be," he said. I responded with a statement on the inseparability of the families; one that I would repeat many times in the days to follow. "It's a common heritage; you can't have one without the other. You always hear "Hatfields and McCoys" as one phrase. The families, basically, over the decades are one. We're joined forever," I said. [38]

The ever-resourceful Roberts was even able to arrange a joint interaction of McCoys and Hatfields for the camera. For my first encounter with a Hatfield descendent, Mark introduced me to a man he had met in the city park. Paul Pruitt was an 82-year-old Hatfield descendant married to a McCoy for 64 years. "You don't hold any ill will against any McCoys?" Mark asked Mr. Pruitt. "Not a bit, said Mr. Pruitt, rubbing his face, mocking the facial hair we three McCoy boys were sporting. If they'd (just) shave them homes for disabled crabs…"[39]

June 18th was also the date of Bo's first visit to Dils Cemetery. Bruce Brown spent the afternoon personally guiding us on a tour of feud sites, beginning with Dils. Following the press conference in the park, Bo, Billy Jack and I made a quick change into blue jeans and matching white *real-mccoys.com* t-shirts and black M2K ball caps that we had made. The caps were the first items in a long line of M2K products.

When I mentioned that I had been unable to locate Sam and Martha McCoy's headstones on prior visits, Mr. Brown was kind enough to direct me to them. Kneeling at the graveside of my grandfather's grandparents was an emotional moment for me. "To actually be here and walk the same hills that they walked and be on the same ground that they lived on is quite something," I told Mark.[40]

Bo's visit was even more compelling. The climb up the wooden steps to the cemetery was difficult and steep. For those dealing with health issues, it was a seemingly insurmountable obstacle, and one that on previous trips to Pikeville, Bo had allowed to dissuade him from visiting the cemetery. On this day, however, Bo was determined to pay his respects. When Bo reached the summit of the climb and saw the graves of Randolph and Sarah McCoy for the first time, his emotions overwhelmed him. For a man of many words, he had few. "It's hard to talk. Pretty hard to talk," he said through the tears. "I've been listening to the legends all my life ... and now I guess it's real."[41]

The balance of the day was spent on a whirlwind tour of feud sites including an unusual stop at the one site deemed off limits: the McCoy Cemetery in Hardy, Kentucky. It was our first visit to the site. Robert's cogent appeal, coupled with yet another of Mr. Brown's introductions, was enough to win the approval of the cemetery property owner, John Vance. Roberts even persuaded the recalcitrant Mr. Vance to make a rare on-camera appearance for an interview. The gracious reception we received that day gave us no indications that just four years later, Bo and I would be facing Mr. Vance in court.

With the whirlwind tour of Pike County complete, Roberts and Young packed up and headed back to Raleigh. Back in Pikeville, the McCoy boys collapsed in our shared hotel room, dazed yet satisfied with how the day had gone. It was our first true exposure to the intense interest the media would show for the reunion, our families and the feud in the months to follow. It was also the first time the trio of Billy Jack, Bo and I had spent an entire weekend together working on the reunion. Billy Jack was an engaging personality with an understated sense of humor, yet equally passionate about his commitment to the family. That night, we discovered that Billy Jack had taken his devotion to the cause to an extreme level. At bedtime, he unveiled his one-of-a-kind custom-made reunion underwear, complete with an M2K emblem on the backside.

Even as we scrambled to organize activities for a Hatfield-McCoy reunion, the event was already beginning to take on a life of its own. Mr. Brown sent me an email stating that the Tourism Commission hoped to vote on formal approval of our reunion, effectively adopting it as an "official" event. In July 1999, Bruce Brown sent us a letter on behalf of Chairman Walter "Doc" Fletcher and the Commission. "The Pike County tourism office wishes to acknowledge the proposed McCoy reunion in Pikeville...we are working closely with the Chamber of Commerce, the Main Street Program, Pike County Fiscal Court and city government to make this a memorable annual event here in Pike County and Pikeville." It was a great leap of faith on Mr. Brown's part. Even though we had yet to hold our first event, he had persuaded the Commission to support our efforts in 2000 and suggested that the event should be recurring *annually*.

Given the media attention the reunion was generating, it was perhaps inevitable that it would evolve into something larger. By August 1999, however, there still was no consideration given to a public festival. Tentative activities planned for the joint-family reunion in Pikeville included an artisans' exhibit in the city park, guided feud site van tours, lectures by feud authors, a charity auction to raise funds for a Randolph McCoy statue and a prayer breakfast on Sunday morning.

My off-the-cuff comment to Kim Hefling about a softball game between the families had sparked a good deal of interest. Everyone, press and family alike, was eager to see the families square off in what we hoped would be a good-natured affair. The Bob Amos Park with its scenic overlook of the Pikeville Cut-Through, picnic shelters and ample parking made it an ideal location for an open-air family picnic. The YMCA facilities there included a play area for children as well as a softball field suitable for a Hatfield-McCoy showdown.

On August 25, 1999, we received a letter from Pikeville City Manager Kenny Blackburn, offering the city's support. "The Pikeville City Commission considers it both an honor and a privilege that the descendants of Randolph McCoy have chosen to hold their family reunion in Pikeville, Kentucky. The activities you have planned are sure to entice a good number of your kinsmen and we certainly appreciate your family's generosity to share your celebration with the residents of our community." The city kindly granted us permission to use the resources of both the Pikeville City Park and the Bob Amos Park for the reunion.

On November 23, 1999, Marilynn Payson, representing the Pike County Judge Executive's office sent us an email offering to lend her office's support: "I have read about your "Reunion of the Millennium" and I am really impressed. Pike County wants to support your initiative and to do our part to help you make it a world-class event." Our family reunion now enjoyed the support of the Tourism Commission, the City of Pikeville and Pike County itself. The wheels of momentum were beginning to turn.

In November 1999, Bo and I were in Pikeville once again to meet with Bruce Brown and Mayor Frank Morris. It was in this meeting that we were encouraged to make the reunion a public festival, along the lines of "Hillbilly Days." Mr. Morris said the City of Pikeville voted to sanction the festival as an official city event and would close its downtown area to accommodate an open-air free-to-the-public celebration, complete with vendors, rides and attractions.

Bo and I were encouraged by the offer. Collaborating with the city allowed us to promote our reunion locally with access to dearly needed resources and manpower. In spite of the national and international media coverage, we had not even begun to advertise the reunion on a local and regional level. With the city's help, we hoped to have advertising inserts enclosed in Sunday editions of the *Appalachian News-Express* as well as billboards and signage on the main roads into town. Sanctioning us as an "official" festival allowed Mr. Brown to print up brochures for distribution locally and to appeal for additional help at the state level. Mr. Brown consented to let us use the tourism office for the registration of vendors and for sales of tickets for our feud site tours and M2K dinner.

The evolution of the event into a festival placed us in yet another unexpected dilemma. While we felt we had a basic understanding of what a family reunion was and even what a joint-family reunion might be, we certainly were not prepared for the advent of a *festival*. We were not even sure what to call it. Was it a reunion or a festival or both? Bo took to calling it a "Reunion Festival," a phrase that is now used commonly to define local events from Idaho to Pennsylvania. Our "McCoy (M2K) Reunion" begat the "Hatfield-McCoy Reunion," which begat the "Hatfield McCoy Reunion Festival." With just seven months to go before the reunion, the task before us was now far greater than we dared admit to ourselves.

M2K

> "Call it a clan, call it a network, call it a tribe, call it a family. Whatever you call it, whoever you are, you need one."
> Jane Howard

The notion of a Hatfield-McCoy reunion was an oxymoron. Before 2000, it seemed like an unlikely, even undesirable, possibility. It was only as we became hopelessly immersed in the planning of the event that we began to consider its potential ramifications. While the reunion was originally intended to be little more than a weekend of fun interaction between the families, we slowly began to realize that a reunion of the Hatfield and McCoys families represented something more.

The 2000 reunion was a deliberate attempt to demonstrate what most family members already knew to be true. The Hatfield and McCoy families were at peace with each other. Most held no ill-will towards the opposing family simply because they did not know they were supposed to harbor any. With the healing passage of time, coupled with the fact many members had moved away from the Tug Valley region generations before, few knew true antagonism towards the "other" family.

Still, there was a degree of trepidation on the part of some leading into the event. Despite our best intentions, the outcome of the largest gathering together of feud descendants was uncertain. "We're trusting everyone to be adult about it and not allow themselves to be drawn into the animosity (of the past), but to look to the future. That's our slogan, 'a new history for an old legend,'" said Bo.[42] In an interview for *Successful Meetings*, the first magazine to carry a story on the reunion, Bruce Brown said, "There's no animosity anymore. I think they'll make friends."[43]

A reunion of the Hatfields and McCoys meant that the families had to take a hard look at their shared histories. "It's a bloody past, but we're embracing it. We can't change the past…life goes on," said Bo.[44] Coming to terms with a history as violent as the feud meant accepting it on a deeply personal level, forgiving those who had committed such acts against our family in the past, and seeking the forgiveness of those to whom our family had inflicted much harm. In so doing, those family members who welcomed the chance to reconcile with a mutually shared past wrote a new chapter into feud history, one that forever changed the way the world viewed the Hatfields and McCoys.

Even before Pikeville and Pike County stepped up to partner with us, officials on the other side of the Tug Fork were taking notice of our plans. Two weeks prior to the announcement of the "Reunion Festival" in Pikeville, Bo and I met with West Virginia State Tourism Commissioner Robert Reintsema and his staff in Williamson, West Virginia. The Hatfield-McCoy Trails project, an all-terrain vehicle trails system, was set to open in October 2000. West Virginia wanted to capitalize on the upcoming reunion to promote the development of the trails and related tourism projects. Local parties in Williamson and nearby Matewan were interested in organizing events in their area, timed to complement those we had scheduled in Pikeville. We were encouraged that West Virginia was interested in our reunion and saw no harm in having additional events happening throughout the region. We welcomed anyone who wanted to participate, no matter what side of the river they lived on. Organizing local festival activities was mutually beneficial to the overall economic welfare of the area. Our only request was that local agencies should work together to coordinate schedules to maximize the opportunities for tourists and family members in attendance.

At the behest of the Pike County Judge-Executive's office, we were invited to a similar meeting with Ann Latta, Secretary of Kentucky Tourism Development in January 2000. The first woman to be elected Mayor of Prestonsburg, KY, Ann Latta was appointed to her Tourism post by Governor Paul Patton in 1995, a role she served in for eight years.[45] My first visit to the state capital was one that I remember well, though for reasons unrelated to the reunion.

Bo and I met in Pikeville on the Sunday before the meeting as scheduling conflicts dictated that we drive separately. Early on Monday morning, Marilynn Payson arrived to pick us up at our hotel. She had volunteered to drive us in her personal vehicle to the meeting that was three hours away in Frankfort.

The weather forecast that day included the possibility of light snow for the area, perhaps two to three inches, which was common for eastern Kentucky. More unlikely, however, was the forecast for the potential of a dusting or light accumulation of snow back home in the Raleigh-Durham area, a region generally unaccustomed to snow. There was nothing in the forecast that threatened the trip to Frankfort or my return trip home the next day.

The drive to Frankfort was uneventful and the meeting with the Secretary went well. Ms. Latta seemed genuinely interested in our plans for the Reunion Festival. She recognized the potential for the reunion to foster increased tourism interest in the area. Ms. Latta's endorsement freed up much-needed resources to promote the reunion at the state level including the printing of brochures and other promotional literature to be distributed through the Commonwealth's network of tourism offices and highway rest stops.

By the early afternoon lunch break, snow had begun to fall in Frankfort. I checked my voicemail to discover several phone calls from home, saying that it had begun to snow there as well. We met with the Secretary until about three o'clock in the afternoon, then settled in for the drive back to Pikeville. By the time Bo and I got back to our motel room that evening, I was surprised to discover additional voice mails from home, each increasingly more frantic than the previous one. I called home to learn that several inches of snow had already fallen in Durham. Weather forecasters had revised their forecasts upwards to say that central North Carolina was to receive between six to eight inches of snow, ensuring a more difficult and treacherous drive home. Weather conditions were deteriorating rapidly with each passing minute, so I made the decision to pack up and make the six-hour drive through the mountains that night.

Driving through the darkness with blowing snow becoming denser and more impenetrable, I inched my way through Kentucky, then Virginia and finally into North Carolina. Surprisingly, the weather seemed to be getting worse the closer I got to home. Thick snow was piling up on the interstate and I knew that if I stopped for any reason, it was unlikely that my mini-van would ever regain traction.

In the wee hours of the morning, I plowed the van into a snowdrift that was once my driveway, relieved and grateful to have made it home alive. By daylight, 20.3 inches of snow had fallen in Durham, setting the record for the largest 24-hour snowfall ever recorded there. North Carolina Governor Jim Hunt declared a state of emergency and dispatched the National Guard to help with recovery efforts.[46] Although Secretary Latta's endorsement was a welcome show of support for our reunion efforts, the memory of the long, perilous trip home is one I will not soon forget.

Someone once said that "Appalachia" is just an old Indian word for "hillbilly." As Hatfields and McCoys, we are accustomed to the exaggerated depiction of a poor, uneducated mountaineer in a straw hat and bib overalls, smoking a corncob pipe and brandishing a jug of moonshine in one hand while cradling a shotgun in the other. One cannot spend any length of time in Appalachia, however, without understanding the truly detrimental effects the epithet has had on the region and the people who live there. Living with the derogatory connotations of the word has created a true aversion to its use.

The relationship between the Hatfields and McCoys and the term "hillbilly" dates to the earliest days of the feud. Though some etymologists have sought to link the word's origin with the Celtic people in the hills of Scotland, the term came to be associated with the people of Appalachia because of the "yellow journalism" coverage of the feud story. Reporters visiting the area from the great northern cities of the country invented the caricature of the "hillbilly" as a means of describing a mountain culture they did not understand.

Outside the region, even among Hatfield and McCoy family members, "hillbilly" is used in jest among those who share an affinity with their mountain heritage. In as much as we are proud to be Hatfields and McCoys, we are also proud to be mountain-folk. Bo even joked at our M2K Reunion dinner in 2000, "there is nothing wrong with being a hillbilly. I know 'cuz I 'r one."

In Appalachia, the term represents a stereotype that the upstanding people of the region have worked hard to overcome. The progressive City of Pikeville with its state-the-art hospital, university, technical schools and training centers is a model for the area's diversification and modernization. "Pikeville is an example of a new Appalachia painstakingly transforming itself from the old days of poverty," said Mike Kiernan, spokesman for the Appalachian Regional Commission.[47] Therefore, it is curious that the town is the host site of the annual "Hillbilly Days" festival, the single, largest public display of the hillbilly-stereotype in the world.

The annual event, begun in 1977 by two Pikeville Shriners, is a benefit fundraiser for the Shriners Children's Hospital. Millions of dollars have been raised over the years as thousands of visitors crowd into the city each year for the three-day event in April. The festival features crafts and music, carnival rides and games and plenty of food and beverage. The festival concludes on Saturday as Shriners dressed in full "Hillbilly" regalia take to the streets in a parade of garishly decorated "hillbilly limousines."

While none can argue with the event's altruistic success, rationalizing its promotion of the stereotype is more difficult. "It's a little paradoxical, but when you can laugh at yourself, that's a healthy sign that you can acknowledge a part of your heritage and be comfortable with it," said Governor Paul Patton. Sandy Runyon, director of the Area Development District said, "We walk a fine line between being very proud of our heritage and trying to dispel the typical idea the rest of the world has….A lot of people would rather not remember the past, but it gave us a heritage to be proud of."[48] Coming to terms with a Hatfield-McCoy feud heritage, however, remains another matter.

As we planned the Reunion Festival, we always did so in the shadow of "Hillbilly Days." No matter one's opinion of it, "Hillbilly Days" was a wonder to behold. Billy Jack was the first to attend in 1999 and Bo and I followed his lead in 2000. Participating in the event was an excellent opportunity to learn more about how a festival was conducted and to hand out flyers and brochures promoting our own.

The spectacle that is the annual Shriner's "Hillbilly Days" left an impression that was equally mesmerizing and mystifying. The sheer volume of people crammed into the city left available hotels at capacity. Winnebagos and RVs lined the side of the roads, as far as one could see. More than 300 vendors, rides and games operated in every available space in town as artisans crowded together in the city park. Shriners in full "hillbilly" gear paraded through the streets, reveling in food, drink and music. It was an Appalachian version of "Mardi Gras."

The "Hillbilly Days" event left me with an uneasy feeling in the pit of my stomach. If the size and scope of "Hillbilly Days" was the barometer by which we were to be measured, we were doomed to failure. Our event was going to be considerably smaller in scope and attendance. Beyond that, Bo and I were certain that "Hillbilly Days" represented the antipathy of what we hoped to achieve. We wanted our Reunion Festival to be a celebration of our Appalachian heritage, embracing the commonalities between our families visiting from the outside and those who still lived in the area. By no means did we intend to make fun of our kin or to enjoy ourselves at their expense. The Hatfields and McCoys are proud of our heritage – and none of us are toothless, ignorant hillbillies.

As plans for the festival grew, so did the demands on our non-existent budget. Expenses for website hosting, database purchases, office supplies, mailing costs and phone bills were paid by us out of pocket. One month, Bo's phone bill for long distance calls alone was $650.00. With our embrace of the time-honored way of doing business in Pike County, Bo, Billy Jack and I made multiple trips to Kentucky for face-to-face meetings, usually of our own financial accord. Travel expenses and vehicle maintenance costs soon took their toll on our already tenuous finances.

The Days Inn of Pikeville was the first venue to step up to help defer our travel costs. Debby Smith, manager of the hotel, always made sure that we had a place to stay whenever we came to town. The tourism office and the Judge Executive's office helped as well, more times than I can adequately quantify. We were their guests on numerous visits to Pikeville and they never failed to take care of us like family.

Given the effort required to make the trek to Pikeville, we viewed each trip as a limited opportunity to get as much work done as possible.

Often, business was conducted while dining with local officials, area event organizers, sponsors or individuals who wanted to meet with us while we were in town. As such, the costs of traveling to Pike County were offset somewhat by our hosts picking up meals. Even when we offered to pay the bill, we were refused by kind and stubborn Appalachian hospitality. Having to pay for a meal happened so infrequently that we began to *assume* that someone else was picking up the tab. However, since the matter was rarely discussed in polite conversation, there were times when we did not know for sure if a meal was going to be paid for.

In the event of such instances of uncertainty, Bo and I developed a non-verbal communications tool, a subtle pantomime that I coined the "McCoy Maneuver." The purpose of the maneuver was not for us to get out of paying the bill, but rather, it was our way of giving our host the chance to pick up the tab if that was his intention. The key to the success of the maneuver was to project a casual sincerity that we were prepared to pay the bill. If the maneuver was overplayed, it seemed disingenuousness. If it was underplayed, we stood the chance of being taken up on the offer to pay for the meal, no small matter to a couple of hungry McCoy boys with little money and worn-out credit cards in their pockets.

Executing the maneuver successfully was all in the timing. When the server brought the bill to the table, Bo and I would shift in our seats slightly, reaching for the ticket and our wallets simultaneously while rising from our chairs as if to stand. The maneuver invariably resulted in our host waving us down, grabbing the check and insisting that the meal was on them. To date, the "McCoy Maneuver" has a 100 percent success rate.

The "Hatfield McCoy Reunion Festival" in 2000 has the distinction of being a public event that developed exactly backwards. While all successful neighborhood festivals build upwards from a foundation of local political and financial support, the "Reunion of the Millennium" began in reverse, with those of us from the outside bringing in an event to the area in hopes of growing local roots. It was a recipe for failure.

One factor that hindered the ultimate success of the festival on a regional level was the divisive splintering of the limited resources available among the local parties that became involved. As word of the festival spread throughout the area, many saw an opportunity to schedule their own events to coincide with ours. Some partnered with us in a symbiotic relationship that served everyone well. Others were less concerned with cooperation, however, planning redundant and sometimes competing events with little regards to what was already scheduled.

Connecting with the local citizens of Pike County was one of the greatest obstacles we faced with organizing the M2K event. Bo jumped at nearly every request he received to speak to local organizations. Marilynn Payson came through with a list of invitations in an email outlining Bo's ambitious itinerary for a January 24-February 5, 2000 visit. Speaking opportunities included the "Pike County Fiscal Court, Big Sandy Area Development District, Rotary Club, Kiwanis, Women's Club, Historic Stone Community, Highway 23 Arts program and local talk shows."

Our appeal for financial sponsorship at all levels, local and otherwise, was less fruitful. Although Tourism was to begin airing public service announcements on local radio stations in the four weeks leading up to the event, additional local advertising was notably lacking. We drafted an ad we hoped to place in local area newspapers, but lacked the resources to pay to run it. I sent a concerned email to Bo. "Our folks are traveling from all over the country to meet their local friends and relations in Pike County. Given that the eyes of the national press will be upon us, we certainly want to ensure that local Kentucky hospitality is clearly on display." Soon after, an exasperated Bo replied with his sense of humor intact. "In the event that we are unable to procure financial assistance from the powers that be, I plan to run naked through Pikeville with the ad taped to my butt. Since space will not be a problem, I plan to "run" a full-page ad, no charge. Once convicted, I assure you that I will make sure that many prison inmates have the opportunity to see said advertisement. I trust this will fulfill your needs."

I sent a more desperate appeal to Secretary Latta's office on May 1, 2000. Citing our inability "to reach the eastern Kentucky area with adequate media i.e. a newspaper advertisement," I implored the Secretary to sponsor an ad in the *Appalachian News-Express*, the Pike County newspaper. "Our counterpart in West Virginia is very well funded and it has made our job somewhat difficult to keep the balance from shifting to West Virginia." It was true. For our M2K event, Bo created a trifold brochure that we printed on plain paper from our home computers. Williamson and Matewan, with the backing of the West Virginia Tourism office, printed two full color brochures, one was ten pages long and unfolded into a map. Thankfully, Secretary Latta's office came through for us, funding a half-page ad that ran for four weeks.

Despite accusations that were leveled at us, our motivation for wanting to host a reunion was never financial. Prior to the event, our total costs for the reunion were estimated at $18,635. The final tab for the event was $24,138, not counting ancillary expenses. Despite a respectable tally of 450 Friday night banquet tickets sold and brisk retail sales of reunion merchandise, the M2K reunion event resulted in a $10,000 loss.

Our intention was always to keep the event as affordable as possible for our family members. We knew that the trip to Pike County would be a sizeable expense for most of our families attending the event. Our true reason for keeping costs down was less altruistic, however.

Unlike our more charitable Hatfield counterparts, as good Scotsmen, the McCoys are notoriously tight with a penny. Not only was it imperative that we make the reunion an event not to be missed, we had to make certain that the price of tickets was reasonable by McCoy standards. We were wary enough about the potential lack of attendance. We certainly did not want the price of a ticket to keep anyone away.

We planned to kick off the Reunion Festival weekend with a gala M2K dinner on Friday night at the Landmark Inn. Fees for the banquet included rental of the Mark II meeting facility and the costs of catering and entertainment. Bo and I fretted over the price of the M2K dinner for months, although there was little that could be done to lessen costs. Adult tickets were set at $25 per person, a substantial price for a meal in 2000. We decided that the alternative to decreasing the price of the meal ticket was to increase the value it provided. Since there were no further required costs to attend the reunion, the ticket to the M2K dinner became part of the general registration price, which included a welcome packet with brochures and maps courtesy of Tourism, a custom lanyard and all the free "goodies" we could muster for our guests. Our guided van tours to feud sites and vendor booths were ticketed, but most Reunion Festival events were free and open to the public. Outside of the cost of travel, room and board, one could attend the first-ever historic national reunion of the Hatfields and McCoys for just $25, not a bad deal even for the McCoys.

Tickets for the M2K banquet were offered for presale through the *real-mccoys.com* website. Tickets were also available through the offices of Pikeville-Pike County Tourism. With a self-imposed deadline to provide the Landmark Inn a headcount for our dinner by March 1, we found that ticket sales were slow. It was no small wonder we were sweating the $25 per person cost. Lethargic ticket sales, however, prompted us to pursue a more creative form of capitalism.

Merchandising the "Hatfield-McCoy" brand was a foregone conclusion. The brand has been used liberally by others over the years to promote everything from dinner theaters to whiskey. During the 2000 event, Bo once casually mentioned to a reporter, "you could slap 'Hatfield-McCoy' on a bottle of water and sell it." It was a remark we saw borne out during the 2001 reunion when we came across "Hatfield-McCoy" water for sale in Matewan, WV. It made sense to us that we should offer "Hatfield-McCoy" merchandise to loosen pent-up revenue streams.

For 2000, we offered a variety of "official" reunion products including softball jerseys, bumper stickers, key chains and pens for sale. T-shirts and hats were color-coded to delineate the families: Hatfield-specific products were red while McCoys wore blue.

While Bo's salesmanship was without question, one product was a cause of real concern for me. Bo had a commemorative coin minted for the reunion. The bronze coins featured an engraving of "Ol' Randall" and "Devil Anse" together on the face with an inscription declaring the unity of the families on the back. Despite the hefty cost of production, the 5000 coins, retailing for $5 each, sold quickly and were one of our most popular items.

More worrisome to me, however, was Bo's idea to have 100 coins minted in silver. The coins were a numbered series with the retail price increasing as the numbers decreased. A select few were held to be auctioned on the night of the M2K dinner. Given the high retail price for the silver coins, online sales were non-existent. I was certain that our venture into high-end merchandising would prove to be an expensive debacle. On the night of the M2K dinner, however, I was happily proven wrong as family members sparred playfully during the auction for possession of the coins. By the end of the night, all the silver coins had been sold and the bronze coins were sold out the next day. Regrettably, in the rush to meet the demand from family members for the coins, I failed to keep one for myself.

Bo and I decided in early 2000 to form an M2K corporation to cover any potential legal liabilities we might incur as part of the reunion. Since our event was taking place primarily in Kentucky, we decided to incorporate there. The person recommended to us by the tourism office to help was Larry Webster. Larry was an established bluegrass musician in the area and he and his "Mule Band" had been an active part of "Hillbilly Days" for many years. Once the Reunion Festival was in place, Tourism asked him to head up the music stage at the city park for our event as well.

In his alternate persona as "Red Dog," Larry was a popular op-ed columnist for the *Appalachian News-Express*. He was also an attorney of considerable reputation in town, noted for his defense of the "little guy." Bo contacted Webster, and Larry filed for the incorporation of "McCoys 2000" (M2K) on our behalf.

The corporation remained in existence until 2002 when it was dissolved for failure to file required annual reports. In 2003, we found ourselves on the opposing side of Webster's legal acumen. As Bo and I began legal proceedings over access to the McCoy Cemetery in Hardy, Kentucky, we were surprised to learn that John Vance had retained the defense services of "Red Dog" himself.

As the Reunion Festival expanded rapidly into a larger, regional event, the demand for information about it was increasing exponentially.

To accommodate the growing demands of the media, Bo and I shared our phone numbers, home and email addresses without reservation. All our contact information was posted on our website, in online message board forums and made available through state and local government offices. We made few restrictions on the disbursement of our personal information or on our availability to do interviews. At times, we were entertaining phone calls from reporters well into the evening, during early mornings and even on the job.

Despite our best efforts, erroneous information sometimes was reported as genuine and further perpetuated by media outlets unwilling to take the time to corroborate the facts. Accurate reporting was made more difficult by the wide range of reunion activities scheduled across the region. With the diversity of local parties involved in planning and organizing these events, there was confusion on the part of the media as to whom to be contacting. Incorrect and contradictory scheduling information was reported liberally through a broad network of media outlets.

To exacerbate things further, Bo and I were often misquoted or misrepresented by whatever news media was covering the story. Frequently, what we said was taken out of context or interpreted in such a way as to support whatever angle the reporter intended on taking. Usually this was done to make the story more inflammatory and to stir the cauldron of some Hatfield-McCoy animosity they hoped still existed.

At times, the media did not even bother to speak with us at all. Instead, they resorted to reworking quotes that had appeared elsewhere or simply made things up. The most blatant and egregious case of news fabrication came in November, 2001 with the publication of a feature article on the pending McCoy Cemetery case that appeared in a supermarket tabloid, the *National Examiner*. Except for one anonymous quote from an "admiring pal" of "Devil Anse" and several non-cited insinuations about our attorney Joe Justice, the only quotes in the article were alleged to have been made by me. "For the McCoys, this cemetery is hallowed ground…thousands of people come to Pike County every year to visit the feud sites, and this is one that must be opened," I was reported as saying.[49]

After the article appeared in the racks of grocery stores everywhere, Bo and others had great fun at my expense, despite my insistence that I had never been contacted by the paper. The levity of the situation faded away several months later when Bo took his turn in the *National Enquirer*. The one-page article featured Bo fretting over the indignity of the cemetery case: "We believe the deeds and Kentucky law are on our side,' blasts Bo" and "I believe I should be allowed to visit the graves of my ancestors," he allegedly fumed." [50] To this day, Bo still denies that he ever talked to the tabloid.

To confront such media misinformation, we began writing our own press releases. While the releases sometimes took the form of schedule updates or informational announcements, usually we issued them in the form of articles, complete with quotes from Bo and me. This self-reporting guaranteed we were quoted accurately, unlike the partial or all-together inaccurate quotes that had appeared elsewhere. We sent out these releases on a regular basis to our ever-growing list of media contacts. Sometimes, we found that our releases would appear in print verbatim and occasionally would be credited to us. Most often, our press releases were used as parts of articles released under other writers' bylines. We took solace in the fact that our story was being picked up and repeated, along with the most accurate information we could convey.

My personal favorite print interview came out of a conversation that, at the time, I thought was entirely bogus. One morning while I was at work, I took a cell phone call from a number I did not recognize. The voice on the line was distant, with a thick accent that was difficult to decipher. "Hello, is this Ron McCoy?" asked the voice with a heavy Celtic lilt. "This is Stephen McGinty from Glasgow, Scotland," the voice continued. I smiled, believing that I was on the receiving end of a practical joke. "If you've got a minute, I'd like to talk with you about the Hatfields and McCoys...." he said. I decided to play along.

McGinty introduced himself as a writer for the *Scotsman*, the Scottish national newspaper. He expressed his country's interest in the Hatfields and McCoys and his own fascination with the families' links to Great Britain. As McGinty began asking his questions, there was a telltale sense of earnestness in his voice, which was enough to cause me to refrain from giving the flippant responses that were running through my mind. I listened closely to McGinty's long list of questions, answering them the best I could, even though I was certain that I was being duped. As the interview dragged on, the gag soon wore thin. If someone was pulling my leg, then he had prepared well for it.

When the call was over, I hung up the phone, not entirely sure if I had allowed myself to be the object of an elaborate prank. A couple of months later, I received a brown-paper package from Edinburgh, Scotland in the mail. Inside was the October 20, 2001 edition of the *"S2 Weekend Supplement,"* a Sunday magazine insert of the *Scotsman*, with a feature article on the Hatfields and McCoys. "In Scotland, we have the Campbells and the MacDonalds, an ancient feud still locked in the DNA of the present generation. In America, they have the Hatfields and McCoys," wrote McGinty.[51] His article remains one of the most balanced and impartial news pieces written about the feud and the battle over the McCoy Cemetery that I have ever read. It almost did not happen because I thought it was a joke.

The inclusion of the Hatfields in our plans for a modest family reunion was the catalyst for an event of historic importance. Whether having dinner together or facing each other on the softball diamond, every joint activity the families engaged in was symbolic of our resolution to demonstrate peace. What surprised us most was how willing and eager the Hatfields were to participate.

Even as we toiled to organize activities in Pikeville, over in Williamson, the West Virginia Hatfield counterpart to M2K was busily coordinating a group of events designed to complement those we had scheduled for Pikeville. The Williamson activities were being organized by long-time director of the Tug Valley Chamber of Commerce, Cecil Hatfield, a retired schoolteacher and descendant of Preacher Anderson Hatfield. Cecil was joined by his daughter, Sonya, an experienced veteran of the West Virginia storytelling guild. Sonya was a persuasive public speaker and adept at handling the media. A strong proponent of the reunion and tourism efforts in Williamson, she was eager to dispel stereotypes about Appalachia. "We are not ignorant, illiterate hillbillies who killed each other over a pig," she said.[52]

On one earlier planning trip, Cecil had invited us to meet him for dinner at the Brass Tree Restaurant, located in the Sycamore Inn in Williamson. The Inn was owned by Cecil's sister, Linda Van Meter and her husband, Doyle. Over dinner, we shared our plans for the upcoming reunion. Like many in West Virginia, Cecil was anxious to see Hatfield-McCoy tourism develop there. "It is part of our heritage to let people know that we are not as notorious, as bad as some people think," said Cecil.[53] We were so impressed by Cecil that that we welcomed him as an "official" part of our team.

There was just one small catch, however. Cecil wanted us to move our M2K banquet to Williamson. On some levels, it made sense. Like the Landmark Inn in Pikeville, the Sycamore Inn provided the necessary hotel facilities and a restaurant to host the dinner. Cecil brought with him the support of the local Chamber of Commerce and the backing of community and political leaders. Whether we were already too far into the planning process or if intuitively we knew that our hearts were firmly rooted in Pike County, we declined his generous offer.

We were duly impressed by Cecil, however and did not want to squelch the burgeoning West Virginia efforts. Bo offered what seemed to be a reasonable compromise. The Sycamore Inn in Williamson would be the site of the official "Hatfields: 2000 (H2K) dinner. The Hatfields would gather in Williamson and the McCoys in Pikeville on Friday night of the reunion and then the two families would meet on common ground over the course of the weekend. It was with the best of intentions that a competing Hatfield dinner came to be scheduled for the same night and at the same time as our M2K dinner, at a different venue 30 miles away.

The ongoing additions of local Hatfield-McCoy events across the region led to confusion on the part of visitors to the 2000 festival. Last minute activities scheduled by third parties were put together at such a rapid pace that we could not keep up with them. With each new addendum to the increasingly overstuffed weekend schedule, the Reunion Festival became more difficult for us to manage.

Bo and I did little to discourage the burgeoning local involvement, believing that every event would serve to promote the others. The truth was there was little we could do about it. The best we could hope to do was compile a single comprehensive schedule of events that we could distribute to our guests. In Pikeville, we remained the "official" M2K Reunion, while the additional local events gave the Reunion Festival a broader, regional presence.

Bo had been soliciting family members of both clans online for months, seeking out those who might be interested in playing on one of the family softball teams. One of the first Hatfields to answer the call was Brenda Bergwitz, a former West Virginia native living in Evansville, Indiana. Much as Margie Annett of San Diego, California did for the McCoy family, Brenda was instrumental in bringing a large contingent of Hatfield family members from across the country to the reunion. She became a prolific poster on message boards and genealogy forums and was a great advocate for what we were trying to accomplish. Her support provided us with a genuine Hatfield seal of approval and certified that the Hatfields would be an integral part of the reunion

Brenda's brother, Bucky Hatfield was one of the most colorful individuals ever to attend a Hatfield-McCoy reunion. Bucky was the owner of the Tennessee State Farrier School in Bloomington Springs, and a master educator and preeminent expert on the subject of horseshoeing and horse foundry. A stout man, made strong by his years as a farrier and as a Marine during the Vietnam War, Bucky had a strong commanding voice with a personality to match. He wore a trademark black cowboy hat that he only took off to exchange for a black "H2K" softball team cap. Quick-witted and boisterous, his outgoing personality made him a welcome subject for the media. In one interview, recounting the story of an encounter with a fellow Marine who had accused him of being "one of them dumb Hatfields," Bucky said that he answered the charge with a worthy response. "I socked him in the jaw."[54]

Ron with Bucky Hatfield in Pikeville, 2000

Bucky was particularly eager to serve as the Hatfield softball team captain. The prospect of a Hatfield-McCoy softball game was no laughing matter to him. Bucky was an active softball player and he had younger nephews and other family members he was interested in drafting for the team. In no uncertain terms, he advised us that he would handle putting together the team for the Hatfield side. If other Hatfield members coming to the reunion were interested in playing on the family team, they would have to go through him. For Bucky, the fun of the game was in the competition.

For our fledgling M2K efforts in Pikeville, there was no source of Hatfield support greater than Jerry and JoAnn Hatfield of Texarkana, Texas. Jerry Hatfield was an Air Force veteran, a retired Federal instructor of nearly thirty years and an accomplished wedding photographer. Jerry and JoAnn were some of the first people to join us in making M2K a reality. Through the media and online postings, Jerry discovered our plans for "McCoys: 2000" and eagerly volunteered to help. When Bo discovered Jerry's acumen with a camera, he asked Jerry to become the "official" photographer for our event. Jerry never refused a plea for help from us, no matter how trivial or inconvenient the request.

For the 2000 Reunion, Jerry became a highly sought-after press spokesperson for the Hatfield clan in Pikeville. Most media requests insisted on giving Hatfields and McCoys equal representation, so Jerry was asked to appear often. He approached interviews with good humor, natural charm and unwavering patience.

Bo was in high demand for media interviews as well. With conflicting and overlapping demands on his time, he was unable to meet every media request for an interview. By default, I became the secondary point-of-contact for the press. As our Hatfield representative in Pikeville for radio and television interviews, Jerry had the unenviable task of working both "shifts," for media appearances. During interviews with Bo or me, Jerry was called on to answer inane or redundant questions, usually those regarding the origins of the feud or the quarrel over the pig. Jerry never complained to us, but we certainly tested the limits of his endurance.

Jerry Hatfield and Ron getting ready for interviews

In an ironic turn for a photographer, Jerry found that he was also a popular subject for media pictures. Whenever I was cornered for a photo opportunity, I always dispatched someone to find Jerry and enlist his services as a model. Tall and lean with silver hair and matching beard, he looked the part of a "Hatfield." Sporting a thick black beard, I fit the press perception of what a "McCoy" should look like as well. Together, Jerry and I made a good team. The Associated Press pictures taken of the two of us in those days have been reused by the press many times over the years.

Jerry's remarkable durability as a press spokesman was put to the test on the Saturday of the Reunion Festival. Beginning early that morning, Jerry met Bo in the city park for the first of many radio, television and print interviews scheduled that day. It was a live appearance for the MS-NBC show, *Morning Blend*, hosted by Soledad O'Brien. The remote broadcast was staged in front of the park gazebo, with onsite camerawork and sound engineering handled by a local crew contracted by the network. Both men, dressed casually, were fitted with wireless microphones and earpieces with which to hear the network anchor's questions. In response to O'Brien's introductions, Bo and Jerry were relaxed and frisky as usual. Jerry commented that someone back home had asked him if he was going to be shooting any McCoys at the reunion to which he answered, "Definitely, I am going to shoot some McCoys. I brought 18 rolls of film." Later, when questioned about the tug-of-war event for which Bo offered to be the anchor on the McCoy side, Jerry was equally droll. "I'm afraid the Hatfields are outnumbered right here, right now. But we are going to give them our best shot. Oh, that was a bad term..."[55]

After enduring a near-endless series of press interviews with little in the way of breaks between them, Jerry was called upon to do yet another live television broadcast later that morning. The anchor was again Soledad O'Brien, but this time, the interview was for NBC's *Today* show. For the second round, the indefatigable Jerry was paired with me, dressed in an unflattering cream-colored dress jacket that was my unflattering trademark look for the weekend. Since I was not part of the previous broadcast, the questions were new to me. For Jerry, they were the same tired questions he had already addressed many times that morning. He stood by patiently as I answered O'Brien's question about the reasons for organizing the reunion, the same question she had addressed to Bo in the previous interview. When she asked Jerry to expound on some of the events scheduled for the weekend, he politely redirected the question back to me. The morning's back-to-back interviews had taken their toll. "I'm the token Hatfield," he quipped. Responding to her final question about the upcoming softball game, he answered with well-earned exasperation: "We're outnumbered."[56]

In our desperate bid to establish a local connection to the Pikeville-Pike County community, one of the corporate sponsors we hoped to secure for the Reunion Festival was an obvious choice. The *Appalachian News-Express* newspaper was published five days a week in Pikeville. It was one of the most widely circulated newspapers in Kentucky and was considered the primary source for news in Pike County. An endorsement by the newspaper would brand our event as legitimate in the eyes of the local populace. We were certain the newspaper would be willing to work with us since it had already benefitted from the early press coverage generated by our upcoming event. We were mistaken.

The publisher of the *Appalachian News-Express* in 2000 was Marty Backus. A native of Beckley, West Virginia, Backus had a long and diverse career in communications that spanned from radio broadcasting to television news.[57] The embodiment of a hard-nosed, no-nonsense newspaper editor, Backus enjoyed his reputation as a hard-charging, aggressive reporter who did not shy away from controversy. He was a "buck stops here" type of man.

Despite the attention the reunion was receiving from the national and international press, we labored in vain to warrant the attention of the *News-Express*. The print-media counterpart on the West Virginia side of the river, the *Williamson Daily News*, was more accommodating. The paper ran a series of articles promoting the H2K efforts in Williamson and Matewan and donated advertising to help promote the events there. In recognition of the 2000 reunion, the *Williamson Daily* reprinted a special commemorative "Hatfield and McCoy" edition, first published in 1982. The special edition, one of the most comprehensive collections of articles, pictures and stories about the feud ever assembled, sold out immediately.

Bo emailed and called the offices of the *News-Express* for months, with no results. As a consummate salesman, Bo was undeterred, certain that a savvy businessman like Backus could be persuaded to be part of the Festival, once he understood the full measure of our intentions. Not one to take "no" for an answer, Bo continued to pursue an appointment with Mr. Backus. Finally, and unexpectedly, his tenacity paid off.

On one of our many trips to Pikeville, Bo received an unexpected phone call from the *News-Express* offices that Mr. Backus would see us. Knowing that it would be our only opportunity to win his support, we tabled our planning activities for the day and hastily made our way to the unscheduled appointment. We arrived at the *News-Express* office early and waited in the lobby for what seemed like an eternity. Finally, an assistant arrived and showed us in to Mr. Backus' office. His office was large and ornate with a massive and intimidating mahogany desk as its centerpiece. The two chairs we sat in across from it were small by comparison.

The room seemed to grow larger and the desk more impressive the longer we waited. After more minutes than I could count, Mr. Backus entered the office and made his way purposefully to his desk. With no exchanges of niceties, spoken or otherwise, Backus sat down slowly, without smiling. His gaze was piercing as he looked us over, like a poker player sizing up the competition. After a long silence, he spoke the only words from that meeting that I can remember him saying. "What are you peddlin'?" he asked.

Silence fell over the room. To his credit, Bo maintained his composure and dutifully recounted the trials and travails of our M2K story. Backus was thoroughly unimpressed by the carpetbaggers in his office. I was sure there was a high price to be paid by the employee who had bothered to set up the appointment with us. We left the *News-Express* offices, dejected and confused, certain that the "Reunion of the Millennium" was a colossal failure in the making.

The threat of our event's impending collapse was further heightened by the sudden and unexpected resignation of Bruce Brown as the Pikeville-Pike County Tourism Director in February 2000. His departure was immediate and without notice. Walter "Doc" Fletcher, the Tourism Commission Chairman, was left to deliver an "official" comment to the press. "The decision to resign was made by Brown and he (Fletcher) could not speculate on reasons for the action." One possible explanation was offered, however. The Board was "not pleased with the way Brown had handled a planned feud driving tour the office was trying to get off the ground." Under Brown's direction, said Fletcher, the office was "having difficulties acquiring easements to property needed for the project."[58]

Since our earliest days of planning, Mr. Brown had been our greatest source of help in Pikeville. He was instrumental in introducing us to key officials who helped us secure permissions and necessary approvals for our event. Indeed, it is unlikely that a reunion in Pikeville would have happened at all had our attention not been drawn to Kim Hefling's 1998 newspaper article about him. Despite our marginal inroads into the local community, we expected that the loss of Mr. Brown all but preempted any hope of success for M2K.

Book

"The past actually happened
but history is only what someone wrote down."
A. Whitney Brown

In the wake of Mr. Brown's abrupt resignation and our ongoing struggle to meet the organizational, financial and media demands of the "Reunion of the Millennium," an unexpectedly intriguing opportunity became available to us. It was something that we had considered from our earliest days of planning, although it was primarily wishful thinking on our part. As with most things we had become involved in, Bo and I had no idea if it was possible or even how to go about achieving it. Given the risky financial straits we were in, it was unquestionably a project we had no business pursuing; but having the chance to have Truda McCoy's family book reprinted was something we could not pass up.

The value of *The McCoys: Their Story* to the McCoy family is immeasurable. Without it, I never would have discovered my own link to the family. The nearly fifty-year struggle to have the book published in 1976, and the effort involved in having it reprinted nearly twenty-five years later, is a testament to the resolve of many unheralded individuals.

The publication of the book was considered a monumental achievement by the descendants of the McCoy clan. For some in the family, the book was a long-awaited alternative to a perceived Hatfield-bias in many feud accounts. While not a true historical text in the strictest sense, it was a priceless chronicle of the oral histories that had been passed down through the family.

Labeling a perspective as "Hatfield" or "McCoy" has been a type of verbal shorthand used by family members over the years to define the point-of-view of a given feud account. The depiction of one family or the other as either the antagonist or protagonist of the feud story is always a matter of perspective. There are still those family members today who avidly defend their positions on their respective sides of the philosophical "river" and few can truly claim neutrality. A close examination of feud history does not lend itself to objectivity.

Perhaps the earliest written account of the feud is *An American Vendetta* by Theron C. Crawford. A reporter for *New York World*, Crawford originally presented his story as a series of articles for the newspaper. These articles were later bound and released as a book, published in 1889. During his reporting on the feud, Crawford traveled to Logan County, West Virginia, escorted by State Senator John Floyd, a friend of "Devil Anse" Hatfield. Crawford was invited into the Hatfield home to conduct the first known interview with the clan leader. The Hatfields extended Crawford all the benefits of mountain hospitality including a hearty meal and friendly conversation. In turn, Crawford found that many of his preconceptions of the Hatfields had changed. He described "Devil Anse" as a "jovial old pirate," an "intrepid, energetic mountaineer," who was "universally regarded in (his) community…in a favorable light."[59] While sometimes criticized for its lurid descriptions and crude portrayals of "hillbilly" stereotypes, Crawford's book nevertheless remains a valuable historical document. It has been cited as a resource in most of the feud accounts that have followed.

Some, like Charles S. Howell of the *Pittsburgh Times*, were able to land interviews with the McCoys during a trip to Pike County. Visiting the home of Randolph and Sarah in Pikeville, he found the two to be bearing the "unmistakable evidences of the intensity of their sufferings." Randolph was described as "bent, almost broken by the weight of his sorrows and grief."[60] Howell's perspective of the Hatfields, shaped only by his visits with those incarcerated in the Pike County jail was less complimentary.

Generally, the McCoys were less accommodating to the media. With the possible exception of Randolph himself, the family was known to be notoriously tight-lipped, reluctant to talk about the feud for generations to come, even among themselves. The Hatfields, on the other hand, enjoyed a certain notoriety following the feud. Staged pictures of the family taken in the late 1890s have become the definitive pictorial evidence of the feud. These pictures of the family, armed and ready, have graced the cover of nearly every book written on the subject.

For some within the McCoy family, the prevailing historical perspective of the feud was decidedly "Hatfield," while the "McCoy" point-of-view was severely underrepresented. The greatest disservice to a balanced take on the feud was the depiction of Randolph McCoy and the critical assessment of his role in the feud. Over a century of feud accounts, "Ol' Randall" has been portrayed as a caricature, usually in a negative light. He has been rendered as a slow-to-act religious fundamentalist, resentful of the economic success of his Hatfield neighbor; a man so consumed by jealously and enflamed by hatred that he was willing to sacrifice the lives of his children to see his own vision of justice served.

By contrast, "Devil Anse" has been regarded as a man of noble character, an intrepid mountaineer, a skilled backwoodsman and pioneering entrepreneur. William Hatfield, Sr. of Greenbrier, Arkansas supports this image of his grandfather. "We make him out to be a gentle soul; very hospitable."[61] In a June 27, 1992 interview, feud author Dr. Altina Waller said of Hatfield; "(he) was known throughout his community for not only his personality, but his commanding presence."[62] Waller went on to describe Hatfield as "heroic and so personally ready to defend his family and his place. He was like a Robin Hood character in a way."[63]

Waller was less gracious in her assessment of Randolph. She described McCoy as an "idiosyncratic" rabble-rouser, a man overwhelmingly bitter and envious, and hell-bent on enflaming public opinion against the Hatfields.[64] In her view, the feud "was mostly perpetuated by (Randolph) McCoy who for many reasons saw the Hatfields as the enemy in the community – many of those reasons economic."[65] Henry D. Hatfield, a great-nephew of the famed West Virginia governor of the same name, concurred. "Really, the Hatfields won the feud. Devil Anse would have ended it anytime. But Randolph McCoy was so irate..."[66]

Historically, Randolph remains a complex figure, sometimes contradictory and difficult to understand. Historian Dr. Otis Rice suggested that Randolph "combined a morose nature with a tendency to talk about his troubles with all who would listen."[67] As such, he has been depicted in widely contrasting styles and seldom favorably. All too often, he has been portrayed as a bitter angry old man, indecisive and powerless, jealous and petty, driven by his raging hatred of the Hatfields. This stereotype of "Ol' Randall" has been perpetuated for more than a century.

It was not until the publication of Truda's book in 1976 that an inimitable resource offered new insights into the feud. For the first time, the story was reconstructed from the oral accounts of McCoy participants and survivors. Familiar feud accounts were told from a fresh perspective, and stories not previously known were revealed. Best of all, a more rounded portrait of Randolph McCoy emerged, detailing his war service, his time in a prisoner of war camp and his commitment to honor, faith and family.

The story of the book's original journey into print was miraculous in itself. Truda Williams McCoy was a schoolteacher in Pike County in the 1920s. She was also a prolific poet, whose works appeared in regional newspapers, literary magazines and three volumes of published works. A descendant of John McCoy, an uncle to Randolph, Truda married Rex Calvin McCoy, son of Sam McCoy (my grandfather's grandfather) in 1924.[68] As a "double McCoy," Truda earned the confidence of the famously taciturn McCoys. This intimacy allowed her to spend years interviewing and recording the oral feud accounts of family members. Many of the stories told to Truda were shared by Sam's wife, Martha, my great-great grandmother.

Truda McCoy (left), circa 1950

New York publishers were uninterested in Truda's book when she began presenting it to them in 1935. After fifteen years of pitching the book to publishers, she retired the manuscript to the confines of her attic in the 1950s, where it remained until her death in 1974. Nearly forty years after its completion, Truda's manuscript seemed destined to fade into the ages.

Truda's children, Paul and Judith were determined to see that the manuscript was published. Paul contacted fellow McCoy descendant, Jimmy Wolford, who was hard at work securing a monument for the McCoy Cemetery in Hardy, KY to enlist his help in finding a publisher.

Wolford stopped by Paul's furniture store to pick up the manuscript, a copy of which he had carried around with him in the trunk of his car for nearly two years. Leonard and Joseph McCoy, the soon-to-be benefactors of the cemetery monument, pointed Jimmy in the direction of Pikeville College and the capable guidance of Dr. Leonard Roberts. However, it was Paul's twin sister, Judith who, after seeing a local television interview with Dr. Roberts in 1976, set the publication of the book in motion.

Dr. Leonard Roberts, the Chairman of Humanities at Pikeville College was a highly regarded writer and editor.[69] In 1974, he edited *The Hatfields*, a book written by a fellow professor and "distant cousin" of "Devil Anse," Dr. G. Elliot Hatfield. Following a distinguished career as a university history instructor, Dr. Hatfield had spent four years researching and compiling the feud stories he had heard in his youth.[70] The Big Sandy Historical Society was instrumental in creating one of the first comprehensive genealogies of the Hatfield family that was included as an amendment to his text.

During a television appearance promoting *The Hatfields*, Dr. Roberts commented that there was precious little written documentation on the events of the feud as told from the McCoy's point of view. Judith remembered her mother's manuscript and contacted Pikeville Preservation Council member Harold Stratton Moore. Dr. Roberts was serving as a Board Member for the Council, whose mission was the "protection and celebration of the eastern Kentucky mountain culture and heritage."[71] After meeting with Judith, Roberts immediately recognized the historical value of Truda's manuscript. He and the Council met with Paul and secured the rights to publish the book, with the provision that editorial revisions be kept to a minimum.

Two enhancements to the manuscript, however, further bolstered the value of the book to the McCoy family. First, Roberts and the Council gathered a collection of rare family photographs to include in the book. Many were offered by Paul and Judith, while others came from family members such as Joseph and Leonard McCoy and Daisy Quick, owner of the Uriah McCoy house in Burnwell, Kentucky.

Taking a cue from the previously published *Hatfields* book, the Council commissioned the first comprehensive genealogy of the McCoy family. Genealogists Betsy Venters and Dorcas Hobbs of Pikeville and Virginia Bare of Ohio compiled a 150-page section that was added to the book. While their effort was not without errors or omissions, it laid the foundation for further serious investigations of the McCoys' family line. As a result, the McCoys of eastern Kentucky, like their West Virginia Hatfield counterparts, are one of the most chronicled American family genealogies.

In the fall of 1976, the Preservation Council unveiled *The McCoys: Their Story*, regarded by one reviewer as "the most important genealogical research ever done on the feuding family."[72] With a cover price of $12, the 330-page book sold out its initial run quickly. Soon after, family members were clamoring for more copies.

Truda's book was an invaluable source of information for McCoy family members, although many had noted mistakes in the genealogy section. Typed pages detailing omissions or revisions were distributed by the Council to owners of the book with the promise that the genealogy section would be amended in subsequent reprints; but the expected republication never happened. The original publication was made possible by a sizable grant from the Preservation Council and funds were no longer available for a second printing. Sadly, the project's arbiter, Dr. Leonard Roberts, who had spearheaded the project, died unexpectedly in a car accident.

For all its value to the McCoy family, Truda's book disappeared again into the abyss of history. The scarcity of the book made it a treasured acquisition in the secondary market. The book became a highly sought-after collectible. Used copies were selling for hundreds of dollars online.

As Bo and I began organizing the M2K Reunion, one of the questions we were asked most frequently concerned the possibility of having Truda's book reprinted. In the days before internet genealogy services, family members without access to courthouse records were limited to posting inquiries on ancestry message boards in online forums in search of family. Those fortunate enough to have access to a copy of

Truda's book were known to photocopy pages to distribute to other family members. Even within the offices of Pike County Tourism, entire chapters of the book were copied and distributed in response to desperate requests for the material.

It was apparent to us that we had received an informal mandate to see to it that Truda's book was republished. At the very least, there seemed to be an underlying confidence that somehow, the M2K boys would find a way to make it happen. Unfortunately, while the sentiment was appreciated, like most of the reunion goals we set for ourselves, we simply had no clue as to how to achieve it.

Phyllis Hunt was appointed to replace Mr. Brown as Tourism director after his departure. Having worked in the tourism office for many years, she was well regarded in the Pikeville-Pike County community. With "Hillbilly Days" just a few months away, she was placed in the unenviable position of managing the new "Hatfield McCoy Reunion Festival" with two organizers who lacked both experience and resources. To complicate things further, we now wanted to venture into publishing.

We brought the issue of Truda's book to Phyllis and Betty Howard, one of the most knowledgeable feud historians in Pike County. Betty suggested we speak with Nancy Forsyth, the current owner of Dils Cemetery, a remarkable woman who had served as a member of the Pikeville Preservation Council that had initially published the book. Nancy explained that the copyrights to the book were held by Paul McCoy, Truda's son. She then provided key information that tipped the probability of having the book reprinted in our favor. The original printing plates, including the entirety of the text, cover and photographs used in the publication of the book, had been stored in the archives of Pikeville College for safe-keeping.

Phyllis Hunt was the person responsible for introducing us to my grandfather's cousin, Paul McCoy, a man we grew to know, love and respect. In a phone call with Bo, Paul was encouraging and supportive of our reunion efforts that he had read about in the newspaper, despite that the fact that he had not met us. Bo asked Paul to consider letting us have his mother's book reprinted. To our great relief, Paul was receptive to the idea. With his verbal consent, it now was imperative that we find a way to find the financial resources to get it done.

Phyllis Hunt put me in touch with Sherrie Marrs, the executive assistant to the Dean of Pikeville College. Sherrie confirmed for us that the plates were stored intact, except for a hand-drawn graphic of a map that appeared as part of the book's interior cover. A few phone calls later, Sherrie had secured the release of the plates by the college for our use in reprinting the book with the caveat that they would be returned to the school upon completion of the project.

With Phyllis's assistance we contacted a local printing company that served regional authors. With the acquisition of the original printing plates, the setup expenses associated with the reprinting were deferred. Having the plates also decreased the lead time necessary for production to about eight weeks, giving us additional time to drum up the nearly $30,000 necessary to place an order for 5000 copies of the book. Given the pent-up demand for the book, Bo expected to exceed this number quickly.

The minimum order quantity necessary to begin the printing processing was 500 copies. He made the book available for presale orders on the *real-mccoys.com* website in January, 2000. Despite a looming deadline in March, Bo was optimistic as he broke the news of the book's upcoming publication. Six weeks after the announcement was made, however, with just 160 copies ordered, it seemed unlikely that the dream of reprinting Truda's book would happen at all.

On February 24, Bo posted a heartfelt appeal online. "I have always believed in the generosity of people. So, I am about to do something I have never done. I am challenging you to make a sacrifice on behalf of the McCoy family. Even, if you are a Hatfield, I am asking you to (accept) the challenge," he wrote. Of the 448 list members on the *real-mccoys.com* website, only 50 had preordered the book. He made an impassioned plea to those sitting on the fence. "I will get on a plane and go to Pikeville personally to take (them) the check (to purchase the books)....Now folks, this is it. Either we are family or we're not. I have not consulted anyone on this, so if I look like a fool, I did this all on my own." With the reunion four months away and still struggling financially, the risk of failure to launch the book reprinting weighed heavily on Bo's shoulders. "After two years of planning (the reunion) consider this payment in full for services rendered. I am not asking for you to give us anything, just preorder this book. That's all I've got, folks. I can't do any more."

Bo's petition to our online family for help was met with a resounding outpouring of support. By the end of March, we had secured enough orders to go to press. The tourism office placed a substantial order for copies of the book with an open-ended promise to purchase more from us. The financial generosity of a local Pike County contributor guaranteed a modified order for 3,000 books.

The books sold quickly for the first few years. Cases of the books were left in Pike County at the home of our patron to accommodate the needs of Tourism and other local inquiries. By 2003, we had about 1,000 copies of the book left to sell. Internet sales had trickled away slowly until there was none. Pike County sales, while steady, were unremarkable. Years later, unable to repay fully the kindness of our sponsors, I made a trip to Pikeville with a mini-van loaded down with all the books I could carry to settle our obligation with barter. Even then, the kindness of our benefactors was unfailing.

In 2012, with the release of the History Channel mini-series, the demand for feud products hit an all-time high. Sales of all books on the feud far exceeded the supply, necessitating the urgent reprinting of volumes that were no longer available. Truda's book was no exception. Copies of the book sold out quickly, until there were no more to be had.

With the death of Paul McCoy in 2009 and passing of his sister year earlier, the rights to the book have fallen into question. To date, these matters have not been resolved. The book remains scarce and nearly impossible to find. Abe Books, an online source for rare books, ranked it number 78 in the top 100 most searched for out of print books in 2013.[73] Seventeen years after its reprinting, the status of Truda McCoy's book is much the same as it was in 2000. Once again, history has come full circle.

Reunion

"History never looks like history when you are living through it."
John W. Gardner

On the night of Friday, June 9, 2000, history was made as the dining room of the Mark II facility of the Landmark Inn in Pikeville, Kentucky became the site of the first national reunion of the Hatfield and McCoy families. The Mark II was a detached building set behind the main hotel and was used for special events and as a club and bar on weekends. The yellow-painted building with a red tile roof matched the look of the main facility. Someone on the hotel staff apparently had missed the news of the previous thirteen months, however. A plain black marquee spelled out "Welcome McCoy M2K Reunion" in white letters, giving no indication of the historical significance of the event that was going on inside.

Befitting the gravity of the night, attendees dressed as formally as they felt comfortable doing. A long line of family members in eveningwear braved the summer heat and humidity as they anxiously waited outside. Nearly 450 family members had purchased tickets to attend the banquet, traveling from as far away as California, Washington, Texas, Florida, Michigan, Wisconsin and Ohio. Edward McCoy, a fellow great-great-great grandson of Randolph had the longest trek, traveling to the reunion from his Air Force duties in South Korea. One resourceful couple, Leslie and Randy Hatfield came all the way from Canada. When the doors finally opened at 6:30 p.m., the crowd politely made their way into a venue that quickly became over-crowded. It was the largest gathering of descendants from both families ever to assemble in one place, and the room was alive with nervous energy.

With Hatfields split between attending our dinner and the H2K affair in Williamson, the balance of the room was stacked in favor of the McCoys. Those brave Hatfields in attendance at the M2K dinner, like Jerry and JoAnn and their family, were a welcome presence. They held their ground amidst a barrage of well-intended humor, and returned fire with a fully loaded arsenal of their own.

The Landmark's staff had outdone themselves in preparation for the event. The dark green walls of the room, combined with the low-level lighting of chandeliers were in keeping with our formal theme. Linen-draped dinner tables were turned sideways to run the length of the rectangular building to accommodate the large crowd.

As dinner was served and our banquet got underway, it soon became apparent that our problems were just beginning. When adjusted to accommodate the capacity of the group, the table arrangement placed the "front" of the room down to one end, a considerable distance away from many attendees. For our dinner, the staff had provided a small podium and microphone unit that sat on the edge of the head table at the front right side of the room. The setup ultimately proved to be woefully underpowered to handle the room size, already overstuffed with an exuberant crowd. Ironically, at the same end of the building, a raised stage used for weekend musical events, complete with a full sound system, stage lighting, microphones and instruments sat dark.

We had spent the better part of that Friday afternoon converting the vestibule of the Mark II into a M2K registration facility. Throughout the day, family members coming to town stopped by to pick up their official M2K welcome packets, stuffed with lanyards, IDs, key chains, raffle tickets and brochures. For the evening, we set up tables to display the M2K merchandise we had for sale, as well as copies of Truda's book, hot off the presses. Local volunteers staffed the tables that evening to give family members the chance to enjoy the dinner. Inside the dining area, we set up a memorial table on which attendees displayed framed pictures of their family members. Bo and I placed pictures of our grandfathers there as well as historic pictures of Randolph and his family. It was our way of ensuring that they would be part of the night. Many family members also brought notebooks filled with pages of genealogy information to share. A makeshift family tree began to grow on the back wall of the room as attendees began taping up pages and comparing notes.

As we had done from day one of our event planning, we worked zealously to exceed our own preconceptions of providing value for our guests. We scheduled a long list of speakers, slide shows, award presentations, music and comedy. While many of those who had helped us organize the event attended, we decided to err on the side of brevity and limit the time allotted for speechmaking. It was a goal we did not achieve.

Paul McCoy, Truda's son, was our guest of honor. Paul, a soft-spoken and reserved man, was making a rare public appearance on our behalf. Other special family members in attendance included Leonard "Mix" McCoy and Joe "Tab" McCoy, former owners of the McCoy Caney Coal Company who had come all the way from Lexington. The McCoy brothers were the financial benefactors of several Hatfield-McCoy projects including the McCoy Cemetery monument in Hardy, Kentucky, Jimmy Wolford's feud album in 1976 as well as the publication of Truda's book that same year.

Our musical guest for the night was Jimmy Wolford, a proud McCoy descendant and famed regional troubadour. Retired from a long and productive music career with Capital Records, Jimmy's appearance, like Paul's, was a rare treat. Jimmy had done much for the cause of the families over the years. His album, *The Great Vendetta* is the definitive musical retelling of the feud story. Jimmy once presented a copy of the album to Richard Dawson, the host of *Family Feud* when Jimmy, Cecil Hatfield and other members of the families appeared on the popular game show in 1979.

Bo also hired a local comedian known for his family-friendly brand of humor. Freddie "Munroe" Goble was a comic staple of the Kentucky Opry, located in the Mountain Art Center in Prestonsburg, Kentucky, about 28 miles north of Pikeville. "Munroe" had the impossible chore of entertaining a crowded room full of Hatfields and McCoys, tired from a protracted evening of festivities. "Munroe's" performance that night gave new meaning to a "standup routine." Taking an earlier cue from me, he performed the entirety of his act while standing in a chair. Despite a listless audience worn down by an itinerary that had dragged on far too long, "Munroe" performed his routine with sincerity and heart. "I had a horsin' accident," he said. "I fell off a horse and got my foot caught in the stirrup over on the right side. And don't you know, the thing kept a buckin' and a goin' and a runnin' and a jumpin' If the Wal-Mart man hadn't come out and unplugged her, I think she'd a killed me."

Wrestling with the myriad details of the Friday night banquet caused me to miss eating the reunion meal. In fact, it was not until the reunion of 2002 that I finally got the chance to taste what we were feeding our fellow family members. There were too many last-minute details to be handled, endless questions to be answered and decisions to be made on the fly. Too many things threatened to go wrong.

Having spent the better part of the afternoon setting up the vendor and family memorial tables and decorating the banquet venue, I was late getting back to my hotel room to get dressed for dinner. At 6:30, my family went on to the banquet without me. With no time to shower or otherwise prepare, I changed quickly from work clothes to dress clothes, and hurried down to meet them, arriving at the dinner at about ten minutes to seven. With no time to do anything about it, I was dismayed to discover that the venue we had worked so carefully to decorate all afternoon was now just a dark, noisy and overcrowded room, packed with family members from all over the country, expecting a good show. It was clear to me that the little podium microphone we had to use was not going to be able to do the job.

My children, Jacob (6) and Rachel (9)

Bo and I generally split most of the organizational duties between us. As chairman of the reunion, Bo was called on to make decisions on the go as he went about shaking hands, welcoming family and posing for pictures. He handled all that he could and then some. The duties of handling the "nuts and bolts" of whatever else there was to deal with fell on me. Although Billy Jack and others were invaluable resources, the tasks to be performed far exceeded the work force we had available to complete them.

The Friday night dinner was no different. The two of us worked diligently to see that the night's program went off with a minimum of glitches. Bo and I took turns at the podium introducing guests, making presentations and keeping the program moving along. Both of us had brief intervals in our seats at the table, just long enough to catch glances of our plates and imagine what the food tasted like.

To begin the program, we put together several video and slideshow presentations that ran as dinner was served. These presentations included a collection of historical feud pictures to remind family members of our reasons for gathering. A compilation of the media coverage of the event was an entertaining way to inform our attendees of the historical relevance of the weekend. These presentations, involving screens, laptops, video players and projectors, kept me sufficiently busy while the families enjoyed their meals.

Watching the interactions of the crowd that night introduced me to a curious dynamic I have witnessed played out by Hatfields and McCoys many times over seventeen years. Since the "Reunion of the Millennium" was a three-day event, most family members had traveled on Friday afternoon, arriving in town just hours before the dinner. Except for some who had made the trip together, few family members knew each other or had the time to be introduced. Many meeting for the first time told closely held family stories, only to find that others in attendance shared them as well. Among the Hatfields and McCoys, there was an immediate camaraderie, a commonality established by a shared history

Some family members offered up Hatfield-McCoy jokes of varying degrees of propriety, usually at the expense of the other family. The jokes and wisecracks were good-natured, however, and the parties involved took them in stride. One I remember us telling was a generality about the differences between the Hatfields and McCoys. "Hatfields are taller, outgoing and more successful than the McCoys. The McCoys are shorter, smarter and better looking." Another of a more dubious quality had its foundation in feud history: "Why do Hatfield men come to the McCoy reunion? To meet McCoy women. Why do McCoy men come to the McCoy reunion? To meet McCoy women."

Conversations that night were lively, high-spirited and more important than the meal being served. The mood of the room was festive and raucous like that of a Friar's roast. It was obvious the Hatfields and McCoys were there to have fun.

Billy Jack was the first victim of the anemic sound system as he stepped up to lead off the night's cavalcade of speakers. He was confronted with a dark room, full of revelers engaged in their own conversations. Reigning them in was no easy task, made even more difficult by his easy-going demeanor combined with the lackluster sound system. As the tide gradually turned in his favor, Billy Jack was met with good-natured but rowdy shouts from the crowd, further exacerbating the sound situation. The ever-genial Billy Jack braved the situation with a smile, thanked everyone for coming to the "reunion they said would never happen," and introduced me as the next speaker.

There was another reason I did not eat that night. It was not the crowd, the pressure of the event, exhaustion or fear that made me sick to my stomach, rather it was a moment of profound embarrassment that made me want to throw off my jacket, rip off my tie and slip quietly out the back door. Stepping up to the microphone, I was unprepared for the damage my improvised remarks would cause.

At the time of the 2000 reunion, Bo was battling obesity, a struggle for his health that he had endured since his youth. In his own defense against derisive remarks, Bo learned to be outgoing, gregarious and downright funny. Instead of having his physical condition be the stuff of behind-the-back whispers, he brought it out in the open with a wicked sense of humor. His making light of it made others feel comfortable and unthreatened. It was normal for Bo to joke about himself. Those who met him were immediately put at ease. His size became a non-factor, something that people noticed at first then never thought about again.

As partners in planning the reunion, people remembered our physical characteristics more than they did our names. Bo was the "big guy" and I was the little guy "with the beard." Over the course of two years of media and public appearances, we developed public personas that were easily identifiable and relatable. Bo was the "heart" of the reunion and I was its "joker." The two of us developed a long-standing shtick that addressed our obvious physical differences. Bo, in his speech to the M2K reunion dinner that night summed it up best: "Together, we're a perfect team. I'll tell you why. He's a "1," I'm a "0"....we're a "10" – a perfect "10."

As a speaker, Bo was always well prepared. Usually, he spoke using notes that he had written out, although he never seemed to be reading or referencing them. The experienced preacher chose his words carefully. He rarely misspoke even when called upon to improvise a media interview at a moment's notice.

I, on the other hand, was a loose cannon. I seldom had time to draft a speech or prepare remarks. Only when reciting the names of the twelve feud victims onstage at the county courthouse on the following morning did I refer to a list of names because I dared not forget anyone. Having had some experience in local theater and as a musician, I was accustomed to performing in front of crowds, though it was not something I was entirely comfortable doing. As an actor and musician, the words and music were scripted. With the reunions, I did not have that luxury. I was usually "winging it," with varying degrees of success.

On the night of the M2K dinner, as we neophyte event organizers took to the podium, we continued the comical rapport with which we had become so comfortable. The family members who had grown to know Bo, Billy Jack and me through the website, email, telephone calls and the media were eager to hear from us. They anticipated our "shtick" as would immediately become apparent to me. Stepping up to take my turn at the small podium, wearing a dark green shirt and the same awful cream-colored coat I wore the entire weekend, I was met with riotous cat calls. In a vain attempt to be heard, I shouted into the microphone, sounding not unlike a local politician on the campaign stump.

At the M2K dinner

The audience was abuzz with discordant jeers coming at me from all over the room. People began standing, peering through make-believe binoculars and gesturing that they could not see me. I realized they knew and expected to see the usual comedic routine Bo and I had devised months before. I began jumping up and down, flailing both arms as if struggling to be seen. "Have you got a box?" I shouted. An obliging stranger to whom I was related stepped forward with a chair for me to stand in. I stepped up on the chair, raised both hands in surrender and gave a royal wave. The family responded with enthusiastic applause. As I stepped down from the chair, energized by the frivolity of the room, I proceeded to make my unrehearsed comments. Recalling the many trips I made previously to Pikeville in planning the reunion, I mentioned that I had driven up on Tuesday of that week, the anniversary of the Allied invasion of France. "Tuesday was D-Day…the anniversary of the allies re-invading Europe and taking Europe back." "They got it wrong—today is D-day and the Hatfields and McCoys are back and we're here to stay." The crowd responded heartily.

Next up was my introduction of Bo, which went much less well. I felt comfortable with the assemblage of family members present. They expected the "shtick" and they understood my intentions, but my words proved clumsy, hurtful and ill considered. "I was going to make a lot of fun at Bo's expense," I started. "But I can't do that and I'll tell you why. In a lot of ways, he's twice the man I am." The crowd laughed again… and then I went too far. "The reason he is as big as he is because (of) his heart and his love for both of these families. He's got to have a body that big to put the heart in it," I shouted, and the crowd responded with gracious applause. With one final nod to the routine, I then introduced my favorite "third, fourth and fifth cousin," Bo McCoy.

The crowd cheered as Bo stepped up to microphone and, without batting an eye, answered "Thank you, *Tiny*." The crowd laughed appreciatively. As Bo spoke to the gathering, I went back to work, determined that something had to done about the sound situation. Collaborating with Freddie Goble who stepped in to help, I secured a microphone stand, microphone and limited use of the stage sound system, though not before Bo and Paul had concluded speaking. I was unaware of the damage my words had done until later in the evening.

As we began presenting a series of awards and door prizes, I introduced Bo as "two of my favorite cousins," a lame moniker I had used many times before. The crowded laughed again, but this time, I noticed that Bo was not laughing. From the look in his eyes, I knew that I had struck a nerve. As far as I knew, we were handling things in the same manner we always had, joking among ourselves. There was no malice intended, implied or considered. As I made my way to the head table, Bo whispered to me in a flat monotone that I remember to this day. "You're not doing yourself any favors here," he said.

It was an unexpected lesson I learned that night. Bo, like many others with a unique physical condition, turned to humor as a defense mechanism. By making fun of himself, he removed the opportunity for others. If Bo made light of himself, it was funny. If others did so, it was not, especially if the remarks came from family. The "shtick" we presented at times was acceptable and funny. On this night and in this setting, however, among other family members, I had gravely offended him.

No other family members said anything to me about my remarks, either because they went unnoticed or unheard. I hope that it was because they understood the lack of malice behind the jests, but it had bothered Bo enough to speak out. Although I would never intentionally hurt or embarrass Bo, I knew that I had done so. I was angry at myself, frustrated at my own insensitivity. For me, the balance of the night was a blur. It was all I could do not to leave the room. Later that evening, I apologized to Bo. He accepted graciously, almost off-handedly, as if it was no big deal. It was just another minor incident in the pandemonium that was M2K…and we never engaged in the "1-0 shtick" again.

The keynote address to the Hatfield and McCoy descendants by the organizer of M2K reunion was simple and heartfelt. Dressed in a black shirt and pants, Bo looked every bit the part of the family ambassador. Stepping up to the podium, the enormity of the moment struck him and the man of a thousand words was at a loss. Someone in the crowd shouted, "Don't tear up on us, Bo," reminding him that our families had come to play. As Bo called out a list of states represented, the crowd responded with a series of whoops and cheers, shouts and applause. "When we started this...we hoped that we'd have about a hundred of you ...in the room. That was our first goal. When we topped a hundred, we said, wow, maybe we'll get 150. When we hit 250, we said, you know 300's not too far away. And when it hit 300, I said something's going on with the Hatfields and McCoys."

As Bo's tone became more solemn, the volume of the room dropped for the first time that evening. "A new millennium has brought a new vision to the Hatfields and McCoys. You...aren't going to put up with (those) sad stories they've been telling about us anymore...let's write a new history for that old legend. I think it's well past time for the Hatfields and McCoys to be remembered for something more than pigs and fighting." The crowd agreed. "This is history in the making. This has never been done like this before...Hatfields and McCoys (have) come together with a singular purpose to renew the history so that (we) can present it back to the world."

Bo at the M2K dinner

Bo concluded with a poem that he had written, titled *We Remember*, a tribute addressed to our ancestors and to their descendants attending the reunion that weekend.

Time has been kind to you, your families have survived.
We hoped that you'd return here so that we could fulfill our vow.
For the blood that was spilled here has purchased our kinship
And we proudly bear your name.

The past will always be, but the pain will fade away
And we will stand as guardians of your yesterdays.
Our vow not completed until the reunion of one and all,
In the mountains of Kentucky or until the homeward call.

We remember, remember yesterday
When your fathers were among us, but those were troubled days.
We saw your fathers fight, we heard your mothers cry
As their sons became the victims of the bitter fight.
We remember.

Having Paul McCoy as the guest of honor for the dinner was one of the true highlights of the entire weekend. Paul was an erudite, well spoken, though rather private, man. He and his wife, Janene operated the "J&M Furniture" store on the outskirts of Pikeville. Paul Ronald McCoy, my grandfather's first cousin and my father's namesake, was one of our reunion patrons, having granted us permission to reprint his mother Truda's book without asking for compensation of any kind. We were honored when he agreed to appear at the M2K dinner.

Bo introduced Paul, doing his best to quiet a crowd that was now facing the fourth consecutive speaker they would strain to hear. He thanked Paul for all that he had done to get his mother's book printed in 1976 and for trusting us with the privilege of reprinting it. Bo stepped back and ceded the podium to Paul who, despite his quiet nature, took to the platform easily.

He thanked Nancy Forsyth, Betty Howard and others for being instrumental in the republication of his mother's book. He spoke gently, in measured tones, about the generational presence of the McCoy family in the hills of eastern Kentucky. He told about the Scottish origins of the family name as a "derivative of the Mackay clan, the oldest Scottish Clan society in existence." He said, "My people, the McCoys, migrated from Northern Ireland, through England, to America into Virginia and finally into Kentucky. This is neither myth nor folklore and can be authenticated by genealogists and historians." Overcoming the shouts of those asking him to speak up, Paul continued. "This first annual Hatfield and McCoy Reunion proves that our generations not only survived but we're actually living better than our forefathers and probably better than royal families of that particular era."

Paul, a well-read man, set about encouraging all of us to value what is most important in life. He did so quoting extended pieces of poetry and writings verbatim, even more remarkable since he carried no notes of any kind. "How few men know their riches, what is ours is ours only insofar as we are conscious of it; so that which we accept without thought or which has no special meaning to it is not a real possession." In conclusion, he quoted the last will and testament of Charles Lounsbury, a Chicago attorney confined to spending his last days in a mental institution, considered to be the "most sensible" will ever written. "(Finally), I bequeath the power to have lasting friendships, the capacity for courage and undaunted faith. To our loved ones with snowy crowns, I leave memory, the peace and happiness of old age, and the love and gratitude of their children before they fall asleep."

Then as unassumingly as he had taken it, Paul stepped away from the podium, to a smattering of light applause. The woefully underpowered podium microphone had done a sad injustice to a noble man. Those people close enough to Paul to hear him did their best to grant him the attention he deserved. Much of the room, however, unable to hear him and perhaps unsure of who he was, missed a once-in-a-lifetime opportunity to hear an eloquent dissertation from the great-grandson of Randolph McCoy.

Another family legend took the stage following Paul, greatly aided by a new microphone and partial use of the stage sound system. While the stage was still dark and off-limits to us, Jimmy Wolford set up at the "front" end of the building with a stool and his acoustic guitar. Jimmy, as usual, sported a style all his own. He had on no tie or jacket and wore a bright yellow shirt that he did not tuck into his baggy pants.

I had the pleasure of introducing Jimmy, a real treat since he was one of our modern family legends. "Jimmy Wolford is one of my heroes. (He) was singing about the Hatfields and McCoys when nobody wanted to hear about it. Jimmy was "McCoy" when "McCoy" wasn't cool," I said. Jimmy stepped forward to a round of thunderous applause, an ovation he took humbly. He mentioned that he too had many heroes there that night, including "Tab" and "Mix" McCoy among others.

Jimmy Wolford accepting the "Real McCoy" award

To the delight of the audience, Jimmy performed several songs from his *Great Vendetta* album. He also told stories about his career as a musician with Capital Records, his travels with Senator Hubert Humphrey and growing up as a McCoy in Pike County. He remembered as a child asking his grandmother about the feud. "Son, that's something we don't talk about," said Jimmy. "I went to Grandpa and I said, "Grandpa, tell me about the Hatfields and McCoys," and he said, "We don't talk about the Hatfields and McCoys."

During his time on the campaign trail with Humphrey, Jimmy was prompted by the Senator to discuss the feud. "He would say, Jimmy, tell me about the Hatfields and McCoys." I said, "We don't talk about that." When Humphrey introduced him to the Prime Minister of England in 1971, Wolford gave the same answer to the same question: "We don't talk about that." Finally, in the early 1970s, Jimmy collaborated with songwriters Larry Johnson and Bob Stanley and spent three years researching the feud story. Wolford spoke with Hatfield descendants, Willis Hatfield, last surviving son of "Devil Anse" and Dr. Henry D. Hatfield, "Devil Anse's" nephew. "They hurt for Roseanna McCoy. They hurt for "Devil Anse" and Ellison and them. They hurt for each other. (The feud) was something that occurred that did not have to happen, but it did."

Jimmy finished his mini-concert and stepped away from the microphone, only to return for an encore, after shouts from family members wanting to hear a beloved song from his *Vendetta* project, *Roseanne* Jimmy concluded his appearance that night with profound words that still reverberate with importance, perhaps more so after seventeen years. He challenged all who were present: "Don't ever let anybody say anything bad about a Hatfield because you're a McCoy. Vice versa. Don't say anything bad about a McCoy because you are a Hatfield. Because that's the way it started."

Following Jimmy's appearance, we began bestowing several awards including one to Wolford himself. We presented Jimmy with the first "Real McCoy" award for his decades of service to the family. Additional awards were given to Marilynn Payson and others for their invaluable service to the reunion. Bo was kind enough to thank me publicly and surprised me with the "Chairman's Award," a blue glass diamond-shaped sculpture that I still have today.

A new chapter in feud history was written that night. Hatfields and McCoys from around the country sat down and ate, talked and laughed together and lived to tell the tale. Except perhaps for my bruised ego and Bo's hurt feelings, the night had been a huge success. The story of the feud would never be spoken of again without referencing the reconciliation between the families that night...and there was more to come.

One of the greatest privileges I have had in my life was the opportunity to pay tribute publicly to those family members who had lost their lives during the feud. It was an important part of the weekend's events. It was also one of the more difficult things I have ever had to do.

As descendants of Randolph, Bo and I knew early on that we wanted to honor his legacy and pay respects to those fallen family members.

It was a somber undertaking and the already-crowded format of the M2K dinner seemed to be an inappropriate venue for such a task. Further, we wanted the reading of the twelve names to be a public event and not limited to a private gathering of the Hatfield and McCoy families.

We decided to present the reading of the names at noon on Saturday, June 10th, on the steps of the historic Pike County courthouse on Main Street. Kentucky Governor Paul Patton, a long-time resident of Pikeville, flew home from a business trip in Japan to address the family members on behalf of the Commonwealth. It was a clear day in the shadow of the courthouse as several hundred descendants of both families gathered to hear the Governor's remarks that morning. Local and state officials, including State Representative Ira Branham and long-time Pike County Sheriff Charles "Fuzzy" Keesee, were on hand to hear the Governor speak.

Large crowd of Hatfields and McCoys at the Pike County Courthouse

As was the case throughout the weekend, the crowd of several hundred Hatfields and McCoys was casual, energetic and lively. Those in attendance at the dinner the night before had been joined by additional family members who had come in for the weekend. Most were sporting M2K Reunion hats and shirts, with the blues and reds of family delineation proudly apparent. Even Bo, as he took the stage was wearing a black M2K hat. I was still wearing the same awful cream-colored jacket from the night before.

Following Bo's introduction, Governor Patton, dressed in a commanding dark suit and dark sunglasses, took the stage with authority. He was accompanied by his grandson and his wife, Judi, a long-time supporter of the reunions and feud tourism in general. Unlike the sound problems of the night before, the courthouse stage was equipped with a wonderful sound system. I imagined that the Governor's booming baritone could be heard all the way down Main Street to the McCoy house. Addressing the McCoys, Patton said, "Your assemblage here with your former adversaries, the Hatfields, I think is very, very symbolic and in many ways, illustrates the "new" Appalachia…we are more than coal and timber. We are as modern as tomorrow."

"By your presence here, you signify that you have retained some of the values that we hold so dear," said Patton to both families. "The same traits that caused your families' conflict over a hundred years ago…we still have those traits, and we are proud of those traits." As the Governor concluded his brief speech, he expounded on a theme that most feud writers have managed to miss as the prime motivating force behind the conflict. "Above all, we value family. In this place, more than any other place in our nation, people still value family, as your ancestors valued their kin…loyalty to family, willingness to help family, willingness to stand up for family."

As he wrapped up his remarks, Governor Patton handed the microphone to me and took his place among the crowd gathered to pay their respects. I stepped up to the platform slowly, humbled to speak on behalf of the families. I pulled out the list of the twelve names that I had been carrying around in my jacket pocket for days. I was not sure that I needed the list but I had to be certain that I did not forget anyone. The names would be read aloud, followed by a moment of silence.

I steadied myself, knowing it was to be an emotional and difficult task. I could already feel my throat tightening and my hand began shaking. The once spirited crowd began to quieten. As I read the first name, "Asa Harmon McCoy," someone in the crowd shouted out their family affiliation. The outburst quickly faded, replaced by an eerie stillness. Despite the size of the gathered crowd, with a festival of music, rides and vendors in full force just two blocks away, a profoundly reverent blanket of silence settled over the courthouse area. There was no sound of any kind, save for the names of those who had been lost. "Ellison Hatfield..."

It was then, ever so subtly, that the magnitude of the moment set in for me. It was not so much an awareness of the venue or the crowd or the deafening silence. In that moment, I imagined my great-great-great grandfather, walking up the very same street on which we now stood, calling out the names of his children and family for anyone who would listen. Suddenly, those very same names seemed to leap from the page. "Tolbert McCoy...Pharmer McCoy...Randolph McCoy, Jr..." The words caught in my throat and I could barely speak. Tears filled my eyes and I could no longer read the words. There were more names to come, but they were names I knew well. "Jeff McCoy...Bill Staton...Calvin McCoy...Alifair McCoy..." I struggled to gasp out the words. These were no longer just the names I had heard mentioned in the familiar feud stories. These were real people, many of whom I was related to, who had fought and died for a cause they felt was just. "Jim Vance...William Dempsey...Ellison Mounts...may God rest their souls."

After I finished reading the names, Bo stepped up to pray for healing, a task he would perform many times throughout the course of the weekend. "We know that the pain is indelibly stained in history but...we ask (God) to wipe away the tears, (and) bring joy in the morning as we look to tomorrow." In the stillness, I was certain that each family member standing there felt as I did. Despite the actions taken by or against our ancestors during the feud, we honored the sacrifice they had made and remembered them as family.

As the group slowly began to disperse, a hushed reverence lingered over the gathering. I felt the weight of history begin to lift from my shoulders. The job was done. Although the unity service and softball game were still to come, with the dinner and the courthouse memorial behind us, Bo and I had achieved what we set out to do. We had accepted Randolph's challenge to us as his descendants to remember the sacrifice of those who were lost. I hoped we had done "Ol' Randall" proud.

Festival

"The past, the present and the future are really one: they are today."
Harriet Beecher Stowe

Just over a year after my exploratory visit to Pikeville, we had watched our idea for a McCoy family reunion evolve to become a regional festival that encompassed two states, two counties and two cities 27 miles apart. Once the announcement had been made that we were hosting a three-day festival in Pikeville to coincide with the M2K reunion, the idea had been quickly emulated by our neighbors across the river. Planning for the H2K dinner in Williamson, West Virginia was already well underway when the town of Matewan began organizing local festival events to coincide with those we had scheduled in Pikeville.

In many ways, Williamson is the West Virginia counterpart to its sister city, Pikeville, Kentucky. Williamson is the largest city in Mingo County, with a population of 3200. The nearby town of Matewan had unsuccessfully campaigned against Williamson for the role of county seat in 1896, leading to a long-standing rivalry between the communities. Williamson boomed with the introduction of the Norfolk-Southern Railroad in 1895 and saw its fortunes rise and fall with the development of coal mining operations. Williamson's landmark Coal House, constructed entirely out of coal in 1933, is a testament to the city's mining heritage.[74]

Bo and I were impressed with the energy and enthusiasm displayed by the Williamson organizers. Their schedule of events was ambitious. For the inaugural Reunion Festival, we fielded more questions regarding events scheduled in Williamson than nearly anything else. While events in Matewan generally complimented those we had scheduled in Pikeville, the Williamson schedule was another thing entirely. By January 2000, schedules for the Williamson festival were posted online announcing activities beginning one week *prior* to the festival events set for Pikeville and Matewan.

The West Virginia Department of Tourism and West Virginia Governor Cecil Underwood's office stepped in to offer much-needed resources in support of the events in Williamson. Brochures and billboards in West Virginia touted the expanded Williamson schedule as the "Hatfield McCoy Reunion Festival," with no mention of our events in Pikeville. This led to a great deal of confusion on the part of family members visiting the area. Some were uncertain whether to arrive on the second weekend in June or the first, or whether the "official" events were being held in Williamson or Pikeville. Our diplomatic overtures and willingness to cooperate with West Virginia had led to the creation of a counterpart festival that dared to eclipse our own.

The "Reunion of the Millennium" in Pikeville has the distinction of being the only Reunion Festival that, despite Williamson's insistence to start a week early, was officially scheduled for a period of three days, June 9 -11. The hours for the festival were 9:00 a.m. to 9:00 p.m. on Friday and Saturday. No public festival events were allowed in town on Sunday. Events at the festival were free and open to the public. Vendor rides and other attractions were ticketed.

Since the Reunion Festival was viewed as *our* event, we were tasked with the duties of soliciting, securing, coordinating and managing vendors for the weekend. This meant overseeing vendor registrations, collecting fees, handling requests for premium spaces and scheduling utility hookups. Bo spent much of his time and energy dealing wrangling with sometimes-quarrelsome vendors.

Securing corporate sponsorships for both festival and reunion events had proven to be a difficult task. Some intrepid businesses supported our untested and unproven abilities to pull off a reunion, festival and/or a Reunion-Festival, however. Community Trust Bank and Bell South Mobility were stalwart supporters. Treasured Crafts, an arts and crafts store operating out of the McCoy home on Main Street in Pikeville, was also a sponsor. Western Reserve Systems of Cleveland was an internet hosting company Bo had worked with and was one of our few out-of-state-sponsors. Debbi Preston at Pepsi Cola Company of Pike County stepped up in a big way and provided our M2K vendor tent. Preston's competitor,

Coca-Cola of Pike County, played an important role in the Hatfield-McCoy softball game, providing team coolers loaded with Coke products.

The Hatfield-McCoy Reunion Festival offered a unique platform to highlight local arts and crafts, food and music. As with the "Hillbilly Days" event each year, the Pikeville City Park at the center of town was the ideal location for the "Village of Yesteryear." The Appalachian Artisan Society, an association of craftspeople, agreed to provide more than twenty artists displaying the skills and craftsmanship of a long-ago time.

The park's central gazebo was a sound-equipped stage commonly used to host local musical talent. Larry Webster and his "Mule Band," one of the area's best-known musical acts, agreed to headline the music in the park. Larry agreed to coordinate the scheduling of other musical acts, a role that he served in for "Hillbilly Days" for many years. He knew the local talent well and saw to it that bluegrass and country music was ongoing in the park throughout the weekend.

One of our hopes for the Reunion Festival was to attract families with children. The primary reason we selected the second weekend in June as the date for M2K was to allow most school systems to be out for the summer. We set up a "Lil' Feuders Village" play area near the park with rides and amusements for the children to enjoy.

Another venue we wanted for the festival was a gospel music stage. Gospel music, like bluegrass, has always played an important part in the Appalachian way of life. Gospel music was something that Bo and I knew well. Bo was a Christian gospel preacher with a classical evangelical style, who had preached and sung at many churches and revival gatherings. I had served as a staff musician for several churches, usually playing bass guitar or drums, for more than twenty years. After years of touring with local gospel groups, I ended my career as a weekend road-warrior and collaborated with a friend to open Crown Recording Studio, one of the first digital project studios in North Carolina. Over eleven years, we had produced and recorded more than 400 musical acts, primarily gospel groups, with styles as diverse as country, rock, rhythm and blues and jazz.

The reunion was a popular subject of conversation during late nights in the studio. Fascinated by the prospect of the reunion, several musicians expressed an interest in attending. The Reunion-Festival was open to everyone, family or not, and we needed all the attendees we could muster. If gospel groups wanted to attend, then the least we could do was provide them an opportunity to perform.

The gospel music stage was set up at the courthouse, just beyond the children's rides and play area, about two blocks from the city park. The stage was sponsored by Crown Recording Studio and Ludwig Drum Company. Rene' Couch, an accomplished drummer and pianist who served as a session player on many of my studio projects, had secured the official endorsement of the drum company for the event. The stage was staffed by host group Servant's Heart from Georgia, and the Chosen Few, True in Heart and the Morris Family, all from North Carolina. Contemporary Christian music was provided by independent recording artist Timothy Tuck with special guest, Rene Couch. One local group, Pastor Michael Blanton & Evidence of Staffordsville, Kentucky also performed.

Despite the festival activities scheduled for the venue, attendance at the gospel stage was, by most reports, sparse. Gospel musicians are a humble and dedicated lot, however, and none felt their work to have been in vain. Since 2000, future events have followed our lead. For the inaugural "Hatfield McCoy Heritage Days" in 2013, the courthouse stage was a popular venue that hosted many local gospel and country musicians as part of the event.

Over the course of the weekend, Billy Jack was instrumental in handling a multitude of tasks, assigned or not. Billy Jack was a master of getting things done, hardworking and never asking for praise or recognition. One of his more interesting assignments was securing the vans used for our site tours. In 2000, there were no organized van tours to feud sites in Pike County. The Tug Valley, twenty-five miles east of Pikeville, was home to most of the sites -from feud history. The route down US 119 North, then south on Highway 319 was a journey that was difficult to navigate for out of town visitors. With no buses, cabs or trains in Pikeville, there were few options for visitors who wanted to visit county feud sites, many of which were then unmarked. For the 2000 reunion, we rented vans, driven by Billy Jack and other volunteers, and hosted the first guided van tours to feud sites in the Tug Valley.

As plans for the Reunion Festival had evolved, it became apparent that the logistics of transporting family members between the Bob Amos Park high above Pikeville and the events in town made its use prohibitive. Abandoning the venue, however, left us without a place to play softball. Sherrie Marrs of Pikeville College quickly found us a viable alternative. The school's softball field was centrally located in town and easily accessible by our visitors. Pikeville College provided use of their equipment while Tourism secured some hardy souls to officiate the game.

In addition to the ball field, Sherrie obtained permission for us to use Booth Auditorium. The 650-seat facility was a fully equipped theater, ideal for lectures, dramatic presentations and film screenings. For the festival, we hoped to bring in a noted feud author to speak and do a book signing.

Back in December of 1999, I extended an invitation to Dr. Otis Rice, author of an outstanding book on the feud, *The Hatfields and McCoys*, published in 1982. His book was one of the most concise, well researched and balanced accounts of the feud I had ever read. I felt that he would be an exciting guest for us, although I was uncertain that he would consider attending.

Dr. Otis Rice and Ron at book signing

While awaiting a reply from Dr. Rice, I contacted the legal department of the Arts & Entertainment network hoping to acquire permission to present a screening of a *Biography* episode on the feud, on which Dr. Rice had appeared as the guest historian. After months of email and fax exchanges, the network granted us a single-day license to show *The Hatfields and McCoys* episode with the caveat that they be listed as the official sponsor of Dr. Rice's appearance. In addition, the network mandated that we purchase a case of videos of the program to sell following the event. The ever-resourceful Sherrie Marrs made certain that a video projector and screen along with a sound and light technician was available at the auditorium to assist with the presentation.

Booth Auditorium also gave us the opportunity to present a dramatic retelling of the feud story. We scheduled a regional theater troupe, the West Virginia Theatre's Acting Company of Beaver, W.V. to present *The Last Hanging in Pike County*, a dramatic presentation written by Hatfield descendent and award-winning screenwriter and playwright, Janice Kennedy. The play was set to follow Dr. Rice's appearance.

A second more controversial choice for a speaker was Dr. Altina Waller of the University of Connecticut. Dr. Waller's book about the feud, *Feud: Hatfields, McCoys and Social Change in Appalachia, 1860-1900*, was published by the University of North Carolina Press in 1988. She was the featured feud historian for an episode of the History Channel series, *History's Mysteries*, in 2000.

Dr. Waller's book offered many previously unconsidered theories on the economic underpinnings of the feud's origins. Her book portrayed "Devil Anse" Hatfield as an enterprising businessman, making his mark in timbering. Dr. Waller's book had been criticized by some on the McCoy side as rife with Hatfield sympathies and unfairly critical in its portrayal of Randolph McCoy. Nevertheless, despite our difference of opinions, I extended an offer for her to attend the M2K reunion as well. Dr. Waller was the first to decline our invitation, albeit politely, due to scheduling conflicts.

In March 2000, we received Dr. Rice's decision to be part of the Reunion Festival. He apologized for his delay in getting back to us and assured me that he had no reservations about being part of our event. Although I was unaware of it at the time, Dr. Rice had been facing serious health issues that could have prevented him from attending. Fortunately, he was feeling stronger and he was encouraged by our invitation.

Dr. Rice arrived on the morning of June 10th for his lecture at 10:00 a.m., having made the drive over from West Virginia the previous night with the help of a dutiful assistant. When the video screening was over and it was time for him to speak, Dr. Rice walked up the stairs to the stage on his own, buoyed by the energetic reception from the crowd of about 300. Steadying himself behind the lectern, he spoke for nearly an hour, giving a history of the feud and fielding questions from the audience. Following his appearance, he greeted family members in the auditorium lobby where he signed copies of his book. A kind and decorous man, Dr. Rice was humbled by all the attention shown him. His appearance in 2000 remains one of my indelible memories of the reunions.

In the weeks prior to the reunion, the much-anticipated showdown between the families on the softball field had escalated into an ongoing exchange of taunts and braggadocio. At the courthouse stage earlier on Saturday, I commented that the "McCoys should win easily," although I thought it was prudent to add, "I've heard that crow tastes a lot like chicken, so I'll let you know." At 4:00 p.m. on Saturday, June 10, expectations were high as Bucky Hatfield and his team made the trip over from Williamson to Pikeville to meet the McCoys on their home turf.

The opportunity to see the Hatfields and McCoys square off in a softball game was a point of interest for the press. Numerous local and national network crews were on hand to cover the event. Bo once compared the media interest in the game to spectators at a racetrack waiting to see a crash. "I think they want to see us slug it out," said Bo.[75]

Community Trust Bank served as a corporate sponsor and paid for custom printed pinstriped baseball jerseys and caps, with the Hatfields sporting red and white and the McCoys in blue and white. A partial list of players registered for the McCoy softball team included those named Bob, David, Allan, Barry, Kenny, Sam, Eddie, Jay, Edward, Robert and Norman (Gibbons). Bo served as manager for the team and I served as coach.

Although Bucky was reluctant to share his line up with us, an email dated May 31 gave us at least a partial list of Hatfields rising to the challenge: John, Greg and Tina Bergwitz, Shannon Byler, Cory Clark, Linda Strevel, and Kevin, Alan and Bucky Hatfield. Although Bucky had stocked his team with an arsenal of young and experienced male players, he also included several Hatfield women on his team, notably Tammy Meister at third base. In 2000, we had no women on the McCoy team.

There was a notable difference in demeanor between the family teams. The Hatfields were a rambunctious and energetic group, obviously enjoying themselves and clearly expecting to win. By contrast, the McCoy dugout was strangely quiet. The group of McCoy men were focused and resolute, determined to shake off the bonds of history. The McCoys were there to make a statement.

One late addition to our team was "Larry," a McCoy family member Bo had met earlier in the week. He was about 60 years old, of medium height and wiry. With a full roster of players, squeezing in an extra man was difficult, especially given that "Larry" had yet to present himself in a non-inebriated state. Bo issued an open invitation for him to play on the team under one condition. If he showed up at the game sober, he could play. To our surprise, "Larry" arrived for the game, sober as a church mouse. With a mounting lead in the latter innings of the game, I was able to work him into the lineup. He stepped up to the plate, hit a standing single and, two hits later, crossed home plate to score. The look of pride on his face as he did so was one of the highlights of the game.

For the McCoys, there was much to celebrate. Despite the Hatfield team's obvious skills and athleticism, the McCoys were a single-minded group. By accident or providence, we had assembled a team of lean, athletic and intensely motivated men. Sam, Robert and others were aggressive batters and fast on the base paths. As runs began to tally up, this created problems of a different sort.

Ace-pitcher Bob McCoy of Spencer, Tennessee proved to be a "secret weapon" for the McCoy team. He and his wife, Marlyn were stalwart pillars of every reunion that we held. As a farmer and retired United States Navy submariner, Bob was a versatile and talented man. He was a skilled woodworker, amateur actor and Baptist lay minister – all talents that would be put to good use at reunions over the years. In 2000, however, his abilities as a softball pitcher were a welcome surprise to us.

Early on, the heralded clash between the families proved to be remarkably one-sided, much to the dismay of the Hatfields gathered to watch the game. As the McCoys jumped out to an 11-0 lead, I could hear murmurs of dissent in the crowd from my position as third-base coach. Though Bo and I never intended the game to be anything but a fair competition, as the hosts, it certainly appeared that we had stacked the deck. Despite years of denials by us, there are still persistent allegations that the game was slanted in favor of the McCoys. "They just killed us because they brought ringers in from Pikeville," said Heather Vaillancourt, great-granddaughter of "Devil Anse" Hatfield.[76]

As the Hatfield's run-deficit continued, Bo and Bucky held a quick conference in the McCoy dugout. The two decided that a "mercy" rule would apply, and the game would end after fifteen runs. Secretly, I hoped that the Hatfields would score, for the pride of the family and out of concern for the well-being of the beleaguered reunion organizers fearing a shutout. Fortunately for us, the Hatfields put together a string of base hits to score in the last inning of the game. After five innings, the McCoys had won the game 15-1.

For the McCoys, the victory was something of a historical catharsis. "We kind of took a beating in the last one (the feud), so we kind of wanted to win," said Billy Jack.[77] The Hatfields were gracious in defeat as both families posed for pictures together. Bo and Bucky wrestled playfully for the cameras over the possession of the game trophy. The "Hatfield-McCoy Softball Challenge" trophy went on display in the winning team's tourism office until the rematch the following year.

The McCoys softball victory in 2000 was bittersweet. Following the game, Bo had both teams sign a pair of game softballs. We placed the game balls, player jerseys, caps and scorebooks in a box that we carried back with us to the city park. With a standing order to have the area cleared by nightfall, we hurried back to the venue to oversee the teardown of the children's rides, artisan's displays and vendor tents. The process went smoothly, but left us little time to pack up our M2K vendor tent. As Billy Jack and others worked quickly to dismantle the tent, Bo suddenly realized that the box containing the game materials was missing. Except for the

Hatfield-McCoy softball trophy, all other keepsakes from the historic game were gone.

One of the best local success stories to come out of the Reunion Festival in 2000 was the Hatfield-McCoy Marathon, staged by the Tug Valley Road Runners club under the leadership of David Hatfield. The race through Kentucky and West Virginia was the first Hatfield-McCoy event to cross the river and involve the cooperation of both Mingo and Pike counties. With little in the way of advertising budget or manpower, the club saw a chance to partner with our festival to promote their inaugural event. Attendance for the race in 2000 was minimal, with only "15 marathon finishers and 11 in the accompanying half marathon," said David Hatfield. "But, the winner came all the way from Vermont!"[78] Today, the Hatfield-McCoy Marathon has survived its humble beginnings to attract thousands of runners from around the world for the annual contest.

Perhaps the strongest advocate for the Hatfield McCoy Reunion Festival was the tiny hamlet of Matewan, West Virginia, fourteen miles south of Williamson. More than any other community, Matewan seized the Reunion Festival as its own and ran with it. Seventeen years later, the town continues to host its annual Reunion Festival in June.

The town of Matewan, in Mingo County, with a total area of 0.56 square miles, has a population of nearly 500.[79] Nestled on the bank of the Tug Fork of the Big Sandy where Mate Creek meets the river, Matewan sits in the heart of what was Hatfield territory during the time of the feud. The Hatfield homestead at the mouth of Mate Creek was nearby.

Matewan has a storied history beyond the feud. In 1920, Chief of Police Sid Hatfield and others battled hired-gun detectives representing the Stone Mountain Coal Company who were attempting to evict families of coal miners. The event, dubbed the "Matewan Massacre" resulted in the loss of ten lives.[80]

One of the town's most distinguishing features is its enormous floodwall. The 2350-foot long, 29-foot high concrete wall, built over a period of five years by the Army Corps of Engineers, was completed in

1997. Prior to its construction, Matewan had been flooded 36 times in 50 years. The distinctive artistic concrete panels of the floodwall, depicting the town's colorful history are of special interest to tourists.

For the Reunion Festival, the entire town turned out to put on a grand show for its visitors. Events included a car show, hayrides, a Civil War reenactment and a Hatfield-McCoy tug-of-war. The events in Matewan were organized by a committee of local citizens including Paula Blankenship. "All of the problems we've had with the coal industry has devastated the area. Tourism is one of our outlets. We have to find something to replace mining," said Paula.[81]

With activities for the "Hatfield McCoy Reunion Festival" spread across the region, organized and hosted by a collection of organizations, individuals and groups, the spirit of cooperation was best exemplified by the events set for Sunday in Matewan. Following the separate M2K events in Pikeville and H2K events in Williamson, we hoped that the weekend would culminate in a joint assembly of the families in a public display of unity. Matewan seemed to be the obvious location for such an event. A two-lane bridge crossed the river there, connecting the community of Buskirk, Kentucky with the town of Matewan. We believed the bridge would make an ideal location for a combined Hatfield-McCoy unity service, with both families coming together at a neutral location over the river that had long separated them.

Such a sentiment would have remained just that, had it not been for West Virginia Tourism and the office of Governor Cecil Underwood. Governor Underwood was a steadfast supporter of Hatfield-McCoy efforts and was a welcome guest at the Matewan events. "I'm happy to be part of this. No other people anywhere have gained such notoriety and popularity such as this," he said.[82] He ordered the closure of the bridge to traffic for the morning of the service. His office dispatched a mobile stage that was erected in the center of the bridge. The prayer service was officiated by Bo McCoy and Rev. Terry Hatfield of Panora, Iowa, with Governor Cecil Underwood, West Virginia Tourism Commissioner Bob Reintsema and other officials in attendance.

Members of both families gathered around the stage in the center of the bridge as Cecil Hatfield welcomed family members and guests. Brenda Bergwitz offered prayers for those in attendance before Cecil introduced Bo to the makeshift congregation. Bo led the congregation in an acapella rendition of the old Christian hymn, "Amazing Grace."

Bo McCoy, Ron and Rev. Terry Hatfield at the Unity Service

Bo's message was a surprisingly low-key appeal for unity, exhorting family members to put "the past behind" them. With no scripted sermon except for three brief phrases he had scribbled on the back of the service program during Cecil Hatfield's opening remarks, Bo's appeal was direct and from the heart. He said, "I'm going to ask you to do something very unorthodox." As family members extended their hands in front of them, Bo encouraged them to both acknowledge and to let go of the past. "I'm going to ask you to put your sins in your right hand, and....to put the sins of (those who have wronged you) in your left." Then he instructed the group to turn around and face the river, and to throw their collective sins figuratively into the waters of the Tug Fork below, there to be forgiven and forgotten. "Don't go fishing," he admonished. "(They're) behind you now...let them stay forever buried at the bottom of the Tug."[83]

Terry Hatfield, an ordained minister in the Church of the Brethren, followed with a message about the promise of possibility saying, "When one door closes, another door opens." He began his message with a phrase that would be used many times by the families in the years to come: "Jesus is the real McCoy." Describing his upbringing on the plains of Kansas as a "small twig of the family tree," his experience in making the trip to the family homeland was like many of the stories I had heard from other family members. "This weekend, I regained some of that sense of belonging—and some of that sense of connectedness—to the larger family," he said. Surveying the eclectic group of relatives from both families gathered there on the bridge, he understood the meaning of unity. "What a blessed demonstration this is today for marriages, for personal relationships and for families and for communities and for nations that need some hope, hope that peace can come, hope that things that have been in the past can set aside. If (those involved in) the most infamous family conflict in America can find true peace, then the grace of God surely abounds."

As Reverend Hatfield concluded his sermon, Bo came forward to pray for him, laying hands on his forehead as he did so. "If you can't love your brother who you can see, how can you love the brother you cannot see?"[84] Pastor Hatfield, in turn prayed for Bo. It was another moment in history as Hatfield and McCoy family members joined hands in a show of unity, as Bo led a closing rendition of the old church hymn, "Bind Us Together." As the service concluded, family members were in no hurry to leave, lingering to bask in the sense of peace that permeated the crowd. "I got to hug Terry and Scott Hatfield and we are forever united…I want this (day) to symbolize the unity of the future rather than the disunity of the past," said Clyde McCoy, a professor from the University of Miami.[85]

Events for Sunday in Matewan included a pig roast, music, crafts and two weddings on the steps of the Town Hall, where the lucky couples jumped a broom as happy family members fired celebratory shotgun blasts into the air. Visitors like Victoria Hatfield Hudson, who had driven 800 miles from the University of Florida, were duly impressed by Matewan's hospitality. "I think it's great and I've had the most wonderful time….I'll be retiring in a few years and this is the right kind of town to retire in."[86] Shortly after lunch, preparations began for the day's battle between the families, the tug-of-war across the Tug.

Tug-of-war across the Tug Fork

For the tug-of-war, the families were divided into teams of fifteen members each. Unlike the softball game the day before, most of the participants in the day's confrontation were local or held close family connections in the area. The Hatfields, still smarting from their loss in Pikeville, were especially motivated to win the event. Bill Vaillencourt of Greenbriar, Arkansas actively recruited volunteers to participate. "We want the big people," he said. "We want to win." Gordon Jorgenson, a Hatfield relative visiting from Nebraska, offered a secondary strategy, should the McCoys prevail. "We let go and let them fall on their butts."[87]

With ample volunteers on hand, neither Bo nor I, still dressed in coats and ties from the unity service, were enlisted to participate. As the Matewan Fire department began wading across the waist-deep water, thick rope in hand, the families began taking their places on opposing riverbanks. The McCoys crossed the bridge back into Pike County while the Hatfields took up position on the Mingo County side. Thousands of spectators gathered along the Matewan floodwall to watch the spectacle.

For some, the site selected for the tug-of-war bordered on sacrilege. The area behind where the McCoy team stood was a sacred feud site. It was the clearing where the Hatfields had executed the three McCoy boys following the death of Ellison Hatfield. Logistically, it made sense to stage the tug-of-war there as it was the lowest and most accessible point of the river. Edward McCoy, great-great-great grandson of Randolph, reconciled himself to the choice of venue. "We are tugging against each other, but we are really pulling each other together. That's what this is all about."

On the West Virginia bank, a volunteer with a bullhorn shouted at the crowd gathered at the floodwall to begin cheering for the Hatfield team. Surprisingly, sentiment was running in favor of the McCoys and cheers rang out in support of the team from both sides of the Tug Fork. The McCoy team, including some members like Sam McCoy from the victorious softball team, sat under the shade trees, pensive and determined, as they waited quietly. The more flamboyant Hatfield team stood confidently in the sun, shouting friendly taunts across the water, egged on by one provocative heckler on the McCoy side. Although the teams were comprised mostly of males, several female family members had joined the teams on both sides of the river.

West Virginia Governor Underwood arrived by black SUV to begin the festivities. Both families dug deeply into the muddy banks as the Governor fired a starter's pistol to signal the beginning of the struggle. In mud up to his knees, lead man Ronnie Hatfield steadfastly refused to budge, to the point that less resolute family members were beginning to be pulled over the top of him. Although the Hatfields were well represented by muscle and mass, the tenacity of the McCoys won out. The Hatfields went for an unwelcome swim in the Big Sandy. In a show of good sportsmanship, the entire Hatfield team made their way across the river to shake hands with the McCoys.

The Hatfield's intention was not entirely magnanimous, however. Tim McCoy of Columbus, Ohio, whose jibes had earned the displeasure of the Hatfields earlier, was picked up by the Hatfield entourage and tossed headlong into the river. Despite early resistance from Sam and other family members, the McCoys relented and gave up Tim in the spirit of keeping the peace…or perhaps, because he had it coming to him. "That felt good, even if we didn't win," said Gordon Jorgenson.[88]

    The close of the "Reunion of the Millennium" on Sunday was more than just the end of a long and hectic week of activity. It was the culmination of a whirlwind journey of exploration into my past that began in 1997. As Bo, Billy Jack and I returned the rental vans to Williamson that night, we enjoyed the reprieve from the frantic pace after two years of planning. It was my first chance to take it all in.

    No matter the measures of success by which the reunion would be judged, I was content that we had completed what we had set out to do. The once feuding families had returned to the hallowed grounds of their ancestors, to pay their respects and remember the sacrifices of those who had gone before us. We reunited with our families' shared history and made peace with it. We were now the Hatfield-McCoy family, forged together by the bonds of a common history.

    On Monday morning, as we packed up our families, said our goodbyes and headed home, we gave no thought to any future Hatfield-McCoy endeavors. With all avenues of our personal and financial resources exhausted, we were certain that we had given the event our best effort. Little did we know we were just getting started.

M2K2

"Those who do not remember the past are condemned to repeat it."
George Santayana

The months following the "Reunion of the Millennium" were a time of recuperation and rebuilding for Bo and me. For two years, the efforts involved in organizing the reunion had reached near obsessive levels, resulting in detrimental effects to our personal lives and finances that lingered for years to come. The nearly fourteen months of frenzied media interest that had followed us relentlessly soon faded into blissful silence. Just as quickly as the story of the reunion had launched us onto the national stage, the Hatfields and McCoys were once again yesterday's news. It was not an entirely unwelcome turn of events for us. As exhausted M2K co-organizers, we needed time to recover the remnants of our "normal" lives and move forward. Photographs, memories and mounds of debt were lasting reminders of an important event of which we were both proud.

While Bo and I were seldom at a loss for ideas, we had given no serious thought to Hatfield-McCoy related plans beyond the conclusion of M2K. Certainly, there was no way that we could possibly attempt a second event, given our ongoing lack of manpower and resources. Mentally, emotionally and financially spent, we had placed all that we had on a single roll of the dice. Incredibly, we had defied the odds and the Hatfield-McCoy family made history.

In the years following M2K, Bo confessed to me a more candid reason for his not planning beyond the 2000 reunion. At the time, his lifelong battle for his health had taken its toll and his prognosis for improvement was not good. He frankly did not expect that he would live to see future reunions. The "Reunion of the Millennium" was the culmination of his life's ministerial work and a fitting conclusion to unresolved family matters. It was a coda to a life well lived. Thankfully, Bo faced his health crisis head on. He has recovered and has gone on to greater academic and professional achievements.

The principal reason for our lack of planning for future reunions was our sincere disbelief in the possibility that anyone might be interested in doing it again. Despite the national and international media attention given the event, we had failed to persuade the majority of our family members to attend, especially those on the local level. Some naysayers were quick to categorize our Reunion Festival as a failure at worst and disappointing at best.

Months after the event, however, the success of the first reunion was sufficient to continue generating email and website inquiries about a 2001 event. Online, a considerable number of family members were professing their regrets for having missed the 2000 reunion and expressing their interest in attending a follow up event. Back in Pikeville, the tourism office was busy fielding phone calls from individuals curious about the details of a 2001 reunion they assumed was going to happen.

Meanwhile, someone failed to mention the fact that we had no future plans to the folks in West Virginia. Before our M2K attendees could find their way back home, Matewan and Williamson were already posting schedules for the second annual Hatfield McCoy Reunion Festival, set for the second weekend in June 2001. Meanwhile, Pikeville-Pike County Tourism waited to hear our intentions.

Bo and I always hoped that the Reunion Festival would take root and become a recurring local event that would outlive our participation in it. In as much as Tourism was not in the business of hosting family reunions, we were not in the business of organizing regional festivals. The Hatfield McCoy Reunion Festival was a curious mix of both.

When Phyllis Hunt contacted us about a 2001 event, we considered the prospect with equal measures of concern and skepticism. Attempting a second Hatfield McCoy Reunion Festival in the shadow of the first was akin to the old axiom about catching lightning in a bottle for a second time. We were faced with following up an event that we could not hope to recreate or exceed. The unprecedented national reunion of the Hatfield and McCoy families was no longer a unique proposition. It had been done before.

Without the benefit of the media attention given to M2K, we knew that promoting the second reunion adequately would be a challenge unto itself. Compelling family members that had come to the 2000 reunion to return for a second was a near-impossible task. Overall, it was a daunting proposition that no one in his right mind should have been willing to undertake.

Judge Karen Gibson, John Gatling, Ron and Phyllis Hunt

With the Eastern Kentucky Tourism initiative of Kentucky Representative Hal Rogers on the horizon, city and county officials were eager to see a reunion take place once again. Enticed by the notion or just too stubborn to concede, Bo and I agreed to helm the event for a second year. We could not stand idly by and watch the Reunion Festival we had worked so hard to build fail in its infancy.

Unlike the first reunion, however, we now had the benefit of experience, a network of local resources and a meager organizational infrastructure that had not existed previously. Some local opposition, certain the Reunion Festival was a one-and-done affair, remained unconvinced by the attention the 2000 reunion had generated. Even with much-needed support on a local level, a second reunion faced a constraint of a different sort. With the M2K event, we had more than eighteen months to plan and prepare – but for 2001, we would have only a short ten months to pull it all together. Organizing a second Hatfield-McCoy reunion proved as challenging as the first.

With the necessary parties on board, the follow-up reunion was again set for the second weekend in June, this time to coincide with the events already scheduled in West Virginia. Following our brief sabbatical, Bo and I dove headlong into the process of organizing the event we dubbed

"M2K2." Even more than the first reunion, we felt that it was incumbent upon us to organize new events for our visitors to participate in, especially for those family members returning for the second year in a row.

Events in Pikeville included genealogy classes, record searches at the Pike County courthouse, local author book-signings, and a display of feud-era artifacts. The tourism office conducted guided van tours that carried visitors from Pikeville to the Tug Valley to witness dramatic reenactments of feud events at the actual sites where they had taken place. 2001 saw the dedication of four new feud-site highway markers, sponsored by the Kentucky Historical Society and the State Transportation Cabinet.

For the 2001 reunion, we embraced the blueprint of the "Reunion of the Millennium" by repeating several popular events, including the author's appearance and book signing at Booth Auditorium, the softball game on Saturday, and the tug-of-war and unity service in Matewan on Sunday. Although we had preliminary discussions about relocating the dinner to a more casual environment, the Friday night banquet was once again held at the Landmark Inn. With about 250 people in attendance for 2001, the room was entirely more comfortable – and this time I brought the sound system. Entertainment for the night was provided by Eddie Nenni and the Jaguars, a local "oldies" group recommended by Phyllis Hunt. The band was so well received that we contracted them for a return engagement in 2002.

2001 was the year the Reunion Festival became a four-day event. At the request of Tourism and the county, the event was expanded to allow vendors an additional day of business and to extend the stay of visitors coming to town. Given the time necessary to allow attendees to visit feud sites in the Tug Valley, expanding the event for an additional day seemed a reasonable request. Scheduling enough activities to fill an extra day proved more challenging.

Without the benefit of the national media interest that the 2000 reunion inspired, it was essential to advertise the 2001 event by whatever means available. West Virginia and Kentucky continued to support the Reunion Festival at the state level, promoting it as an "official" tourism event in brochures, billboards and publications. Fortunately, Pikeville-Pike County Tourism was actively promoting the reunion through its offices, producing an assortment of professional brochures and schedules.

Although our advertising budget was non-existent, one avenue I felt might give us some exposure on a national level was running a small advertisement in *USA Today*. Space for an advertisement in the national publication was highly valued. Since the newspaper was only published during the week, an ad that appeared in the Friday edition would be seen throughout the weekend. On April 13, Tourism sponsored a small one-inch announcement for the 2001 Reunion Festival in the "Notices" section of the newspaper. The unremarkable listing did little for our marketing efforts, but it represented an achievement of a different sort. For the first time in history, a national publication had run an ad for a "Hatfield-McCoy *reunion*."

The financial prospects for our hosting a second-year event were dire. I sent an email to Bo addressing my concerns: "As we begin organizing the 2001 Festival, I must express some concern at the projected financial burdens that the festival will entail. Unlike last year's effort, we do not have the two-year lead-time... required to raise the capital for the "Reunion of the Millennium." I believe that additional support and assistance will be needed from Pike County authorities in order to raise the necessary support in the next few months. As per last year, I believe that ticket sales, solicited corporate donations and vendor sales can be used to offset some of these costs." It was unfounded optimism on my part.

Merchandise sales through the M2K vendor tent were the saving grace of our rapidly imploding corporate financial situation. Products for M2K2 included embroidered shirts and hats, t-shirts, coins, key tags, sipper bottles, coffee mugs, pens, mouse pads, books, CDs and videos. By 2001, however, reunion merchandise was no longer exclusive to us. Quality Hatfield-McCoy merchandise was available in a multitude of outlets from Pikeville to Williamson to Matewan.

The aftermath of the 2000 media frenzy resulted in one substantial benefit for us. For better or worse, people knew who we were. While we held no place of influence in the local community, we no longer had to take the hat-in-hand, door-to-door salesman approach that was the hallmark of our previous sponsorship campaign. Securing corporate sponsors was never an easy task, but getting introductions and scheduling appointments was now considerably easier. Several sponsors invited themselves to the event.

A catalog writer for Land End's, a manufacturer of custom apparel, contacted us and requested our participation in a campaign they were planning. As we were "the most famous family reunion in America," the writer hoped that we would agree to promote the company's new mesh polo shirts, color-coded to denote the two families. The company offered to donate shirts in exchange for pictures they could use as part of their catalog.

While we welcomed the company's interest, their involvement led to a frantic beginning very early on the first morning of the festival, when I received an urgent telephone call from Bo. The Land's End representatives had arrived unannounced at the tourism train with boxes of Land End's shirts in hand, embroidered with a "Hatfields and McCoys" logo of their own design. The Land End's representatives were on a tight travel schedule, so Bo was on the phone, desperately rounding up "models" willing to participate.

In a scene repeated many times over the years, I violated my share of Pikeville's traffic laws, arriving downtown at the tourism office in record time, to find the ever-ready Jerry Hatfield already dressed in the traditional "Hatfield Red" and ready to go. Quickly, I grabbed a dark "McCoy Blue" shirt and ducked behind the Tourism train to get dressed. This was not the first time, nor the last, that I changed clothes semi-publicly in Pike County. Too often, Bo and I required to run from a coat and tie formal event to an informal family affair to a business casual media event to a period costume dramatic reenactment, usually within a short span of time. Arriving for an event properly dressed meant changing wherever was convenient. Apparently, I was never as discreet as I imagined myself to have been. I have seen more reunion photographs of me in various states of public undress than I dare to mention.

With the morning costume change behind me, Jerry Hatfield and I posed for a series of pictures, as did Bob McCoy and others. After an hour, the Land's End representatives seemed happy with the results and went on their way as quickly as they came. To my knowledge, the company never used the photographs they took or made mention of their contributions to the 2001 Reunion Festival. Their donated shirts have lived on, however, in Associated Press pictures that have appeared countless times over the past sixteen years in publications around the world.

Following her ground-breaking article that launched our M2K efforts and subsequent articles that followed it, Kimberly Hefling was promoted and reassigned. She was replaced by another Associated Press reporter, Roger Alford. Alford covered some of the most significant Hatfield-McCoy events in the following years including the McCoy Cemetery court case and the Hatfield-McCoy truce signing. Alford had dispatched an AP photographer to the park on the morning of the Land's End shoot to gather file photographs for upcoming stories. The photographer requested to take some pictures of Jerry and me together.

The photographer asked for a recommendation for an appropriate location for a Hatfield-McCoy picture. I suggested that we pose in front of the highway marker at Dils Cemetery, the only marker that reads "Hatfield McCoy feud." The marker site was located on a steep incline at the base of the cemetery.

At the marker location, Jerry and I stepped gamely over the guardrail and took our places under the sign. The photographer stood on the wooden walkway nearby and prepared the shot as Jerry and I tried to secure our footing on the steep hillside. Because Jerry is significantly taller than I am, I suggested that he should stand on the lower side of the hill. Stationing Jerry on the left side also placed us both under the respective family surnames as listed on the marker. In retrospect, I should have been more considerate of my compatriot, thirty years my senior, who was perched precariously on a hill that dropped twenty feet to the parking lot. Jerry, tough Texan that he is, did not complain as he dug in his boots and posed for the picture. Days later, when the picture appeared in conjunction with Alford's Associated Press article, it was obvious that posing on the hillside had been a mistake. Because of our positioning on the hillside, the picture showed the proud, tall Texas Hatfield to be a full foot shorter than the McCoy boy from North Carolina. Try as I may, I have never convinced Jerry that it was not my intention for the picture to turn out as it did. To make matters worse, this particular Associated Press file photo has been used repeatedly over the years to accompany Hatfield-McCoy articles in a variety of media from *USA Today* to the *National Examiner*.

Another sponsor that participated in a big way in the 2001 Hatfield-McCoy Reunion Festival was Pike County Coca-Cola. We campaigned unsuccessfully in the previous year to enlist their financial help. As with many of our solicitation efforts the first year, we were unable to convince them of our ability to produce an event that was beneficial for both families and the community. When the 2001 event rolled around, however, Coca Cola was determined to be part of it.

On June 4, Pikeville Coca-Cola held a press conference in the Landmark Inn banquet room to announce the release of a commemorative Hatfield-McCoy Coca-Cola bottle. They had enjoyed success regionally with a "Hillbilly Days" tie-in and felt that the Reunion Festival would be an ideal platform from which to launch a Hatfield-McCoy bottle. The Coca-Cola press conference reached across political and geographic divides by inviting Governor and First Lady Paul and Judi Patton, Judge-Executive Karen Gibson, Pikeville Mayor Frank Morris, "Doc" Fletcher, and family members Bo McCoy and Cecil Hatfield. Sales manager Joe Adams announced that a share of the proceeds from sales of the bottles, with an established minimum of $15,000 would be donated to Pikeville-Pike County Tourism. "Collecting these Coke bottles is a worldwide phenomenon," said Patton. "This is a win-win situation." Cecil Hatfield offered a bit of wisdom we had been advocating since the beginning of our reunion efforts. "We have to ignore the river and work together," Hatfield said.[89]

For the launch of the bottle, Coke unveiled a pair of Hatfield and McCoy representative cartoon characters that were stereotypically "hillbilly." They wore bib overalls, plaid shirts and straw hats, not unlike similar characters created for the "Hillbilly Days" bottles. The characters were featured in all of Coke's marketing efforts and appeared frequently in print and online marketing materials in Pike County and West Virginia.

The bottles were an immediate hit and sold out before the weekend was over. 2001 and 2002 were the only years the bottles were created. In 2003, as a cost-saving measure, Coke released commemorative six-pack cans in lieu of bottles. While not the collector's item that the bottles were, the colorful cans were popular and more plentiful. By 2005, as attendance to the Reunion Festivals began to fall off, Pike County Coca-Cola discontinued the line altogether.

In addition to the lack of media attention, shorter planning time and the absence of financial and personnel resources, the 2001 Reunion Festival was plagued by an altogether unexpected and invincible adversary: rain. Although the weather in the Tug Valley region in the month of June was generally hot and humid, the area had seen record levels of rain preceding the 2001 event. Creeks and streams were swollen to the point that even a small amount of additional precipitation could send them flooding over roads and bridges.

The week leading up to the 2001 Reunion Festival continued the pattern of heavy rainfall. Attending area events in advance of the reunion, Bo and I were escorted in vehicles that crossed over roads already inundated by stream waters. We hoped the waters would let up enough to allow for the van tours and other festival events scheduled in the county. While some of the creek waters did subside, the rain did not. Thursday of the Festival was a complete washout. The rain continued sporadically on Friday and well into Saturday. Some events did take place as scheduled, although the year's softball rematch was not one of them. The Hatfields would have to wait until 2002 for a rematch. Sunday was the finest day of the weekend, with blue skies and not a cloud in sight.

The 2001 festival offered a greater variety of historical and genealogical events for our attendees, which was something sorely missing from the M2K event. Visitors were granted unprecedented free access to the historical records of the Pike County courthouse for the purposes of genealogy research. Historians Connie Maddox and Betty Howard assisted visitors there with research.

The old train station on Hambley Boulevard in Pikeville was the host site for a makeshift Hatfield-McCoy museum exhibit. McCoy descendent John Daniels of Felton, Delaware loaned the tourism office an old rope bed that once belonged to Asa Harmon McCoy for display. The bed was the centerpiece of the exhibit that featured pictures, documents and other items related to the feud and regional history.

A wealth of authors with books on local interest was on hand for book signings as well. A free class on the use of the internet for genealogy research was conducted at the Pike County Library. The library was also the host site for a display of rare, historical feud pictures. Walking tours of downtown Pikeville guided by historian and author Ed Maddox were sponsored by the Pike County Society for Historical and Genealogical Research.

The Thursday night of our first-ever four-day event allowed us to organize a low-key affair that was as historically noteworthy as anything we had done previously. Over the years, Randolph and Sarah McCoy's final home in Pikeville had assumed many identities. In 2001, the Garden Café, a small family-style restaurant, was housed there and offered a limited menu of home-cooked meals. For Thursday night of the reunion, we chose the café to be the host site of the first "Chairman's Gala" dinner. About two dozen McCoys, along with a dozen Hatfields gathered in the front and middle rooms of the house for dinner on June 7. The Hatfields were guests of unprecedented importance. History was made that night as the Hatfields and McCoys broke bread together in the home of Randolph McCoy.

Bo and I remained committed to having a "L'il Feuders" play area for the festival, with rides and activities for our youngest attendees. A company used for "Hillbilly Days" signed a contract with us to serve as the

Reunion Festival ride provider for 2001. By Thursday night, however, they had yet to arrive. Frantic phone calls from Bo and the Kentucky State ride inspector determined that the vendor had a history of not showing up for an event, especially if he expected not to make money. Bo was undeterred. "The focus of this Festival hasn't changed," he said. "It would take more than a cancelled carnival to stop the festival."[90] Fortunately, Phyllis Hunt came to the rescue, using her contacts with the Shriners to secure a carnival with games and rides for the children.

For the duration of the Reunion Festival, rain continued to plague the city park venue. Vendors and artisans battled rain and mud to sell their wares. Hardy musicians and singers took the stage at the gazebo, offering bluegrass and gospel music as weather permitted. By the time we dismantled the M2K tent late Saturday afternoon, we were standing in ankle-deep water.

For M2K2, the county offered us a special treat, one that permitted Bo and me greater ease of access to the many activities around town at which we were expected to appear. Golf carts were provided for our use, on loan from a local golf course. Having the carts freed us from having to find parking near the city park where our M2K vendor tent was located, and greatly assisted us with the frequent trips we made back and forth to our vehicles.

One incident involving the golf carts remains engrained in my memory. My daughter Rachel, then aged eleven, accompanied me on one of the numerous trips to the family mini-van to pick up more M2K paraphernalia. After considerable pleading on her part, I consented to let her drive the golf cart on the return trip to the park. The carts were not particularly fast and were easy to maneuver, so little harm could come of it.

As we made our way back to the park, I directed Rachel to park the cart behind a food vendor trailer, beside a utility pole. Rachel had done well driving the cart to this point, not yet having been called upon to stop the vehicle. As we approached the pole at breakneck speed, I tried in vain to help her slow down. Rachel did not realize that the secret to stopping a golf cart was letting up on the accelerator. The pedal was not a break. As we reached the point of no return, Rachel made one last desperate attempt and pressed the pedal hard to the floorboard. Until that day, I was unaware that golf carts possessed the capability of vertical ascent. Somewhat miraculously, she had managed to run the cart straight up the side of the utility pole. As Rachel eased off the pedal, I hopped out to help guide the cart back down to earth. Remarkably, the golf cart and its occupants were unscathed. Perhaps not coincidentally, it was the last year we were allowed use of the golf carts.

Dramatic feud recreations were something that we had hoped for since the earliest days of reunion planning. John Gatling of the Judge Executive's office was the first to suggest the idea. He had seen actors in character walk the cemeteries of Birmingham, Alabama, telling stories about the historic events of their lives. He felt that a similar approach to reenactments would work well in Pike County.

Ron with Betty Howard

Selecting the characters to be brought to life and scripting the words they would speak was a task taken up by the very capable Betty Howard. An avid researcher and devout records-hound, Betty had been a genealogist and amateur historian for more than forty years. A descendant of both the Hatfields and McCoys, Betty was an outspoken advocate of feud preservation efforts and a great supporter of the reunions. There was no finer expert on the subject of the feud in Pike County.

Working from her extensive library of notes and research, Betty began writing first-person monologues to be performed at selected sites. Stephanie Richards, a prolific director in the Pike County artistic community, worked to find local volunteers to play the roles. For the second reunion, the presentation of feud reenactments was a risk. It had never been done before, nor did anyone really know what to expect. The gamble paid off and the monologues were well received.

Pikeville-Pike County Tourism organized a group of 15-passenger vans and drivers to make the four-hour round-trip tour of the Tug Valley historical feud sites, beginning at 8:00 on Saturday morning. The Valley shuttles made stops at local crafts and quilt shows along the way to allow visitors the opportunity to support local artisans. Tickets for the tour were $5, which was less than the cost of the gas it took for an individual to make the drive himself. In addition, Tourism offered an in-town shuttle that ferried visitors to points-of-interest around the City of Pikeville, from Dils Cemetery to the Pikeville Cut-Through. Tickets for the in-town shuttle were $1.

Character monologues for the first year were performed at three designated feud sites. Local volunteer actors in costume met the arriving vanloads of visitors four times during the morning and early afternoon. Visitors in 2001 were introduced to "Aunt Betty" and "Roseanna" at the Uriah McCoy house, while at the Paw-Paw tree site, the three McCoy brothers told of their sad fate. At Blackberry Creek, visitors were met by "Asa Harmon McCoy," his wife, "Patty Cline McCoy" and his slave, "Pete."

Given the success of the book signing by Dr. Rice the previous year, we followed up with a guest who proved to be a provocative choice. Unable to participate in the M2K reunion, Dr. Altina Waller agreed to join us in 2001. For Dr. Waller's appearance at the Reunion Festival, A&E agreed to a screening of *"Family Feud: the Hatfields and McCoys,"* to be followed by Dr. Waller's lecture and a question and answer session.

Unlike Dr. Rice's practical and measured approach to the feud, Dr. Waller's position was regarded as "pro-Hatfield" by some in the McCoy family. In an interview given for the documentary film "West Virginia" recorded shortly after the publication of her feud book in 1992, Dr. Waller gave the following basis for her enmity with the McCoys. "One of the reasons the McCoys don't like me as much in the Tug Valley as the Hatfields do is that I seem to suggest that Randal McCoy, the patriarch of the family, was sort of irrational and flamboyant and did jump into wanting violence more than, say, Anderson Hatfield," said Waller.[91]

My contentious selection for a guest lecturer arrived at Booth Auditorium on Saturday morning, promptly on time. In person, I found Dr. Waller to be well spoken, intelligent, thoughtful and gracious, an unlikely target of ire for those in the McCoy camp. Her matronly demeanor; however, was in stark contrast to the inflammatory things she was prone to saying.

Dr. Waller's lecture and book signing proved to be quite popular. Several hundred people turned out to hear her speak, many of them Hatfields. There was also a surprising contingent of McCoys in attendance as well including some who were vocal opponents of Dr. Waller's views. I knew that the potential for an altercation was great.

Following the video presentation, I introduced Dr. Waller to the waiting crowd. The audience was polite and receptive during her lecture. As she opened the floor for questions, I held my breath, dreading the possible outcome. To my great relief, Dr. Waller fielded the tough questions adeptly. The exchanges were lively and engaging but remained cordial. Although members of both families were on their best behavior that day, I was relieved when the event was over. Dr. Waller's appearance at Booth had gone off without a hitch, but it was the last author event we scheduled there.

In 2001, Pike County, Pikeville-Pike County Tourism, the Kentucky Historical Society and the Kentucky Transportation Cabinet began a series of new highway marker dedications that continued for years to come. 2001 saw the unveiling of four new highway markers, denoting locations of historic feud events. Sites selected included Randolph McCoy's home off Highway 319 on the Blackberry Fork of Pond Creek, the McCoy Cemetery in Hardy, the site of Asa Harmon's killing near Ransom and the location of the hog trial and Election Day fight, near the post office in McCarr. In 2001, the ruins of Preacher Anderson Hatfield's home, site of the infamous "pig trial," were a thick plot of undergrowth and trees. The cabin had disintegrated long before and only the stones of the cabin's chimneystacks remained.

On Sunday at 9:00 a.m., the markers were dedicated in a ceremony presided over by Walter "Doc" Fletcher, with an invocation given by Bo. A crowd of local media including prominent local radio personality, "Dr. Don" Bevins of WXLR gathered as Kentucky Governor Paul Patton stood side by side with long-time political rival Pike County Judge Executive Karen Gibson for the dedication of the new marker. The Judge watched politely as the Governor, dressed in his usual dark suit, pushed his way through the undergrowth and explored the remains of the cabin site. By 2004, the lot would be cleared and a replica of the cabin rebuilt, funded by grant monies received as part of Kentucky Representative Hal Roger's initiative to bolster eastern Kentucky tourism. The cabin recreation stands as a shining example of cooperative efforts in feud site preservation.

Following the marker dedication, the families gathered again on the Buskirk-Matewan Bridge for a service that commemorated unity of a different sort. Newly elected West Virginia Governor Bob Wise extended an invitation to Kentucky Governor Paul Patton to attend the event in Matewan. "We have common bonds and borders," he said. "We need to work together on this area." In a rare joint appearance, the two Governors posed for pictures together, shaking hands and agreeing to work cooperatively for the benefit of the region.

With the abundance of political dignitaries in attendance, the unity service was less of the spiritual affair that it had been one year prior. In addition to Bo McCoy and Cecil Hatfield, speakers at the service included a lengthy list of politicians. Despite the change in tenor, the theme of unity prevailed. One speaker, Bob Wolford, referring to the mammoth Matewan floodwall, said "it was once only particles before it brought together to form an anchor of hope and comfort. We too must come together to form a wall of peace, comfort and unity."[92]

The town of Matewan turned out in full force for the weekend of the Reunion Festival, as it had the previous year. With record rains swelling the waters of the Tug Fork, the tug-of-war event was relocated to a field near the Matewan town hall. Spectators looked on as teams comprised of mostly local Hatfields and McCoys fought it out. For the second year in a row, the McCoys were victorious, though the Hatfields would return undaunted the following year.

The 2001 Reunion Festival ended as a decided victory over the impossible. Despite the obstacles of lower turnout, less media interest, little advertising, uncooperative vendors and copious amounts of rain, we had proven it was possible to produce a Hatfield McCoy Reunion Festival event on an annual basis, a tradition that continues in the region to this day.

2002

"Study the past if you would define the future."
Confucius

The third annual Hatfield-McCoy Reunion Festival was a time of reinvention and a return to the heart of our original idea of hosting a family reunion. The tragic events of September 11, 2001 mandated a different tone for our 2002 event. Our county was in a time of reaffirmation of the important things in life. For us, it was a time of renewed focus on family. From an informal Friday night dinner, to a Hatfield wedding in the city park to the much-anticipated rematch on the softball field, every event was a renewed celebration of family. 2002 was also the year that "Bad" Frank Phillips returned to walk the earth …and nearly got me arrested.

The dramatic monologues for 2002 called for an expansion of the cast of feud characters as well as the number of sites selected for presentations. Betty Howard and Stephanie Richards decided to open the selection of volunteers to include those family members attending the reunion. Betty selected Bob McCoy of Spencer, Tennessee for the role of Asa Harmon McCoy. He was the quintessential southern gentleman, whose dignity and strength of character translated well into his portrayal of Asa Harmon. Bob was also a dead-ringer for Asa Harmon's brother, Randolph.

Since the monologues were performed on the Kentucky side of the Tug Fork, Betty had chosen characters associated with the Pike County sites. One of the early criticisms leveled at the monologues was that there was not enough "Hatfield" representation in the presentations. Betty responded in 2002 by adding the character of Wall Hatfield, brother of "Devil Anse," a colorful character made even more so as portrayed by Jerry Hatfield of Texarkana, Texas.

One character Betty was eager to bring back was the larger-than-life Frank Phillips. Betty knew exactly whom she wanted to play the role. She asked *me*. When Betty first emailed me about the part, I was honored but uncertain about taking it. I felt that I was far removed from the qualities necessary to do justice to one of the definitive feud characters. Apparently, Betty saw something in me that I did not. While I had performed in high school, church and some community theater productions, I could not envision myself as "Bad Frank." Frank Phillips, the bold, fearless man of action was the polar opposite of me. Betty was insistent that I take the part, however, and I could not say "no" to her. I was not as intimidated by the character as I was daunted by the prospect of facing Betty if I failed to do the part justice.

Frank was a passionate, brave, conflicted and imperfect man. In her depiction of the character, Betty did little to dampen Frank's enthusiasm for his work in taking on the Hatfields, nor did she rein in his temperament or alcoholism. He lived hard, worked hard, and played hard – and died young. As written by Betty, Frank was a staunch defender of his actions during the feud.

"Bad" Frank Phillips

"I was the first man to step forward to lead the McCoys in an honest-to-goodness fight. I do not think I deserve the reputation of being a cold-blooded killer. The two men I killed each were wounded – but they each had a gun. They were shooting. Can the Hatfields say that? Did Tolbert, Pharmer and Randolph, Jr., have guns when they were killed at the Paw Paw trees? Did Alifair have a gun when she was killed running from a burning house? Was Sarah shooting at anyone as she was beaten trying to crawl to the body of her dead daughter?"

The chance to portray Frank Phillips was one of the finest acting opportunities I have been given in my lifetime. Best of all, Betty seemed happy with what I was able to bring to the part. I was fortunate to play the role for three years.

We decided that the Friday night dinner on June 7 would be an informal affair, with a renewed focus on American patriotism. A dedicated group of volunteers worked throughout the day decorating the Pikeville College gym, setting up tables and chairs and blowing up red, white and blue balloons for decorations. The meal for the night was a barbequed pig provided by Bobby and Karen Boyd of Bob's Mountain Barbeque. The ownership of the pig was a fun topic of debate for the night.

Our logo for the reunion, featured on hats, t-shirts and assorted other products, echoed the country's post-911 sense of pride. As designed by Bo, the logo was a joint "Kentucky-West Virginia" banner with a tri-color "USA" in the center over a silhouette of the mountains. Like the 2002 event itself, the logo reflected the cooperative spirit that prevailed throughout the country and the region. The Jaguars, a local band specializing in oldies-style music, made their second consecutive reunion appearance to serve as the evening's entertainment. The Jaguars did their part in upholding the evening's theme as well, wearing white pants and shirts that looked like the flag of the United States.

The 2002 reunion marked the first time I could enjoy the dinner being served. With our third reunion, Bo and I were more capable of balancing the details of the event. Overall, the night was a lighter affair than in years past. Bo, in blue jeans and t-shirts, was in rare form as the Master of Ceremonies for the night. He stepped into the role of gameshow host as he persuaded family members to participate in a homespun trivia contest he called, "Are You Smarter than a Hatfield/McCoy?"

The dramatic reenactments were part of van tours to feud sites in the county, conducted once again by Pikeville-Pike County Tourism. To help generate interest in the tours, we decided that several of the characters would be presented at the Friday night dinner. The characters of Patty Cline and one of the McCoy boys were selected to appear that night. Frank Phillips was also set to make his debut.

For nearly fifteen years, I had worn a thick black beard. My daughter, Rachel was twelve years old and had never seen me without it. Frank wore a long 1880s-style mustache but no beard, so accepting the part meant a sacrifice of a different sort. For the Friday night banquet, I felt that Frank should make a dramatic entrance worthy of the man he was. I decided that I would take part in the night's events as I usually did, then exit the dinner covertly to shave and get dressed. Ron would leave the room and Frank would return to make his grand entrance in style.

Ron as Frank Phillips

For the first year, portraying Frank held an added bonus. John Gatling of the Judge Executive's office had been contacted by local descendants of "Bad Frank" after they got word of the reenactments. They offered the use of a unique artifact that ensured historical authenticity – a rifle once owned by Phillips himself. For each performance as Frank that year, John handed the rifle to me, just before I stepped forward to perform the monologue. Following each presentation, I returned the weapon immediately back into John's hands for safekeeping.

Following the dinner, I excused myself after fulfilling my hosting duties. In a distant bathroom, I shaved, dressed all in black as Frank and then met John in a back hallway to retrieve the weapon. When Frank made his first appearance before the crowd of family, I heard audible gasps, followed by murmurs of astonishment. While my actor's ego hoped they were dazzled by my performance, I was certain they were more shocked by the fact that I had bothered to shave my beard.

Some did not make the connection, however. When the character reveals were over, I returned to my normal less-macho persona, though without my usual facial hair. Dressed in blue jeans and t-shirt, I came across a table of friendly, saintly ladies. They were all complimentary of my performance, even to the point of being happy to meet "Frank" in person. One lady, however, was less interested in speaking to me. She had a question for "Ron" and was concerned that she could not find him. She kept asking me where he was.

The early years of reenactments were bare bones operations. Volunteer actors were responsible for providing their own makeup, props and costumes. Required to be onsite for the duration of four performances slated for the day, there were few opportunities for the actors to rest or retreat from the stifling humidity of summer. Those who came to watch the reenactments fared no better. After disembarking the air-conditioned vans, most audience members were left to watch the dramas while standing in whatever shade was available. In following years, Thacker Funeral Home donated chairs and tents for the comfort of audience members.

The actors were not so lucky. The site selected for our group of monologues was the Blackberry Creek Elementary School parking lot. The weather forecast was for summer temperatures in the 90s with humidity to match. The actors were positioned facing into the sun so that tour groups attending the reenactments could stand with their backs to it. Beginning at 10:00 a.m., our presentation lasted about 45 minutes with new vanloads of visitors arriving about an hour apart. The first van arrived promptly on time, but successive rounds were less punctual.

Portraying Frank Phillips was an unusual experience. At times, it seemed as if I was a third party to the performance, both speaking and listening to the poetry of Betty Howard's words. The transcendence of the moment was most likely the result of the intense heat coming off the blacktop parking lot. It was not a good day to be the man dressed in black.

As played by me, Frank was an over-the-top character, full of pith and vinegar and an ample helping of whiskey. While trying not to be melodramatic, I did my best to give him the intensity and strength of character that I believed he deserved. Playing Frank was a physically and emotionally draining experience for me. Standing in a blacktop parking lot on a 90-degree day and dressed entirely in black, it was also a hellish one. As Frank was busy retelling his story with all the swagger I could muster, I was doing my best not to pass out.

Members of both families always responded well to Frank. As a McCoy, I found there was much to like about him. He was both sinner and saint, hero and villain. His was a personal vendetta against the Hatfields and he took to it with abandon. Frank's enthusiasm endued him with a roguish charm that made him especially appealing to some.

Bo was in the audience at one of the early performances in Blackberry Creek and I was eager to get his assessment. I found his comments to be both surprising and unexpected. Bo leaned in with a sly smile and asked me if I understood the effect that Frank was having on some of the ladies in the audience. I shook my head, puzzled. He patted me on the back and summed things up with a remark he had heard from one of the women there: "Frank Phillips, what a man!"

On September 11, 2001, our country had endured the first enemy attack on our home soil in 60 years. Hatfields and McCoys, like the rest of the world, had watched the events unfold as airplanes crashed, buildings toppled, and innocent men and women lost their lives in an unprovoked terrorist attack on the United States. The tragic events of 9-11 set the stage for what would become another defining chapter in the history of the Hatfields and McCoys in 2003.

Reo Hatfield was a businessman, living in Waynesboro, Virginia. He was the great-great grandson of "Bad Elias" Hatfield, whose fistfight with Tolbert McCoy over a debt owed for a fiddle led to the Election Day attack on Ellison Hatfield in 1882. Raised in Mingo County, West Virginia, Reo was the grandson of famed Matewan Chief of Police, Allen Hatfield. Chief Hatfield had been involved in an infamous occurrence in 1947, decades after the last gunshot of the feud was fired. When Chief Hatfield and another officer raided a local bawdy house, an angry patron grabbed the officer and shot Hatfield twice in the back. "My grandfather turned and shot him dead," says Reo. The man who fired the shots was named "McCoy."[93]

As President of Reo Logistics, a company managing supply chain logistics and transportation services for manufacturers, Reo was actively involved in his local community. He had served as Vice Mayor, City

Councilman and Chief of Police for the reserve division of the Police Department.[94] Following the 9-11 attack, Reo deployed five tractor-trailer loads of supplies donated by local citizens to assist ongoing relief efforts. Through his leadership, more than $14,000 in cash contributions and supplies were delivered to first responders in New York City. "The citizens of Waynesboro and Augusta County came together and donated everything from canned goods to pet food and bottled water to help the people in New York City. It was so touching what they did," said Reo.[95]

Impressed with his work during the crisis, Bo began to correspond with Reo and the two became fast friends. We decided to honor Reo for his charitable work at the 2002 reunion dinner. The "Real McCoy" award that night was particularly fitting. It was a resin statue of a firefighter, rescuing a small child. The uniform nameplate of the fireman read "Hatfield."

The one and only time he declined an invitation from us, Reo was unable to attend the Reunion Festival that year, due to previous business commitments. Stalwart Jerry Hatfield accepted the award on his behalf. Reo was proud to be honored by the families, however. To this day, the award holds a place of prominence in his offices at Reo Logistics.

Weddings have been part of the Hatfield-McCoy reunions since the first festival in 2000. Like moonshine, vittles and bluegrass music, "shotgun" weddings are a popular part of Appalachian mountain lore. Following the unity service in 2000, Judge Mike Thornsbury conducted a "shotgun" wedding for two local couples on a stage outside of the Matewan City Hall.[96]

In 2002, Bo was asked to officiate the wedding of two individuals who had met two years before at the "Reunion of the Millennium." Greg Bergwitz of Evansville, Illinois was the son of Brenda Hatfield Bergwitz. Greg, like his Uncle Bucky Hatfield, was a fierce softball competitor and one of the many "ringers" we accused Bucky of recruiting for the classic M2K showdown.

Marie Harman, a Hatfield descendant from Traverse City, Michigan attended the 2000 Reunion intending to learn about her family heritage. She attended the H2K Hatfield family dinner in Williamson, hoping to meet fellow family members there. At the dinner that night, she took the only empty seat available and found herself seated next to Greg. "It was love at first sight," she said. Greg was also smitten. "I could see myself spending the rest of my life with her."[97] On Saturday, June 8, Greg and Marie were married at the Pikeville City Park gazebo with Bo McCoy officiating, Jerry Hatfield taking pictures and a crowd of Hatfield and McCoy family and friends in attendance.

The festival portion of the 2002 reunions was the most elaborate and locally inclusive of all those that took place in Pikeville-Pike County. Community involvement was at an all-time high. In Pikeville, for the four days of the festival, the Pikeville library hosted a gallery of feud exhibits. Connie Maddox, Betty Howard and others were stationed at the Pike County Courthouse for guided public records searches and "Orientation to Genealogy" classes were taught there twice daily. Downtown, Coca-Cola sponsored a "Carnival of Fun" area for the children as well as an antique car show. The Mayo Technical School was the site of an "Old Time Music Workshop" and an "Appalachian Heritage Days" celebration was held at the Pike County Extension Office. The city park played host to bluegrass music acts, local talent shows and a large collection of arts, crafts and food vendors.

Clifford Whitt, a local Hatfield descendent, was the organizer of the festival events held in Pike County. Activities scheduled there including a carnival, horseshoe tournament, square dance, beauty contest, hot-air balloon rides and a play. The Blackberry Senior Center was the site of a Hatfield-McCoy worship service on Sunday morning, presided over by Johnny Hatfield, pastor of Toler Freewill Baptist Church and Bo McCoy.

It was my involvement with "Bad" Frank Phillips that nearly led to my arrest. During the first year of expanded dramatic presentations, the complicated logistics of transporting vanloads of visitors from Pikeville to tour sites in the Valley led us to fall quickly behind schedule. The delays compounded throughout the afternoon, making the prospect of me getting back to Pikeville for the annual softball game unlikely.

By late afternoon, I wrapped up my last portrayal of Frank for the day, grateful for having survived a long day of heat and humidity. As I made my way back to my van, I knew that making the trip back to Pikeville in time for the softball rematch was nearly impossible. I thought with the proper combination of luck, grace and lead-foot, that it might be possible to catch the last few innings of the game. With no time to change into the shorts and t-shirt I brought with me, the man in black put the pedal to the metal, making the trip to Pikeville in record time.

Arriving back in town, I drove the van to a parking lot of a vocational school building that sat adjacent to the college softball field. From that distance, I could see that the game was in the eighth inning. I did not know which family was represented by "home" or "away," but I hoped that the McCoys were winning.

As I hopped out of the van, it dawned on me that I needed some place to change. The game was so near the end that there was no time to find a place. It also did not make sense to run to the ball field in full costume and try to change in the dugout. The van itself was packed with a sound system and leftover materials from the reunion dinner from the night before, so changing clothes inside the vehicle was not an option.

With few choices available, I opted for the most expedient one. Making my way to the passenger-side door, I carefully surveyed the parking lot. It was empty of vehicles, without a person in sight. The players and spectators at the ball field a safe distance away were fully engaged in the spectacle of a Hatfield-McCoy grudge match. I decided that I could shield myself from their view by keeping the passenger door open. I figured I could change quickly then run over to the ball field to catch the closing few minutes of the game.

Frank's costume was made up of pieces of clothing that I had picked up at local second-hand shops. Trying to find materials that looked authentic to the period of the 1880s proved difficult, but I had managed to put together something that bore a resemblance to the outfits Frank was photographed wearing. The outfit looked good, but it was not entirely well fitting. The long-sleeved black shirt fit my arms and chest well, but hung down to my knees. Tucked inside Frank's black pants, though it did not matter much. That day, I discovered the oversized shirt was handy for cover while changing clothes in the parking lot.

With no need of them at the ball game, I put my wallet and cell phone in the glove compartment of the van for safekeeping. I slipped off Frank's black dress pants and tossed them into the back of the vehicle. As I quickly reached for a pair of shorts, my imagination was racing with thoughts of me reaching the game just in time to contribute the winning run in the bottom of the ninth inning. Before I could bask in the glory of my own invented success, however, my sports fantasy was interrupted by a stern voice, asking "Sir?"

I looked around but saw no one. "Sir?" the invisible voice asked again. As I slowly looked back over my shoulder, I noticed that a Pikeville City police cruiser had suddenly materialized behind my van from who-knows-where. The vehicle sat idling quietly, parked just behind my van.

The cruiser's passenger-side window was rolled down and I could the officer still seated in the driver's seat. The officer pointed an accusatory finger at me and beckoned me over. As I moved slowly towards the police car, I realized that Pikeville's finest was being represented that day by a grim-faced *female* officer. She did not look as amused as I was at the ridiculous sight of Frank Phillips, the embodiment of masculine virility, coming face to face with the long arm of the law, while wearing no pants.

My mind was racing with possible reasonable explanations for my predicament. "What are you up to?" asked the officer, in a low, dispassionate monotone. Her lips moved but her expression remained unchanged; her stare was penetrating and intimidating. Suddenly, it occurred to me that she must be familiar with the Hatfield-McCoy events going on in town that weekend. "My….n-name…is Ron McCoy…I'm one of the organizers of the Reunion Festival," I stammered.

"I don't care who you are," responded the officer as she cut me off, obviously unimpressed. "What are you up to?" she asked again. In my mind eye's, I was sinking quickly. "I…was headed to the game…it's probably about over by now…"

"You have some I.D?" asked the officer. I smiled weakly, anxious to comply with her request. "Yes ma'am, I sure do," I answered before realizing that my wallet was in the glove compartment of my van. I smiled again, this time more sheepishly. "Ma'am...I...I put my wallet....in the glove compartment..."

The officer did not flinch. Uncertain whether I had received permission to do so or not, I made my way ever so slowly back to the van, retrieved my wallet, then returned and handed it to the unfazed officer. For a long moment, she looked at my license. Her face was impassive and unchanging. Then slowly, with the same unemotional response she had shown throughout the episode, the officer handed my wallet back to me.

"Next time, find somewhere else to change clothes" the officer said flatly. I nodded affirmatively; relieved as I watched the officer drive away as quickly and quietly as she had arrived. Squeezing as far into the passenger's side of my van as I could, I swapped Frank's shirt and vest for a "McCoy" softball shirt and tennis shoes. As I stepped out of the van, I could hear the sound of cheers and applause in the distance, coming from the softball field. The game was over. In 2002, it was a Hatfield sweep. For the first time, the McCoy team had lost to the Hatfields on the softball diamond, followed by a loss the next day at the tug of war in Matewan. All things considered, though, I was a happy man.

The extent of community involvement in the 2002 Reunion Festival proved to us that the event had grown local roots. Events in Pike County and Pikeville had been well coordinated and executed. Activities scheduled in Williamson and Matewan continued to flourish. A cooperative spirit between the communities had begun to develop, even though 2002 was the first year without a joint-service on the bridge over the Tug Fork.

Having concluded our third successful Reunion Festival, Bo and I felt the time was right to hand the event off to local authorities who could better manage and sustain it. The local infrastructure was such that we were confident that the festival would continue for many years to come. We would continue in advisory roles, supporting tourism and feud preservation efforts in whatever capacity they deemed fit.

Meanwhile, Reo Hatfield was putting together an idea for a reunion event that would necessitate our participation once again. He wanted the families to sign a formal peace treaty as a way of demonstrating American resolve and unity to the world. It was an idea that we embraced and supported fully. We decided that the Hatfield-McCoy truce would be the centerpiece of the reunion for the following year.

2003 was also the year that our commitment to the families would be subjected to its most extreme test. Two years earlier, Bo and I had initiated an unpopular course of action that would land us squarely in the middle of opposing views of justice, public opinion and the scrutiny of the press. In 2003, the Hatfields and McCoys would be fighting it out in court.

Court

> "We are made wise not by the recollection of our past,
> but by the responsibility for our future."
> George Bernard Shaw

Reconciliation with one's history brings with it an inherent duty of stewardship. It is an obligation to preserve and to perpetuate the legacy of family for those who will follow us as the next links in the ancestral lineage. Enjoying the benefits of my reunion with my family's history conveyed with it a responsibility to accept it as my own and to stand by it when put to the test. For me, this commitment to family faced its greatest test over the issue of access to the McCoy family cemetery in Hardy, Kentucky.

High on a knoll that once overlooked the old home place, the tiny cemetery had been part of the McCoy farm, property that once extended across Blackberry Creek and beyond. It had fallen victim to time and was nearly lost to history until family members recovered it in the 1970s. The property was purchased by its current owner in 1984. In the years since, the cemetery has become the focal point of an ongoing dispute over the rights of family to visit the cemetery versus those of the landowners. The long-simmering stalemate threatened to erupt because of the renewed interest in feud sites spurred by the annual family reunions. By the end of the third Reunion Festival, it was obvious to us that we needed to find a resolution to the matter.

In 2003, after two years of legal proceedings, we were faced with the prospect of taking the cemetery property owner to court. It seemed entirely incongruous with the theme of unity we had advocated for the past three years and it was an action that we always hoped would not be necessary. We expected that the potential fallout from the affair would be severe. Our ambivalence was warranted. Hatfields and McCoys alike questioned the sincerity of our commitment to peace between the families. "This was designed to get national headlines and designed as a way to get free advertising for people who hope to make a profit from these things," said attorney Larry Webster.[98] No matter our good intentions, we stood alone in our decision to pursue an unpopular course of action that threatened to undo everything we had worked to build.

Our first visit to the McCoy Cemetery was on June 18, 1999. Bo, Billy Jack and I were in Pikeville for a press conference with Pikeville Mayor Frank Morris. A CBS affiliate in Raleigh, North Carolina, WRAL, dispatched a reporter to cover the story. Mark Roberts was an energetic and personable individual, never one to shy away from conflict. After a guided tour of other feud sites, Mark was intrigued by the one site noted as "off limits." We had never visited the place. The ever-persuasive Roberts was insistent that the McCoy boys should be allowed to visit and convinced Mr. Brown to make a phone call to the owner on his behalf. After a few moments on the phone with Mark, John Vance surprisingly agreed.

We understood the rare opportunity we were being offered. Even before the reunions, the McCoy Cemetery was not a place that was visited often. Locally, the property was closed to visitors and few polite Pike County citizens dared to violate a neighbor's right to privacy.

As we visited Mr. Vance's property that Saturday, we found our preconceptions to be unwarranted. Mr. Vance was polite and cordial as he personally escorted us up to the cemetery site. A Hatfield descendent, Mr. Vance even delivered a well-intended jab at the McCoys, offering an old family explanation for why the three McCoy boys were buried in a single grave. "The McCoys were too lazy to dig more than one hole," he said.

Mr. Vance was accommodating to us; consenting to a rare on-camera interview and even inviting me into his home to show off a new computer he had recently purchased. I was perplexed and wondered if somehow the situation surrounding the cemetery had been nothing more than a misunderstanding. The small, peaceful site with its friendly host hardly seemed worthy of its reputation. As we left the cemetery that day, we shook hands with Mr. Vance, exchanged pleasantries and thanked him for his kindness to us. Sadly, it would be the last time we did so.

To the McCoy family, the cemetery in Hardy was hallowed ground. It was the burial ground for five sons and one daughter of Randolph and

Sarah McCoy, five of whom were killed by the Hatfields during the feud. In 1882, following the execution of the three McCoy boys at the "Paw Paw" tree site, Tolbert, Pharmer and Randolph "Bud" McCoy, Jr., were buried in a common grave on the mountain hillside, said to be placed there so that Sarah could see them from the front porch of her home.

A fourth son, Bill was buried there soon after. Bill had been the third McCoy boy involved in the Election Day assault on Ellison Hatfield. Following "Bud's" death in his place, a guilt-ridden Bill retreated into the woods alone for days at a time. Ultimately, his remorse overtook him. He died of grief and the family buried him in his rightful place alongside his brothers.[99]

Following the attack on the McCoy cabin in 1888, Calvin and Alifair were buried in the cemetery as well. Randolph's sons Jim and Sam then relocated the family to the relative safety of Pikeville, 25 miles to the west. Randolph buried Roseanna in Colonel Dils' cemetery in 1889 and Sarah a few years after. He followed them in 1914. No further burials took place in the McCoy Cemetery in Hardy. For nearly ninety years, the McCoy Cemetery remained undisturbed, left to the forces of nature and the passage of time.

The McCoy farm was sold to John B. Farley in 1889. Upon his death in 1957, the property, including the cemetery located off Highway 319 in Hardy, was subdivided by Farley's heirs. The cemetery was once offered to Pike County free of charge by Mrs. S.A. Mitchell, one of the daughters of John Farley. For reasons unknown, the transfer of ownership failed to happen. By 1976, when an application was made by Pike County to place a number of historic feud sites on the National Register, Mitchell was still listed as the owner of the cemetery.[100]

In 1975, local troubadour and McCoy descendent Jimmy Wolford, was concerned about the deteriorating state of the cemetery. The road to the cemetery was overgrown and impassable. The cemetery's original grave markers, four small pieces of stone, one etched with the letters "C-A-L," were nearly lost in the undergrowth. Wolford contacted Joe "Tab" McCoy and Leonard "Mix" McCoy, descendants of Asa Harmon McCoy by way of his son, Larkin. The owners of the McCoy Caney Coal Company in

Phelps, Kentucky were successful businessmen and actively involved in helping the community. Previously, the two philanthropists had donated funds for the construction of the McCoy Athletic Center in Phelps.

Monument at the McCoy Cemetery, dedicated in 1976

The brothers had the road leading to the cemetery cleaned up and purchased an $8000 granite memorial for the site, manufactured by the Hatfield Monument Company in Sarah Ann, West Virginia.[101] The monument, nearly six feet long and three foot high, was carved in the shape of an open Bible. It listed the names of the McCoy children buried there and featured a quote from one of Wolford's songs: "There is no secret why they died so young; pride took control – youth's song was never sung." The monument was dedicated on a rainy May 1, 1976 as 300 witnesses looked on. Willis Hatfield, aged 88, the last surviving child of "Devil Anse" Hatfield, was there to pay his respects and to meet Jim McCoy, 92, great-grandnephew of Randolph McCoy and the grandfather of Wolford. At the buffet luncheon following the dedication, the two oldest living feud descendants cut the cake together.[102]

On April 25, 1984, John Vance and his wife purchased a nearly 20-acre tract of land on the Blackberry Fork of Pond Creek in Hardy, from its previous owner, Gregory Dotson.[103] They erected a home on a flat portion of the property, effectively blocking the view of the cemetery from the road below. The cemetery road was adopted as their driveway. Given the steep, rugged terrain, the gravel road was the only means of access to the gravesites.

Vance's ownership of the property was steeped in historical irony. John Vance was the great-great-great grandson of "Devil Anse" Hatfield's uncle Jim Vance. Jim Vance, one of the most brutal and notorious feud protagonists, was believed responsible for the death of Randolph's brother, Asa Harmon McCoy. Jim Vance allegedly led the attack on the McCoy home and was said to have brutally assaulted Sarah McCoy.

Given its importance to the McCoy family, it was no wonder the cemetery had become the center of a hotly contested dispute over legal rights to it. Since purchasing the land, John Vance had exercised his rights as a property owner to limit access to his property. He expressed due concerns about permitting visitors to the cemetery. "If someone falls and gets hurt on our property, then we are liable. I question their right to force their way through my property."[104] In his court testimony, Mr. Vance stated that he welcomed the occasional visitor to the cemetery. His testimony, however, was at odds with the generally held opinion that he was not amenable to having visitors to his property. Certainly, the constant interest in accessing the property was burdensome to one well within his rights to value his privacy. From time to time, there were expectations that Mr. Vance was prepared to rid himself of the property. On one trip early in 1999, I remember seeing a hand-painted wooden "for sale" sign posted on the Highway 319 roadside.

After the publication of Kimberly Hefling's article in 1998, the impending "Reunion of the Millennium" had begun to generate rekindled interest in all-things related to the feud. Even as many local parties welcomed us and stepped in to assist with planning the event, others held concerns about the sudden revitalization of interest in the feud and the influx of visitors to the area. Apparently, as implied in his court testimony, John Vance was one of the latter.

Despite his friendly reception of us in 1999, by the time the reunion rolled around in June 2000, Vance had taken measures to make sure that no one could visit the cemetery. Monitors placed on either side of the access road activated chimes inside his home that alerted him to anyone coming up it. At times, he parked loaded pickup trucks in the road to impede access. He posted warning signs down at the highway plainly stating that there was no public access to the graveyard. It was obvious that the McCoy Cemetery was clearly off-limits to visitors.

Attempts were made through official channels to reason with Mr. Vance, to listen to his misgivings and to appease them if possible. Mr. Vance argued correctly that parking was non-existent and that visitors attempting to park on either side of Highway 319 presented an impending road hazard. Further, he stated that his rights as a property owner superseded any obligation to permit access to his property or to oblige any perceived obligation to the public good. Compromises were sought to have the cemetery open on a restricted basis, at least during the time of the reunions. In 2000, Pike County had anticipated the influx of first-time visitors to the area and wanted to put their best foot forward.

By the time the first Reunion Festival rolled around, however, it was apparent that the cemetery would not be available for visits by family members. There was no mention of it made by us or by the tourism office in any promotional materials or brochures, nor did we disclose its location. There was no need to prompt any type of altercation between Mr. Vance and our visiting family members.

Hatfields and McCoys are an informed, resourceful and determined lot, however. The well-kept location of the McCoy Cemetery site did not remain a secret for long. Despite warnings to the contrary, some family members failed to heed Mr. Vance's admonitions. As incursions onto his property became more frequent, he became understandably more protective of it. Following the 2000 reunion, new highway markers were erected to denote feud sites in Pike County. One intended to mark the location of the McCoy Cemetery was steadfastly opposed by Mr. Vance and removed.

The success of the 2000 reunion prompted Mr. Vance to issue an ultimatum to us. In an email sent to me, dated June 23, 2000, Vance wrote, "(I) just want to say that my family and I have taken care of the McCoy Cemetery for over 16 years and we have never treated anyone that came here with anything but respect. We have never asked anyone including the tourism department for a dime, nor asked anyone to cut a blade of grass or weed. What have we got for it other than threats by the tourism department to take our land that we lawfully own? You are no longer welcome in my house or on my property." It was obvious to me that Mr. Vance's level of tolerance had been breached.

Pikeville-Pike County Tourism contacted us in 2001 to apprise us of the steadily deteriorating situation with the cemetery. Increased demand to visit the site was being met with belligerent resistance. It was apparent to us that nothing good could come of it. While we understood Mr. Vance's reasonable concerns about being deluged with tourists, we did not believe that he had the right to obstruct access to the cemetery by family members.

Since restricting access to a cemetery by family members was in violation of Kentucky law, the logical recourse against Mr. Vance was a legal one. "Relatives have an unquestionable right to visit the graves," said attorney, Della Justice.[105] Since the issue was a family matter, it was necessary for the McCoys to spearhead the fight. As the organizers of M2K, Bo and I found ourselves to be established representatives of the McCoy family. Our position as "outsiders" made us the sensible choice to take legal action since no one locally was willing to do so. If there were anyone going to take on Mr. Vance, it would have to be us.

The McCoys' involvement in legal proceedings in Pike County dates to the earliest days of the feud. It was Perry Cline, supported by Colonel John Dils, who acted on behalf of the McCoys, prompting warrants to be issued against the Hatfields involved in the New Year's raid. "Detectives" sought bounties that were placed on the heads of those involved and Frank Phillips had crossed state lines with abandon in the pursuit of "justice.". In the case of the McCoy Cemetery, the McCoys were called upon once again to take legal action on behalf of the family, supported by local public officials and guided by premier legal help in Pikeville.

A preliminary title examination of the McCoy Cemetery property was begun in early 2001 by the Pike County Tourism Commission. A letter dated February 23, 2001, signed by Ed Maddox on behalf of the law firm of Stratton, Hogg and Maddox confirmed the rightful ownership of the property by John Vance. The letter detailed the long history of the property and its succession of ownership from Sarah McCoy to Thomas Farley on May 20, 1889 through to James Dotson in 1976, to his son, Gregory in 1982 and finally to the Vances in 1984. It was clear that John Vance was in full possession of the property and that the legal battle for access to the cemetery was to be with him.

The Tourism Commission said that they could not be part of the case against Vance, for good reasons. Beyond the bad form of a government agency taking on a Pike County citizen to gain access to his property, the matter of the cemetery was a family matter and needed to be addressed from that perspective. The decision to take legal action was not one that Bo and I made lightly, however. We understood the volatility of the situation and its potential ramifications. No matter our motivations or justifications, there was simply no way that we would appear to be anything more than interlopers trying to deny a Pike County private citizen the fair use of his own land. We knew the national press would run with the story of the McCoys suing a Hatfield (Vance). Most importantly, we stood the very real chance that the case would undermine the Hatfield-McCoy unity that we had worked so hard to achieve.

For the 2001 Reunion Festival, the cemetery was again off limits to visiting family members. On May 22, 2001, an online post by Mr. Vance made it clear that the "MCCOY CEMETERY IN HARDY, KY REMAINS CLOSED TO THE PUBLIC." To stem further escalation, I posted a follow-up advisory to those planning to attend the reunion that year. "Given the inaccessibility of the cemetery, we realize that honoring

Mr. Vance's rights infringes on the rights of those who wish to visit the cemetery. However, in an effort to maintain the peace, we would like to encourage those visiting the Tug Valley in the next few weeks to comply with Mr. Vance's wishes until a future settlement is reached." Mr. Vance's posted response was less conciliatory. "It is not against federal or state law to limit use of private property such as my driveway. I will protect that right to the limits of the law."

Bo and I truly were reluctant to pursue legal recourse. Instead, we opted for a final effort at dialogue. Our emissary of choice was a Pikeville barrister by the name of Joseph W. Justice. Joe Justice, a McCoy descendant, was recommended to us by Tourism and the Judge Executive's office. He was an established attorney in Pikeville, with a stellar reputation. An amiable and intelligent man, Joe was also resolutely fearless and the only man in Pike County willing to take on our case. We held out hope that a resolution benefiting all parties could be had, so Joe agreed to send one final appeal on our behalf.

In a letter to Mr. Vance, dated October 2, 2001, Joe Justice wrote, "I understand that you have an objection to family and others having access to this cemetery. I have done some research of the records in the Pike County Clerk's Office and find that in the deed from Gregory A. Dotson and Jeannie Dotson to you and your wife, a right to land adjoining the McCoy Cemetery was reserved for their use. I further found that John B. Farley recorded a plat in the clerk's office which he exempted a 30-foot road, which would be a public dedication. I know that you can appreciate the importance that this cemetery has to the McCoy family and to the public. The purpose of this letter is to see if we could sit down and talk with you and see if something could be amicably worked out to everyone's satisfaction." Bo hoped for the best. "I'd love to get a phone call saying they've decided to sit down and negotiate a settlement," he said.[106] The letter was received with silent indifference.

Thankfully, the reluctant McCoy cousins had "justice" on our side. Joe and his cousin, Della, representing the law firm of Justice and Justice, took our case pro bono and did what others would not. Representing "outsiders" taking on a local interest was an act of sheer bravery in Pike

County. Della was a petite, mild-mannered woman with glasses, her appearance cleverly masking her abilities as a no-nonsense attorney with nerves of steel. Joe was, and remains, a man of great character. Together, they were an indomitable team.

Justice filed a complaint against Mr. and Mrs. Vance on behalf of the McCoy family on March 29, 2002. As a minister, Bo was disappointed at having to take legal action. "We've been put in this position where, as family members, we have been told we cannot have access to this cemetery. We had no choice but to file suit. We regret that it was necessary," said Bo.[107] Over the course of three pages, the complaint outlined the storied history of the McCoy family cemetery. In part, the complaint alleged that the Vances had "denied access to the McCoy descendants and others who (had) come to visit the cemetery. They have gone so far as to erect "no trespassing," signs on the public road leading to the cemetery from State Route 319." Point 11 of the complaint declared that the Vances "should be enjoined and restrained from interfering with the rights of the Plaintiffs and others to access and visit the McCoy Cemetery."[108]

On May 15, 2002, an "answer to complaint" asking for dismissal of the case was filed by counsel for the defense, Lawrence R. Webster. Larry "Red Dog" Webster was a Pike County attorney, newspaper pundit and musician. He was also someone with whom we were acquainted. In 1999, Larry Webster had helped us establish "McCoys: 2000" as a Kentucky-based corporation and had served as music coordinator for the city park venue during the 2000 Reunion Festival.

In point one of his rebuttal, Webster contended that our legal "action should be dismissed for the reason that the Plaintiffs are not authorized by law to bring the same, have no standing to bring the same or to make the claims herein."[109] From the very beginning of the case, Webster sought to portray us as interlopers. Our case against Vance was invalid because our status as "family" was invalid. "These people are trying to charge people admission to visit my clients' property," said Webster.[110]

On May 9, 2002, affidavits were sent by Joe Justice to Bo and me to be signed in front of a notary and returned to him as soon as possible.

It was a final declaration of our intention to move forward with the proceedings. Once signed, there was no turning back.

By order of the Pike County Court, a temporary injunction was granted on June 7, 2002. The Vances were ordered to "permit access to the McCoy Cemetery…during the hours of 9:00 a.m. to 7:00 p.m. and so long as no more than five (5) people visit said cemetery per visitation." Curiously, this injunction allowed more visitors to visit at any given time and over a greater number of hours than had been permitted by Mr. Vance previously; but the injunction was short-lived.

A preliminary conference was held before a judge in Pike County on August 9, 2002 to discuss the merits of the case. In a letter to us dated August 19, 2002, Justice advised us that the case had been assigned for a jury trial on January 22, 2003 at 9:00 a.m. For the first time in nearly 100 years, the Hatfields and McCoys were headed back to court.

As preparation for the legal trial began, we made multiple trips to Pikeville. Our attorney decided that Bo would take the stand to represent the family. Bo was a gifted, intelligent speaker and a passionate man who wore his heart on his sleeve. He would make the personal case for the family well.

Joe compiled a list of witnesses to be submitted to the court by December 2, 2002. He felt it was paramount that the historical significance of the cemetery be included in our court presentation. Doing so meant telling the story of the feud in detail. As far as we were concerned, there was one person in all of Pike County fully qualified to do the job. To our great relief, Betty Howard stepped up, without hesitation, to help.

On Wednesday, January 22, 2003, for the first time since the trials of the late 1880s, the family of Randolph McCoy was represented once again inside the Pike County courthouse. Just three years prior, the Hatfield and McCoy families had stood together on the steps of the courthouse to pay respect to those family members lost in the feud. The proceedings were presided over by the Honorable Charles E. Lowe, Jr. Despite the general unpopularity of the court case, in attendance to lend their moral support that day were Jerry and Jo Ann Hatfield and Bob and Marlyn McCoy.

From our vantage point, the case was just a matter of the property being designated as a family cemetery and that rightful family members were being denied admittance. Vance, on the other hand was the wronged landowner set upon by unscrupulous foreigners with personal interests in the development of tourism. As with most things Hatfield-McCoy, the reality of the matter was more complex. There was little middle ground for compromise and no easy resolution would satisfy all parties concerned.

Graceful and poised, Betty Howard took the stand to explain the historical relevance of the McCoy family cemetery. Following a few questions by Justice to establish Betty's status as an expert witness on the matter of the feud, an assertion uncontested by the counsel for the defendant, Betty methodically began to lay out the feud story in vivid detail. For the first time in history, the complete story of the feud was entered into the Pike County court records. As I sat listening, I imagined that Randolph was looking down on us, smiling.

When Bo took the stand, Webster attempted to play upon our decision to form the M2K Corporation as an indication of our ulterior motives to profit from Hatfield-McCoy tourism. Bo assured him that "McCoys 2000, Inc." was a legitimate corporation, intended for the benefit of the family. Webster quickly called this into question as he provided us with information we were unaware of: "McCoys 2000" no longer existed as a corporation. It had been dissolved administratively by the Kentucky Secretary of State in 2002 for failing to file required annual reports.[111] Bo was surprised by Webster's revelation but parried well. Since he lived out-of-state, he was unaware that annual reports had not been filed, stating that he expected to be apprised of the situation by the agent representing the corporation, Larry Webster.

Under tense examination by Webster, Bo detailed his personal story behind organizing the "Reunion of the Millennium." Discussing his relationship with his grandfather, Clyde, Bo became choked up. The memory of his grandfather was a primary motivation for his involvement with the reunion as it had been for me. Bo proved to be a sympathetic witness. Webster's attempt to present us as carpetbaggers hoping to benefit financially from opening access to the McCoy Cemetery had been unsuccessful.

Joe Justice took a more pragmatic, factual approach to his presentation of the case. The dispute boiled down to a single point of contention, the true status of the only means of access to the cemetery. If the road to the cemetery was a public road or a dedicated one, then Vance could not restrict the use of it. If it was a driveway as he contended, then he was within his means to do with it as he wished.

From our point of view, the truth was obvious. Justice produced a plat of the property filed by the heirs of John Farley in 1957 upon the subdivision of the property. The plat marked the cemetery and denoted the single road leading up to it from Highway 319 as "30' reserved."[112] The lots adjoining the cemetery, sold in later years to other parties, also referred to the plat in their deeds. Pike County, in the past, had declined to recognize the road as a county road, possibly to remove itself from the obligation of maintaining a "public" road on "private" property. It was a matter of fact, however, that nearly thirty years before the Vances purchased the property, a road to the cemetery had clearly existed.

John Vance would have none of it. Under examination by Webster, Vance went to great lengths to convince the court that his existing driveway could not be the road indicated on the plat because, he said, it was in a different location. Given the topography of the lot, this seemed unlikely to us. There was, and still is, only one means of access to the property.

Vance was persistent in his opinion, however. He claimed, "The existing road cut across the hillside at a sharper angle, deviating on the uphill side from the platted road toward the switchback by several feet."[113] Further, he insisted that the upper portion of the road, that portion nearest to the cemetery, had been rebuilt by him and was presently closer to the cemetery than was indicated on the plat. Joe Sloan, a neighbor of Vance's and owner of an adjoining property, testified that the lower portion of the road had been modified by the previous property owner, S.A. Mitchell, though for purposes unknown.

Based on Sloan's testimony, the trial court ultimately decided that the current road was "in a different location (from that) shown on the plat."

In his rebuttal, Joe Justice argued our position that the "evidence clearly established that the existing road follows the same course and directions as shown on the plat. Although the existing road may deviate slightly in places from the platted road, there is no evidence that the road is in a substantially different location than was designated on the plat."[114]

The case ended that day with Judge Lowe deferring on a final decision that was not announced until April 9, 2003. Judge Lowe upheld the existing easement that permitted access to the cemetery for Bo and me. The scope of the easement, however, was restricted to us, although it was implied that other legitimate family members had the right to visit the cemetery as ancillary parties to the lawsuit. Both sides claimed victory. "The McCoys win," said Joe Justice. "The McCoys have access to the cemetery now." Vance claimed victory as well, stating that the cemetery would remain closed to tourists, protecting it from any "commercial exploitation."[115]

A few months later, during our visit for the 2003 reunion, I wanted my daughter, Rachel to have the chance to visit the cemetery. As we made our way up the cemetery drive, I knew that we would trip the sensors and that Mr. Vance would be there to meet us at the top of the hill. It was the first time I had visited the cemetery since the court ruling. Mr. Vance stepped out from his home with a friendly wave and a smile. "Where you folks from?" he asked. I was puzzled by his reception, then realized that he did not recognize me as I had shaved my beard for my annual role as Frank Phillips. "Mr. Vance," I said, rubbing my bare cheeks. "It's me." Mr. Vance's air of congeniality quickly vanished, replaced by an angry scowl. He waved his hand in disgust, then retreated inside. Rachel and I finished our brief visit without further incident. It was the last time I set foot on the property.

The April 9, 2003 ruling by Judge Lowe set aside the arguments over the status of the cemetery to conclude, "While the road had been dedicated on the 1957 plat, (it) had never been used by the public and thus could not be considered a public road." The McCoy family's right to visit the cemetery was upheld, though left as indeterminate as ever. McCoy family members were permitted visitation rights, with reasonable consideration given to the rights and privacy requests of the Vances as the property owners. It was left unclear, however as to how and by whom the identity of McCoy descendants was to be determined. The ruling, as given, was impractical and unworkable.

On February 1, 2005, Joe Justice entered a motion to vacate the judgment, an appeal that was struck down by Judge Lowe's successor, the Honorable Steven Combs. On March 3, 2006, Judge Lowe issued a reversal, seconded by Judge Robert W. Dyche, stating, "The trial court did not have the authority to limit rights to the dominant estate only to the named parties in this action." With the 2006 ruling, legitimate McCoy family members were permitted access to the cemetery, although how such a determination was to made and at whose discretion was left uncertain.

The fate of the McCoy Cemetery remains a concern. Unsubstantiated rumors, allegations and stories continue to circulate among family members. On February 8, 2013, John Vance posted the following on the social media network, Facebook.

National Historical Site for sale
Burial place of the 5 McCoy Children killed in the feud
McCoy Cemetery and surrounding Property, House, Outbuildings
Approx. 20 acres
Possible $30,000.00 plus income depending on proposed uses.
About ½ way between Williamson, WV. and Matewan WV. Hatfield and McCoy
ATV Trailheads
At Hardy, KY. $250,000.00
Serious inquiries only call

On April 29, 2013, Vance enlisted the help of Jim Gabbert, a historian with the National Register of Historic Landmarks, to draft a letter to Marty Perry with the Kentucky Heritage Council. Mr. Gabbert stated that Mr. Vance wanted the cemetery removed from the Hatfield-McCoy Feud Historic district expressing concerns "about trespassers and potential damage to his property."[116] The request stated that "the boundaries for the listed property were improperly drawn and do not reflect the true boundaries of the eligible property" designated in 1976.[117]

At present, Mr. Vance has posted an imposing white sign with black letters by the roadside, clearly stating his position regarding access to the cemetery. "McCoy Cemetery is closed to the public. Those related to the McCoy children buried in the McCoy Cemetery may visit on Memorial Day weekend and the third weekend of September each year. No parking will be allowed on the property while doing so. We reserve the right to ask for proof of descendancy and time to verify it. This is within the court rulings concerning private cemetery visitation! Trespassers may be prosecuted!" Handwritten addendums to the sign read "limited access" and "no tours!"

Despite the public spectacle of Hatfield and McCoy descendants taking each other to court, the case of the McCoy Cemetery has become another anecdotal chapter in the long history of the families. Bo and I risked our personal reputations and those of both families in the hopes of achieving a mutually beneficial outcome for the family and the property owner. Fifteen years after our case against John Vance, the matter of the McCoy Cemetery remains unresolved.

Truce

"The wise man must remember that while he is a descendant of the past, he is a parent of the future."
Herbert Spencer

In the wake of the legal battle surrounding the McCoy Cemetery case, the 2003 Reunion Festival was a welcome occasion to shore up the positive aspects of the Hatfield-McCoy reunions we had been cultivating since 2000. While Bo and I felt the fight to open the cemetery had been a worthy cause, the negative press coverage of the case had done much to reinforce old misconceptions of antagonism between the families. Although activities scheduled for the festival that year were not especially noteworthy, the 2003 Reunion produced a defining moment in the history of the families. The signing of a truce between the families was an achievement that permanently annotated the saga of the Hatfields and McCoys.

The Hatfield McCoy truce of 2003 was a testament to the power of forgiveness. The symbolic act of unity between the clans provided lasting proof that reconciliation between once-warring enemies was possible. Among the acts of such notable historic figures as Jesus Christ, Pope John Paul II and Nelson Mandela, the truce signing was listed by the John Templeton Foundation as one of the "ten great moments in forgiveness history."[118]

The truce was the inspiration of Reo Hatfield. As the first Hatfield recipient of the "Real McCoy" award, Reo considered it an honor to be acknowledged by the descendants of the McCoy family. In his mind, the feud was a conflict that had never been formally resolved. Growing up in Mingo County, Reo "disliked the McCoys on principle, and never had any intention of making amends with them: 'Never even considered it'."[119]

For Reo, the truce was a chance for the descendants of the feud to stand united as Americans. "We argue about this and that. But when it comes to attacking us, we're all one family, one community of Americans," said Reo.[120] The Hatfield and McCoys coming together to declare a formal peace between the families was both an acknowledgment of a shared history and a determination to overcome it. "We are one family now. I think that sets an example for the world that if we can come together, anybody can." said Reo.[121] It was a simple message,

Reo Hatfield, Jerry Hatfield, Ron & Bo McCoy

profoundly delivered to the world on June 14, 2003 by a group of nearly 70 Hatfield-McCoy descendants from all over the country.

    The origins of the truce began in the shadow of the worst attack on our country since the Pearl Harbor assault in 1941. In the months following the 9-11 attack and his community's relief response to it, Reo felt a lingering desire to do something more. He came up with an idea he felt would honor his heritage and inspire the country in a way that only the Hatfields and McCoys could. In the fall of 2002, Reo contacted Bo to discuss his plan for a truce between the families, an affirmation of strength through unity. "We're not saying you don't have to fight because sometimes you do have to fight," said Reo. "But you don't have to fight forever."[122]

    When the truce signing was announced for 2003, it was ridiculed by some as a publicity stunt and unnecessary since the families had buried the hatchet many years before. While we expected the truce might renew interest in the reunion, orchestrating the truce signing as a media stunt never crossed our minds. For Reo, the truce was personal. "I wanted to show that even the Hatfields and McCoys would come together, because we believe in the same principles. I wanted to show that in America we are one family," he declared.[123]

The importance of formalizing peace between the Hatfields and McCoys did not escape me. Just five years earlier, the feud was a chapter of my family history of which I knew nothing. Now, I was being asked to join Bo as ambassadors for the family, teaming up with a Hatfield to declare that the whole matter of the feud was over and done.

Despite its historic implications, little thought had been given by us as to the content of such a document. Reo emailed Bo and me to solicit our input. In my mind, the task of drafting a Hatfield-McCoy truce was especially daunting. The words had to be chosen carefully with a sense of gravity and solemnity worthy of the occasion. Trying not to be intimidated by the blank slate before me, I sat down at the computer and slowly began to write. I just hoped to get some words on the page that might serve as a foundation from which we could build.

(1)   We the descendants of William Anderson Hatfield and Randolph McCoy, as well as the descendants of other ancillary participants in the historic feud between the Hatfield and McCoy clans from 1865-1890, do hereby and formally declare an official end to all hostilities, implied, inferred and real, between the families now and forevermore;

The opening paragraph was an introduction to the families. It was both a recognition of the feud and our official declaration of its end. The second paragraph was intended to outline our ongoing commitment to our families' rich heritage.

(2)   Whereas we, the families do remain resolved and committed to the preservation of our common heritage, to the perpetuation of its relevance to our individual, corporate and national history and to the protection of the veracity of the feud and the lessons learned from it;

The third section, later to become the fourth paragraph of the final document, offered a formal conclusion to the truce, written in the pseudo-legalese style of the first paragraph. It was a public affirmation of the harm done to and by our respective families. As witnesses, we acknowledged the actions of our ancestors, while relegating them to the past. We also determined to preserve the legacy of our family heritage for future generations.

(4) Do affirm by our signatures affixed below, that the injuries and wrongdoings inflicted to and by our ancestors in years past are now committed henceforth to history, and that, from this day forward, the Hatfields and McCoys stand united, forever bound by our sacred legacy.

With no legal training or background in writing, I nonetheless thought it made sense to give the document the semblance of a formal binding agreement being entered into by both parties. The paragraphs as written were wordy, flowery and more than a little over-the-top. I hoped they could serve as a good beginning from which we could edit, once Bo and Reo offered their input. I emailed them my rough draft text, anxious to see what they would make of it.

Both men were supportive in their comments. We managed some cleaning up of the extraneous wording and further clarified the mission statement of the second paragraph; but it was, in my opinion, nowhere near a "final" form. I expected the document would continue to improve as we edited it further during rewrites. While Reo, Bo and I would provide the principal signatures on the truce, we added a second signature page as a declaration of agreement to be signed by the family members in attendance as witnesses.

Reo's outstanding contributions came in the form of the third and fifth paragraphs of the truce. These paragraphs represented the heart and conclusion of the truce, with a 9-11 emphasis as he had always intended. They were a concise and well-written testament of his personal commitment to family and country. The paragraphs were entirely his workmanship, without editing or input from Bo or me.

(3)   *"United we stand as Americans against an opposing foe to our freedom. Our families stand as a symbol of unity to let the world know that we will not allow our freedom to be taken from us. We stand together to oppose any forces that would threaten our country, a country made of people from all nations in a common bond of freedom.*

(5) "We ask by God's grace and love that we be forever remembered as those that bound together the hearts of two families to form a family of freedom in America."

Reo's resolution epitomized the core of his character and brought the purpose of the truce down to a personal level. While I was preoccupied with the historical relevance of a Hatfield-McCoy truce and sought to over-inflate the value of its content, Reo wrote from the heart. His words spoke volumes beyond anything I had drafted previously. Inspired and humbled by Reo's prose, I resolved to pare down the verbosity of the opening paragraphs. I intended to make it a more honest, compelling and personal effort on my part; but it was not to be.

In his enthusiasm, Reo had taken the ball and run with it. He had three copies of the truce printed up for the families to sign. The documents were then matted and framed, with the three principals signing again on the glass. For better or worse, the words of the Hatfield McCoy truce were preserved for all posterity…in triplicate.

In the years since the 2003 signing, Bo, Reo and I have been asked to appear together to discuss the truce, usually in support of a charitable or public event. For most of these occasions, there is a public reading of the truce text. To this day, I still cringe when I hear the phrases "ancillary participants," "perpetuation of its relevance" and "protection of the veracity of the feud" read aloud.

News of the impending truce between the families spread as we began conducting a series of radio and television interviews early in 2003. A popular running gag arose from an obvious question that had surfaced in nearly every media interview: why were there two McCoys and just one Hatfield involved in the truce effort? Reo was the architect and driving force behind the truce and had collaborated with Bo to push the project forward. Bo was kind enough to keep me involved, given our history with organizing the Reunion Festivals. He insisted on my participation in the truce signing and Reo agreed. It made sense that the three of us tackled the truce together. Whenever the question about the balance of power came up, we answered with a quip: "it takes two McCoys to equal one Hatfield."

Interest in the pending truce signing reached New York City and Reo was contacted by CBS' *The Early Show*, a national weekend news program, about covering it. The network was granted exclusive permission to carry the truce signing live on the morning of Saturday, June 14, 2003. Because *The Early Show* ran from 7:00-9:00 a.m. on the East Coast, it was necessary that the truce signing be scheduled for early in the morning. Given the impossible task of having family members on vacation awake, dressed and ready for a national television appearance early on a Saturday morning, we opted to have CBS schedule our appearance as late as possible. CBS agreed to 8:30.

For the truce signing, the wooden gazebo in the Pikeville City Park was selected as the ideal platform on which to stage family members and spectators. Tourism and the city had worked diligently to decorate the facility for the broadcast. A "Hatfield McCoy Reunion Festival" banner hung overhead. A table draped in a blue tablecloth on which the copies of the truce were laid out was set up in the center of the platform.

On the morning of June 14th, more than 70 family members – men, women and children – made their way to the park. Most were dressed casually, although Bo, Reo and I were attired in our usual coats and ties. Local dignitaries, politicians and those representing the offices of the two governors were on hand to witness the event.

Governor Paul Patton of Kentucky and Governor Bob Wise of West Virginia issued proclamations declaring June 14 as "Hatfield McCoy Reconciliation Day." In his proclamation dated June 6, 2003 and witnessed by West Virginia Secretary of State Joe Manchin III, Governor Wise reiterated the themes of unity and freedom that Reo wrote about and that the families stood to exemplify that day. Governor Wise wrote:

"Whatever the cause may have been, the feud brought heartbreak and tragedy to the area for nearly 30 years, exemplifying the best qualities of courage and devotion and the worst aspects of sorrow and loss;

And whereas the present day descendants of these two proud families have long buried the passion that ignited their feud and have embraced one another with mutual respect and friendship;

(And whereas) the descendants of the Hatfields and McCoy families believe their example of reconciliation, love of country and mutual respect for the principles of democracy and freedom will strengthen the same goals among our fellow citizens."

As airtime grew closer, CBS technicians were busy adjusting lights and preparing the single camera used for the broadcast. Bo and Reo, fitted with wireless microphones and earpiece receivers to hear the on-air hosts in New York, were seated in the two chairs at the table. Following a quick sound check, all was set for the historic broadcast except for one minor detail. The production crew had apparently missed the memo that there were to be *two* McCoys seated at the signing table.

Bo gave me a quick, anxious glance, wondering why I was still standing. I shrugged, pointing to the absence of another chair. Bo gestured hurriedly to the production staff, insisting that we needed a third chair at the table. The crew moved quickly to comply, equipping me with a microphone, ear receiver and a place to sit.

Reo, the consummate statesman in his dark blue suit, was positioned on the right side of the table. Bo, in his dark coat and navy tie, looked every bit the part of a minister and the rightful spokesman for the McCoy clan. Bo occupied the center seat and I was seated to his left, dressed in my familiar well-worn cream-colored coat. The family members in attendance were placed standing behind us. Those present that day included many faithful reunion attendees such as Billy Jack McCoy, Jerry and JoAnn Hatfield, Bob and Marlyn McCoy and Margie and Bill Annett among others. Jerry Hatfield stood directly behind me, holding the Kentucky Governor's proclamation. My 13-year-old daughter, Rachel, stood at the other end of the table beside Reo. In a t-shirt and shorts and chewing gum, she was unfazed at the prospect of her national television debut. My son, Jacob, then a small shy boy, stood center stage behind his favorite cousin, Bo. He spent most of the broadcast on his tiptoes peering over Bo's shoulder, fascinated by the television lights and camera.

Getting to the truce signing that morning was the beginning of long day for me. Besides dressing for the truce-signing event, I had to be certain that "Bad Frank" Phillips was ready to make his second annual appearance following the broadcast. The vans carrying the actors to the

Truce signing on CBS. Seated at the table: Reo, Bo and Ron, surrounded by family

feud site locations had already departed for the Tug Valley. With my mini-van loaded, I was prepared to make the trip into the valley to meet them once the truce signing was over. It was a tight schedule, as the trip from Pikeville took about forty-five minutes.

Preparing for the arrival of Frank Phillips meant carrying the black costume and weapons that were the trademarks of the character. That morning, I opted to forego wearing my contact lenses that would become irritated from sweat later in the day, choosing instead to wear my glasses for the television appearance. It also made the transformation into Frank more fun later, much like Clark Kent taking off his glasses to become Superman. Appearing as Frank also meant shaving my beard down and leaving his signature 1880s style long moustache, a look that worked well when dressed in period costume. For a live broadcast on network television in 2003, however, seated next to the statesman and the minister, my glasses, long mustache and cream-colored sports coat made me look like the like the epitome of 1970s fashion sense.

With the last-minute addition of the "third man" and with the family crowded closely around the table, the stage was set for the historic broadcast. There was no preparation for the interview and no introduction to the person with whom we would be speaking. For remote broadcasts, a local producer or technician sometimes would stand by the camera and provide helpful visual cues for us. Often, the production staff and the interviewees were entirely dependent on the voice of an off-site producer speaking through the ear receivers. The off-site producer provided general information, instructions, encouragement and notification that the broadcast was about to go on the air. Curiously, on the day of the truce broadcast, the "voice" in my ear was strangely quiet.

As the three of us sat waiting patiently, it occurred to me that I did not even know the identity of the person to whom we would be speaking. As Reo and Bo sat smiling and talking amongst themselves, I assumed they were engaging in some good-natured jousting to break up the long wait. I was about to step into the fray myself when I realized that the two were not speaking to each other at all. They were apparently responding to questions from someone else. I suddenly realized, to my dismay, that we were already live on the air, being broadcast from coast to coast – and I could not hear a thing.

Jon Frankel, now a correspondent with HBO's *Real Sports with Bryant Gumbel*, was serving in the role of anchor for *The Early Show* on the day of the truce signing. A reporter with a long history at CBS, NBC and ABC, Frankel stepped in to help with the program on Saturdays.[124] He had a reputation as a serious reporter with a sense of humor, both of which served him well in covering the Hatfields and McCoys.

Frankel introduced the CBS television audience that morning to the subject of the truce, declaring that the feud "officially ends this morning on parchment. The Hatfields and McCoys are ready to sign a truce to formally end the feud that has lasted more than a century." Still hearing nothing, I realized that in the sudden rush to get me ready for the broadcast, there had been no time to check the levels on the ear receiver. For the first few moments of the broadcast, I sat smiling, nodding my head in agreement, all the while frantically and as discreetly as possible, searching for the volume control on the receiver on my belt. As Frankel continued with his introductions, I searched for the volume control in vain. Thankfully, the voice of the anchor arrived in my ear just in time to bid the family and me good morning. "I'm assuming you all checked your guns at the door," said Frankel to no one in particular. Reo answered, "Yes, we did," followed by Bo's quick response, "We've got a few hidden."[125]

Frankel addressed his first question to Reo, the obligatory inquiry that Jerry Hatfield usually fielded. Frankel cited disputes over "land ownership, inter-clan romance and a pig" as possible reasons for how the feud between the families got started. Reo, in his measured, diplomatic style, proceeded to recount a brief, concise and balanced synopsis of the feud's origins, listing "the Civil War (and) the death of Ellison Hatfield by the three McCoys and their death (as to) what started the feud." Bo countered, "of course, in true Hatfield style, he did not give you *all* the details." After a brief laugh, Bo's tone was more contrite. "It was bloody on both sides," he said. "We're just happy that it's all come to an end…and today will signify that."[126]

Finally, the mystery man directed his question to me. "Why has it taken so long to sign this treaty?" asked Frankel. It was a good question with an obvious answer, though I may be the only McCoy ever to have said so publicly. "Well, it just took a long time for the McCoys to get over the whuppin' we took," I answered. [127] The family members gathered around me took it in good humor and laughed. To my great relief, there was to be no public lynching on national television that day.

Frankel acknowledged that the truce was Reo's idea and invited him to read a portion of it. Thankfully, Reo chose a portion of the concluding paragraph, bypassing some of the document's more florid language. Following the reading, Reo, Bo and I signed the first page of the truce, just above the state seals of West Virginia and Kentucky, to the applause of the families and witnesses in attendance.

Frankel's next question addressed the relationship of the truce signing to the events of 9-11. "If we could put aside our differences, we felt like the rest of the world could do the same thing. And, we felt that it was important enough to make that message known to the rest of the world," said Reo. Bo agreed, summing up the historical importance of the day's event. "From hence forth, when they mention the Hatfields and McCoys, they'll have this document as a piece of the history, so it won't just be the feud, it'll be the peace and the proclamation that came after it." After suggesting that we could help resolve the conflicts in the Middle East, Frankel followed with a question of ownership. "You guys signed this proclamation, how much fighting is there going to be over who gets to keep it now?" he asked. "There are three copies," answered Bo, to which I added, "It will be signed in triplicate."[128]

Following the five-minute telecast and a quick removal of microphones and earpieces, the three of us signed the second page of the truce document. Before making a speedy exit for my appearance as "Bad Frank," I took a moment to watch the steady line of Hatfields and McCoys as they carefully signed their names to the truce. The signatures of which I am most proud are those of my children, Rachel and Jacob McCoy. Jacob, as the great-great-great-great grandson of Randolph McCoy, was the youngest family member to sign the truce. He was nine years old at the time.

The truce was the culmination of nearly 120 years of efforts to produce a final, lasting and tangible resolution to a conflict that once seemed to have no possible end. The generations of families represented by the signatures were a testimony to a lasting desire for peace, a message that reverberated worldwide. "We were glad it did, because we wanted to tell people, this is no joke. We're serious about this. To this day, we will stand together and fight anybody who attacks us. We're not going to put up with it," declared Reo.[129]

Those family members who affixed their signatures to the truce considered it an honor to represent the generations of Hatfields and McCoys who had come before them and to set an example for those who would follow. No longer would the families be remembered for the feud alone. Newspaper editorials following the truce signing agreed. "If the Hatfields and McCoys can do it, anybody can do it. That was the message at yesterday's signing of a truce between the two infamous feuding families. And it was a good message….the truce signing sets a good example for the rest of the country and the world," wrote the editor of the *Appalachian News-Express*.[130] The *Los Angeles Times* was a bit more perplexed by it all: "This solution probably makes way too much sense for intractable disputes elsewhere. Everyone surely takes a shine to one less feud in the world. But how are we going to describe long-running disputes now, when "like the Hatfields and McCoys" means picnicking and coed tug of war?"[131]

Ascribing a monetary value to the truce was not something we had ever considered. In 2004, the three of us were asked by Theatre West Virginia in Beckley, West Virginia to take part in a fund-raiser dinner for their theater. The outdoor theater, opened in 1955, was a popular tourist venue, running summer musicals and dramas annually. Their *Hatfields and McCoys* was a musical that opened in 1970.

The truce signing had gained the attention of the fund-raising committee who decided that a copy of the truce might make an excellent item for their auction. Reo offered to have a reproduction of the truce framed, a copy that the three of us would sign again and present to the winner. Following dinner, when the truce came up for auction, it sold for $900. The auction winner then donated the truce back to the theatre to be placed on display at its facility.

Sadly, the theater succumbed to financial troubles and closed its doors in September 2013. Props, costumes and other artifacts were sold to help settle the theater's debts. The theater was given a reprieve when the West Virginia legislature offered a grant of $125,000 to reopen the facility, beginning with the 2014 summer season. While the *Honey in the Rock* show was tabled indefinitely, the *Hatfields and McCoys* would live to fight another day. The whereabouts of the auctioned copy of the truce, however, are unknown.

Sequels

"The past is the beginning of the beginning
and all that is and has been is but the twilight of the dawn."
H. G. Wells

Following the national attention, both acrimonious and favorable, given the remarkable Hatfield-McCoy events of 2003, subsequent reunion gatherings continued on an annual basis, although with gradually diminishing attendance. While we attended and supported the yearly events, Bo and I stepped back from leadership positions to tend to personal affairs long overdue. Others like Margie Annett worked diligently to ensure that the reunions would continue for years to come. For all of us involved in the reunions, it was a time of change.

The personal effort necessary to produce the first four reunions was herculean. As a result, our commitment to ensuring that the reunions would be successful at times bordered on the near obsessive. Consideration for the needs of our immediate families was overshadowed by the concerns of the greater family unit. Beyond the obvious financial losses, the reunions taxed our physical and emotional resources as well as our time and energies. Whether by coincidence or as an indirect result of the lingering effects of the reunions, all the principals involved in organizing the reunions suffered repercussions to their personal lives. The years following the frenzy of the reunions were a time of introspection and rebuilding. Meanwhile, the adventurous path on which my journey of discovery had placed me continued to unveil its share of surprises.

Given that elections are an intrinsic part of feud lore, it should be no surprise that Hatfields and McCoys have a genuine respect for the political process. Feud history is rife with the influence of politics. More curious, however, is the notion that on the eve of a pivotal presidential election, the media would contact us for our opinion on the matter.

The outcome of the Bush-Gore election of November 7, 2000, hinged on the manual recount of ballots in the state of Florida. The contest was too close to call nationally, so the final tabulation of Florida votes was critical and decisive. With Republican candidate George W. Bush 600 votes ahead of Democratic opponent Al Gore, Florida ordered a machine recount of the ballots. Bush's lead narrowed to 327 votes. After a manual recount of questionable ballots, however, Bush was declared the winner with 537 votes, prompting legal action by the Gore campaign. The Florida Supreme Court then ordered a statewide manual recount of all votes. Bush's lead dwindled to 154 votes, forcing the Bush team to appeal for intervention by the United State Supreme Court on December 9.[132]

It was a trying time for the nation. Remarkably, on the eve of a national political crisis, the media contacted the Hatfields and McCoys for reassurance that the situation was going to be resolved. Bo hoped for a peaceful outcome. "Maybe by looking at our families, it will help," he said. Speaking on behalf of the Hatfields, Mingo County Sheriff Tennis Hatfield echoed Bo's sentiment. "We've buried the hatchet. We associate together, and we help each other. I think the nation could learn from it."[133]

Apparently, the Supreme Court heeded our plea. On Dec. 12, the same day the article appeared, the Court decided by a 5 to 4 vote to reverse the recount decision of the Florida Court. Bush was declared the winner in Florida and won the Electoral College by one vote, despite Gore having won the national popular vote. To this day, we stand by our contention that the Hatfield-McCoy involvement in swaying the 2000 election was purely coincidental.

Following the reunions, I received many email testimonials that corroborated the positive effects of the events. While some email messages were from family members who had attended, most were from individuals who had read or seen accounts of the events in the media. Many felt motivated to write and explain what the sight of the Hatfields and McCoys reconciling publicly had meant to them. One of those individuals was a man named Martin.

Martin's story taught me that the definition of family often extends beyond the boundaries of heritage and blood relations. Neither a Hatfield nor a McCoy, Martin felt an affinity for the families, although he did not know any family members personally. He was hesitant, almost apologetic, to ask permission to attend an upcoming reunion, as if he was inviting himself to someone else's party. I reassured him that his concern was unwarranted. He was as welcome as anyone was to attend.

Martin was one of the most enthusiastic attendees I have ever seen at any reunion. A middle-aged, soft-spoken and modest man, he seemed to have an unbridled energy for all-things Hatfield-McCoy. He wanted to take part in as many of the weekend's events as possible. With the easy mobility of his motorcycle, he joined in numerous events from Pikeville to Matewan to Williamson. He attended our dinner on Friday, then on Saturday made his way to the Tug Valley for the start of the Hatfield-McCoy Marathon, then went on to Blackberry Creek and multiple feud sites to catch the feud reenactments and finally back to Pikeville for the softball game.

Unlike some who gravitated to the reunions because of a lack of family attachments, Martin had a family of his own, although he did not talk about them much. I inferred from our conversations that, although he was estranged from his own, family was important to him. He demonstrated his affection for our Hatfield-McCoy family at every event that he attended. As the weekend ended, I told Martin how pleased I was that he had taken part in the reunion. He told me how honored he was that the families had welcomed him as if he was one of their own. With tears welling in his eyes, he stopped abruptly, unable to speak. He nodded at me and I nodded back. I understood what it was like to be unable to say "goodbye." Without another word, he boarded his motorcycle and rode away. I have never heard from Martin again.

2004 was the year I met Jerome and Norma McCoy. Jerome, a military veteran living in Philippi, West Virginia was one of the finest family members I have had the fortune of meeting over the years. His story, as with so many others, was indicative of what the Hatfields and McCoys had come to represent to so many. During his service in Vietnam, Jerome had been exposed to the "Agent Orange" defoliant used during the war and he suffered chronic health issues as a result. His wife, Norma, also endured more than her share of health challenges. The prospect of attending a

Hatfield-McCoy reunion was financially and physically prohibitive, but making the trip to Pikeville was something that Jerome had always longed to do.

While uncertain of his connection to the "feuding" McCoy lineage, Jerome felt a kinship with the family he had discovered in the media and online. He frequented the *real-mccoys.com* website and came across my contact information posted there. Although he was not a proficient computer user, in late 2002, Jerome reached out to introduce himself to me through email. His email was one I remember well because I almost overlooked it. Jerome was not an especially good speller or typist nor was he fond of capitalization. Following the onslaught of M2K, it was common for me to receive large volumes of email. I had become adept at scanning and deleting "junk" email quickly. I would sometimes get the occasional "odd" inquiry, generally from someone alleging to be some-degree of family member, usually wanting to argue some obscure facet of Hatfield-McCoy history.

Most often, the email I received was from family members curious about their heritage or eager to introduce themselves and their specific feud lineage. I nearly always answered email from individuals who wanted to make contact. There were many extended family members throughout the country, most of whom I never had the opportunity to meet, who just wanted the chance to say "hello." Poorly written email or those lacking a proper subject heading were sometimes overlooked by me or lost in the purging of "junk" email.

Jerome's first email to me was nearly deleted. There was something about Jerome's short message, however, with its poor spelling and lack of punctuation that caught my attention. In his introduction of himself, there was a complete lack of pretense or ulterior motive, a genuineness that prompted me to reply to him. Over the months that followed, Jerome and I began a series of email exchanges that lead to recurring phone calls and finally to a lasting friendship.

Of the people I communicated with over the years, there was none more sincerely longing to attend a Hatfield-McCoy reunion than Jerome McCoy. As much as I knew he wanted to attend, there was always an expressed reluctance on his part about doing so. It was only after I invited Jerome to attend the 2004 reunion that I realized the financial and medical burden it would place on Norma and him. While Jerome listed all the reasons it would be impossible for them to attend, he never asked for special consideration or financial assistance. Although I had yet to meet him in person, I could think of no one more deserving to be part of our festivities that year.

Getting Jerome and Norma to Pikeville was no easy task. Both had personal medical assistants that needed to attend the reunion with them. Both had medical equipment and wheelchairs to be transported, necessitating the rental of a van large enough to accommodate them, their helpers and equipment. Their attendance at the reunion meant it was necessary to hire a driver, compensate the medical staff, book hotel accommodations for the weekend and acquire tickets to events for all involved.

We needed to get Jerome and Norma to the reunion, although as usual, I was uncertain as to how to make it happen. Jerome knew the physical effort that the trip would require of him but he was undaunted by the prospect. He was certain he could talk his medical aides into driving the van and attending the reunion with them. If it were somehow possible, Jerome was committed to making it to the reunion and I was determined that he should have the opportunity.

With reunion funds tight as always, Bo and I struggled to find some way financially to make it happen. With several hundred people already interested in attending the 2004 reunion, it seemed the solution to getting the Philippi McCoys to Kentucky was right before our eyes. We announced the need to our family members online and passed the digital hat.

I received immediate and positive reactions to the solicitation I emailed to family members. They began donating money to the cause, along with their purchases of reunion tickets. One family member in New York mailed a check that covered the full price of the van rental. Within two weeks, family members had contributed more than enough money to bring Jerome, Norma and their two aides to Pikeville for the 2004 reunion.

Ron with Norma and Jerome McCoy, 2008 Reunion

On Friday, June 11, 2004, it was my honor to welcome Jerome and Norma to Pikeville after nearly two years of email and telephone calls. A quiet man, frail from a decades-long battle for his health, Jerome had the steely resolve of a veteran soldier that shone in his eyes. He was also a profoundly earnest man, proud of his wife, his military service and his heritage. In 2008, Jerome and Norma attended a more scaled back Hatfield-McCoy reunion, this time of their own accord. On Friday the 13th of that year, in a banquet room at the Landmark before a group of about sixty family members, I watched Jerome as he set aside his oxygen tank to share a dance with my then-fiancé, Bobbi. Two years later, he and Norma made their way to a mountaintop in western North Carolina to attend our wedding.

On November 26, 2011, Norma called us to inform us that Jerome had passed away from complications due to his lengthy illness. Bobbi and I packed up and made the trip to Philippi to attend his funeral. It was a snowy day in Grafton, West Virginia as Jerome Barton McCoy was buried with full military honors in the National Cemetery there. Following the funeral, Bobbi and I walked the granite concourse, picking up expended shells from the twenty-one gun salute. Along with Norma, we were the only members of Jerome's McCoy family in attendance.

By 2006, the effort to keep the annual Reunion Festival energized and growing was severely waning. Although we endeavored to continue our outreach to family members across the country, compelling relations to make the trip to Pikeville year after year had become an increasingly difficult task. Interest in the Hatfield-McCoy reunions in Pike County was declining, as were the numbers of those attending.

On the West Virginia side of the Tug Fork, the prognosis for the health of the Reunion Festival was significantly more optimistic. Matewan continued to promote the Reunion Festival and the annual Hatfield McCoy Marathon as their own and attendance for both was gradually increasing. On the Kentucky side of the Tug Fork, however, the news was dire. Despite the Hatfield McCoy Reunion Festival being named a "top 10 event" by Kentucky Tourism Council and a "top 20 event" by the Southeast Tourism Society, support for the festival at the local level was on the decline.[134] Judge Executive Karen Gibson left office and county support for the festival went with her. Corporate and business sponsorships had become non-existent.

The City of Pikeville continued to allow use of its facilities and to provide public services for festival events. Pikeville-Pike County Tourism never relented in their support, although their resources were strained, promoting both "Hillbilly Days" and the Reunion Festival. After the 2005 event, however, I received the following email assessment of the situation from one Pike County official. "It doesn't make sense to have a festival with poor attendance such as 2005. It was a failure and very embarrassing." Facing the inevitable, Bo and I resolved to table the reunion for 2006 and 2007 and resume with a gala event in the following year.

The McCoy boys were not retiring completely, however. Since the truce signing in 2003, Bo and I had entertained the idea of taking the reunion on the road. Interest in the Hatfields and McCoys on a national level remained high. We thought that the cost of traveling to eastern Kentucky prevented some family members from attending the reunions. By organizing a "Hatfield-McCoy Goodwill Tour" to venues around the country, we felt we could build upon the notoriety of the truce signing to promote and encourage interest in the families. Hosting Hatfield-McCoy family gatherings in major metropolitan centers such as Orlando, Las Vegas or New York City would foster interest in feud history and encourage people to make the journey to feud-country for themselves. While the idea had merit, the logistics of organizing the conflicting schedules of the principals involved hampered enthusiasm for it, so the "Hatfield McCoy Road Show" never saw the light of day.

Margie Annett's determination and steadfast refusal to let the reunions die kept the events going in Pikeville during the lean years from 2005-2008. Following the 2001 reunion, Margie Annett had begun soliciting recipes from family members for a long-gestating project on which she had been working. Margie had been instrumental in organizing annual family gatherings at the Uriah McCoy home place for many years, a site that her branch of the family had always cared for and maintained. In 2002, she published *Cooking with the Real McCoys* and used the sales proceeds for the upkeep and restoration of the property. Rebuffing the idea that the reunions in Pikeville were over, she parlayed her organizational talents and cookbook revenues into hosting family activities there as well.

For 2006, Margie organized a Friday night family dinner at the restaurant owned by "Bob's Mountain Barbeque." The entertainment for the crowd of fifty included trivia contests and music by Bob Brooks and other family members. While I attended and brought the sound system for the night, it was nice just to be part of the audience for the intimate family affair Margie had put together.

2006 was the first reunion that Bo missed attending. His professional life had begun to take off and the demands on his time had increased significantly. I missed the reunion for the first time the following year, as my daughter Rachel's high school graduation and other considerations prohibited my attendance.

The "history" of the feud is replete with its own mythology. Some stories have been repeated often enough to become inherent parts of the feud legend. Sometimes, purveyors of feud "history" have strung together unrelated details to create a "new" perspective on a feud event, real or imagined. More common in the modern age of feud-enthusiasm, however, is the use of the feud as a vehicle of convenience to raise attention to an issue. Such was the case with the "discovery" of a McCoy "genetic disease," said to be an underlying factor in the Hatfield-McCoy feud.

In 2007, the Associated Press reported on doctors at Vanderbilt University treating dozens of McCoy family members in Tennessee with Von Hippel-Lindau disease, a rare disorder linked to tumors in the adrenal glands. It was a condition alleged to have been in the family for generations. Symptoms associated with the disorder included "hair-trigger rage and violent outbursts" linked to the over-stimulation of adrenaline. The article alluded to a "1998 medical journal article tracing the disease through four generations." Reports of family members with the disease stretched from Virginia to Oregon.[135]

While linking the disease to the feud required a great leap of logic, testifying to the renowned McCoy disposition did not. "The McCoy temperament is legendary. Whether or not we can blame it on genes, I don't know," I was quoted as saying. "(But) there are a lot of (other reasons) that are probably a more legitimate source of conflict," I added. Reo Hatfield concurred. "I would be shocked if doctors blamed it on illness," he said. Even though she conceded, "an argument could be made for seeing the McCoys as the more aggressive of the clans," feud author Altina Waller agreed with us. "Medical folks like to find these kinds of explanations....the rage and violence as such was not confined to McCoys."[136] While I am certain that framing the story of the disease within the context of the feud did much to help newspaper sales, I hoped there was a more positive benefit of raising awareness for those suffering with this affliction.

For nearly a century, McCoys have suffered from statue envy. When "Devil Anse" Hatfield passed away in 1921, the family erected a six-foot Italian marble visage of the patriarch that was placed atop his grave in the Hatfield cemetery in Sarah Ann, West Virginia. "Devil Anse's" funeral was a grand affair, attracting hundreds of visitors from around the area. His statue, estimated to have cost several thousand dollars, was no small monument in its time. Like the man it represents, the statue has stood proudly atop the hilltop cemetery, watching over his family for nearly one hundred years.

In contrast, Randolph McCoy was buried alongside his wife, Sarah in Pikeville in 1914 in a small, private ceremony, in a plot donated to the family by the eminent Colonel John Dils. Until 1977, the grave was marked by only a stone with the initials "RM" on it. That year, the stone was replaced with a large granite headstone, donated by Paul McCoy, the son of feud author Truda McCoy. While the granite marker was beautiful, it paled in comparison to "Devil Anse's" statue. Some in the McCoy camp over the years have felt that "Ol' Randall" should get his due.

Bo and I decided to adopt the cause of giving Randolph a statue of his own as the charitable mission of the 2000 Hatfield McCoy Reunion Festival. Although we had no drawings or plans for the statue in place, "Give Ol' Randall a Statue" became the rallying cry for the mission. Funds donated by attendees were collected by the tourism office in hopes of one day raising a statue.

With limited funds in hand, I began working with Phyllis Hunt in planning a Randolph McCoy memorial. The ideal location for the statue was undetermined, although the city park seemed the logical place for it. Pikeville officials were insistent that the statue should be on display within the city limits. Although I was not opposed to the statue being set up in town, I felt that Randolph's heart truly was back in the Tug Valley with his children. Sam McKinney, a local artist who had worked on other statues on display in Pikeville, began the design work for the statue. I suggested that no matter where the statue was placed, Randolph should be depicted looking in the direction of the Tug Valley.

Local resistance to a Randolph McCoy statue in Pikeville was stiff. One Pikeville resident suggested that placing the statue in the park would be romanticizing criminal behavior. "I don't believe we should be putting up the statue," the citizen declared. "Killing is killing. It doesn't matter how (or why) you do it."[137] After three years of fund-raising and planning, a Randolph McCoy statue on public property in Pikeville was not to be. We declared an official end to our efforts to have the statue placed on public property, but we had not given up on the idea of a statue entirely.

Nancy Forsyth, owner of Dils Cemetery, offered us the chance to place the statue there. Although space in the cemetery was limited, there was a plateau to the left of the main steps leading up the hillside that was an ideal location for the statue. Setting the statue on private property negated any resistance to having the statue placed on public lands. Placing the statue at Dils also provided us other new and exciting possibilities as well. The cemetery was the burial site of five feud participants including Randolph and Sarah McCoy, daughter Roseanna and son Samuel and his wife, Martha. I suggested we design a McCoy family statue that would honor the family buried there and portray the struggle that the family had endured. A series of sketches were drawn up, capturing the family in a dramatic moment in time: Sarah was pleading with a withdrawn Randolph, his back turned to Roseanna, clutching her baby, Sarah Elizabeth closely to her as a concerned Sam and Martha looked on.

As preliminary design sketches for the statue were reproduced and circulated by the tourism office in hopes of raising awareness of the project, reactions by family members was decidedly mixed. Although the rough sketches were intended for early consideration and discussion, the drawings were made public as approved designs for the statue – an idea that did not sit well with those who felt Randolph never would have turned his back on his family. As debate over the look of the statue continued, the increasing costs to produce it and the ongoing argument over its final location led to the project miring down. To date, plans for the statue have failed to move forward. Tourism dutifully continues to collect funds for the project in hopes of one day seeing it come to fruition.

The 2008 reunion was notable for several reasons. For all intent and purposes, it was the last "official" Hatfield-McCoy reunion as organized by the original M2K crew. We celebrated the event with a Friday the 13th dinner in a small banquet room at the Landmark Inn with an attendance of about fifty people. Jerome and Norma McCoy were attending their second reunion. Libby Preston, an Internet genealogist whose *www.libby-genealogy.com* website was a popular online resource at the time, attended her first reunion along with her twin sister, Susie. Both brought laptops and collected ancestral data for family genealogy trees that they printed on the spot. Family icon Paul McCoy and his wife, Janene were on hand for what would be his final appearance at a Hatfield-McCoy reunion. The setting was intimate as we reminisced about reunions past. Although little was said about it, there was a palpable sense of change in the air.

For the 2008 event, Reo suggested that we commemorate the fifth anniversary of the 2003 truce signing. To mark the occasion, Reo purchased a quartet of shotguns that he dubbed the "Hatfield-McCoy Peacemakers." The guns were signed by Bo, Reo and me at "high noon" on Saturday in a

Bo McCoy, Reo Hatfield, Bob McCoy, Jerry Hatfield & Ron with governor's representative

ceremony reuniting family members at the site of the truce signing. Bo joked that only Reo would bring shotguns to a Hatfield-McCoy reunion.

Two of the signed shotguns were presented to the governors of Kentucky and West Virginia, Steve Beshear and Joe Manchin, who had representatives on hand to receive them. The third shotgun was to be presented to President George Bush later to honor him for his continued support of the military. The fourth shotgun remained in Reo's hands for safekeeping. Following the signing, family members including many who had faithfully supported the reunions over the years gathered for a final joint-family portrait.

The story of the shotgun presented to then West Virginia Governor Manchin has a curious epilogue. Following the success of the History Channel's *Hatfields and McCoys* mini-series in 2012, Reo suggested that a special exhibit honoring the feud should be established in the West Virginia State Museum. When no exhibit came about, Reo asked about the status of the shotgun he had donated four years before. To his surprise, the shotgun could not be found. Although all gifts with a value great than 35 dollars received by the governor on behalf of the state must be catalogued and recorded, a thorough search of the registry from 2008 showed no listing of a "commemorative shotgun." History Commissioner Randall Reid-Smith, in response to Reo's inquiry suggested that the "shotgun was stored in a safe in the Governor's Mansion upon receipt and is probably still there."[138] The gun has yet to be recovered.

Hollywood

"The most important thing is family."
Walt Disney

Over the course of a century, the story of the feud has taken on all the qualities of an American myth, fostered in no small part by the media's ongoing fascination with it. The families' conflict has been displayed in various forms, from music to cartoons to television to films. In the modern era, the enthusiasm for the story of the Hatfields and McCoys has not waned.

Beginning with the "yellow journalism" print coverage of the 1880s through the invention of moving pictures to the advent of modern era cable television, the Hatfields and McCoys have become engrained in the fabric of modern American storytelling. "Devil Anse" was said to have portrayed himself in a turn-of-the-century silent film version of the story. Among the many variations of the feud tale are the 1949 MGM film *Roseanna McCoy* with Joan Evans and Farley Granger, a 1975 ABC television movie *The Hatfields and McCoys* with Jack Palance and a recent 2012 Lionsgate film, *Hatfields & McCoys: Bad Blood*, starring Perry King and Christian Slater.[139] In 2013, the History Channel produced a short-lived "reality" series, *Hatfields and McCoys: White Lightning*, featuring a cast of purported local "family members," pitted in a heavily orchestrated and disingenuous battle over moonshine.

As characters, the Hatfields and McCoys are archetypal representatives of humanity. Their story presents a ready-made dramatic backdrop on which to display the broad tapestry of the human experience. Actor Robert Duvall once described the feud story as "American Shakespeare."[140]

The most successful media portrayal of the feud story occurred in 2012, when the History Channel premiered the six-hour, three-episode mini-series, *Hatfields and McCoys*, starring Kevin Costner as William Anderson Hatfield and Bill Paxton as Randolph McCoy. Shot on location in Romania, the multi-million dollar production debuted to record numbers. On the night of May 30, 2012, the mini-series commanded an audience of 14.3 million, making it the highest rated cable television program in history.[141]

Critics, like Mary McNamara of the *Los Angeles Times* praised the production, writing, "*Hatfields & McCoys* transcends the confines of its age by revealing the feud's posturing, resentments and callous violence that mirror the dynamics of modern urban gangs."[142] Nominated for sixteen Emmy awards, the production won five awards including those for Kevin Costner as Outstanding Lead Actor for his portrayal of "Devil Anse" and Tom Berenger as Outstanding Supporting Actor for his role as "Jim Vance."[143]

Given the mammoth ratings and overall positive reception, the Costner mini-series likely will remain the definitive Hollywood account of the feud for years to come. Most family members have supported the project, despite reservations about its mischaracterizations of feud participants and misrepresentations of historical facts. Others have complained that the series gave little consideration to the existing generations of Hatfield-McCoy descendants and sought no input or approval from either family. Some were displeased that, for budgetary reasons, the series was shot on location in Romania and not Appalachia, a region that could have benefitted from the jobs and financial resources a Hollywood product would have brought into the area.

My awareness of Mr. Costner's interest in the project began in 2001 when his company, TIG Productions purchased a copy of Truda McCoy's book from us. The order was paid using a company credit card, but the shipping address in Burbank, California caught my attention. After confirming the address of the production company, I let Bo know that the company was buying a book. Under the guise of validating the order, Bo called the company's office to corroborate our suspicions. Excited that the company might be considering a film based on Truda's work, I drafted a letter that I enclosed with the book that included an open-ended offer to help as needed. We never heard from them again.

In 1999, when the news broke that we were planning the "Reunion of the Millennium," Hollywood came calling. The earliest inquiry I received was a script submitted to me via email from a producer whose name I do not recall. The script was laughably bad. In the first ten pages of the work, Randolph and Sarah stood idly by the banks of the Tug Fork while up-river, a grandfatherly "Devil Anse" entertained a group of Hatfield and McCoy children. Suddenly, a McCoy child was swept away by the fast-moving river waters of the Tug. Hearing the child's frantic cries, the McCoys watched helplessly as "Devil Anse" dove into the river to save him. What became of the poor child is uncertain. At this point in the story, I deleted the file and committed the script to the digital abyss.

The first serious overture came shortly after. We were approached by "Plan B Productions" of Sherman Oaks, California about making a movie about the reunion. Company President David Ronald Franzke contacted Bo by phone, then followed with a quickly drawn up agreement that was faxed on May 19, 1999. The offer as presented by Plan B was for an "option to purchase motion picture feature and television rights of "Hatfields and McCoys: the M2K Reunion" (working title)." Plan B agreed to "acquire a one-year option to purchase motion picture, television, book and allied rights for the sum of $1.00." They also reserved the right to extend the option for an additional two years, for the price of an additional dollar. Retaining the "right to make changes to the story line for creative purposes" Franzke offered to employ Bo as an "advisor" during production and was prepared to pay an undisclosed fee to him for the story rights if the project ever went into production.

Intrigued by their interest in our story, Bo responded to Plan B with a letter of his own. While consenting to serve in an advisory capacity, Bo balked at the idea of selling the option rights for one dollar, especially the "allied" rights, which controlled our ability to promote our event in the press and to produce and sell M2K merchandise. Plan B responded the same day, explaining that the dollar option was business as usual in Hollywood. "There are no guarantees, which means that there is a chance that even though we might sell the project; it still might not get made."

On May 25, 1999, Bo replied with his final letter on the subject. He stated that while we were still considering their offer, he planned to have it reviewed by a former high school classmate of his, now an attorney, named Mark Hatfield. Bo respectfully declined the one-dollar option. "We are the story. Our work is what has put (the) McCoys:2000 reunion in the press. Our family name and heritage is what allows us (to) produce such an event," he said. We did not hear from Plan B again.

In 2003, another company with a similar sounding name made an announcement to the national media. "Plan B Entertainment," then owned by actors Brad Pitt, Jennifer Aniston and current CEO of Paramount Pictures, Brad Grey, declared that *The Hatfields and McCoys* was to be a Warner Brothers production, written by Oscar winner Eric Roth, directed by Michael Mann and starring Brad Pitt in an unspecified role.[144] For reasons unknown, the project never went into production. In 2010, "Plan B's" plans surfaced once again when actor Robert Duvall leaked the news during an interview. *The Hatfields and McCoys* remained an active Warner Brothers project, scripted by Roth, and directed by Scott Cooper, with music produced by another Oscar winner, T-Bone Burnett.[145] After languishing in production for years, the dormant project was trumped by the Costner mini-series. It will likely remain in the dustbin of unproduced Hollywood projects.

Curiously, the second offer to purchase the options to M2K arrived at nearly the same time as the first. David Garrett, an experienced television and film producer, was president of "On Time and Sober Productions," named after one producers' assessment of Ronald Reagan's secret to his longevity as an actor. The company based in West Hills, California had purchased the rights to feud accounts written by Dr. Altina Waller and Dr. Otis Rice and a novel, *Days of Darkness* by John Ed Pearce. Garrett saw the press surrounding the M2K reunion as an opportunity to promote his project, which was still being written. Likewise, as notices of his project were scheduled to appear in *Variety* and the *Hollywood Reporter*, we thought our event could benefit from the publicity as well.

On May 20, 1999, Bo signed a marketing agreement with the company. For the term of one year with options to extend beyond the initial period, the agreement gave both parties the "right and power to market, promote and publicize the other's project by any means, including but not limited to the Internet, press releases and television and print interviews." Each could consult on the other's projects on a "non-exclusive, non-compensated basis," although the agreement was not to be "construed as creating a partnership or joint venture between the parties." It seemed a win-win agreement for all parties involved but it did not shackle us with the constraints of the previous "Plan B" offer.

Our first and only joint press release on June 14, 1999, however, indicated the flawed concepts of the Hatfield-McCoy projects the company was considering. Promising a film "in the vein of *Fargo* and *Bonnie and Clyde*," Brian Sawyer, an executive with the company, intended to "present a unique take on the characters and incidents that a strictly factual telling could not." The company also announced a syndicated action series set in eastern Kentucky described as a "*Young Guns* meets *Dawson's Creek*" following "orphaned teenage members of both families, who must reconcile and team up in order to survive in the lawless region…all the while dealing with problems faced by typical teenagers everywhere."

The third and final project announced in the press release was a complete surprise to us. "On Time and Sober" announced an "as-yet-untitled film" dramatizing the events leading up to the reunion, in which "stalwart family members from both sides refuse to forgive and forget the past. In the spirit of *Field of Dreams*, however, the spirits of the ancestors killed in the feud appear to work a reconciliation between the family members."

Bo and I were stunned by the nature and poor quality of the projects the company had announced. Following the press release, we moved quickly to distance ourselves from them. Although "On Time and Sober" survived until 2012 producing a steady output of documentaries and low budget films, the company is no longer active. Mercifully, their Hatfield-McCoy projects never saw the light of day.

The most promising opportunity for a family-focused, thoughtful and character driven Hatfield-McCoy presentation came in an email sent to me, dated February 20, 2007. Rachel Klein, a sports producer for HBO living in New York, had recently purchased a copy of Truda's book and was enchanted by the "personal story (which is) far more interesting than the historical accounts from outsiders." Although her background was primarily in live-broadcast sports, Klein wanted to delve into producing scripted dramatic work. Klein collaborated with Wendy Neuss, co-producer of the *Star Trek: the Next Generation* and producer of *Star Trek: Voyager* television series to form "Wicked Lord Entertainment," in hopes of developing non-sports related projects. In the late 1990s, Klein had worked as a production supervisor for *HBO Boxing* and *HBO Boxing After Dark*. Her experience with HBO led to a position as post-production supervisor for the film, *Rocky Balboa* in 2006. In 2009-2010, she served as production supervisor for the television series, *Steven Seagal: Lawman* and as a producer for many *Ultimate Fighting Championship* events.[146]

In early email, Klein demonstrated a commitment to ensuring that the feud story was told with a respectful sensitivity to the families, past and present. Throughout our communications, I found myself increasingly supportive of the type of project she intended to produce. "I must admit that I am excited about the direction you are taking with the project. I believe this project will be something of significance, on the order of a *Roots* type of event. With little exaggeration, I believe you may be on the verge of producing an important, historic piece of work," I responded in an email on February 26, 2007. During follow-up phone calls, we discussed various facets of production including the possibility of shooting on location in Appalachia and involving family members and local citizens as background actors.

The basis of Klein's Hatfield-McCoy project was to be Truda McCoy's account and she hoped to secure the rights to the book. To do so, she needed to attain the permission of the rights-holder, Paul McCoy, an endeavor that proved more challenging than Rachel had expected. Paul was a private individual, not easily accessible to a Manhattanite HBO producer to whom he had not been introduced.

From her earliest inquiries, I was impressed with Rachel. She was always considerate of our family history and understood the value we descendants placed on our shared heritage. In comparison with previous incarnations of Hatfield-McCoy projects, her approach to the story was refreshing and implied a genuine affection for the families. I had great confidence in the integrity of her proposal and felt that once it was presented to Paul, he would too.

Hoping I could help to bridge the divide between the Tug Valley and New York City, I offered to broker a meeting between Paul and Rachel. In April, 2007, her attorneys drafted a mutual non-disclosure agreement for me to sign, ensuring that all discussions regarding the subject matter would remain confidential and would not be passed on to a competing entity. Signing the agreement put me into the curious position of working with an HBO producer I had never met with the expectation that I could convince Paul to sign on to the project, while being contractually unable to talk to anyone else about it.

Meanwhile, Klein was assembling her team. She had completed an HBO project for Cal Ripken, the great Baltimore Orioles third baseman, in partnership with Matt Apfel, former Head of Development for True Entertainment. Well-regarded with ample connections in the industry, Apfel seemed to be the perfect partner for the Klein's Hatfield-McCoy project. Klein set up a meeting to present the project to one of HBO's competitors, Showtime. The deal was contingent upon securing the rights to Truda's book – and a new and unexpected condition.

Rachel intuitively understood the symbiotic relationship between the families. Since the earliest days of discussing the project, she insisted on the involvement of the Hatfield family, a position I supported. "I definitely have some Hatfield resources we can call upon for input. While I think we should keep this as close to the vest as possible, I think we should get some Hatfield opinions on the project. If we err in having this project too pro-McCoy, then we will have done a great injustice to a noble family," I wrote. In my mind, enlisting Hatfield support was not as difficult a prospect as securing Paul's permission to use his mother's work. I assumed that, should we enlist Paul McCoy's support, the Hatfields would soon follow.

By May 10, 2007, Klein had become more insistent about the issue. She wrote, "I am about to pursue the other side of the feud, so if you have any direction to approaching the Hatfields, please fire away!" Apparently, Hatfield family support of the project alone was not all that Klein was hoping to secure. Unbeknownst to me, Klein had been in touch with Dr. Coleman Hatfield, a great-grandson of "Devil Anse" Hatfield in Logan, West Virginia, about acquiring the rights to his book, "Tale of the Devil" published in 2003. According to Klein, the Hatfield representatives were excited about the prospect of signing a deal.

Although securing the rights to a Hatfield book was not something I considered all together necessary, it made good negotiating leverage for Klein in dealing with the McCoys. On May 13, 2007, Klein wrote, "Heard back from (the) Hatfield side already! They are interested in talking about the book rights deal. I think it is very important to speak to Paul ASAP to complete both sides. My contact at Showtime is ready to set a meeting in July, but I would need the rights buttoned up on both books before I can write the pilot (script) and head to the meeting."

Despite my reservations, Klein's tactics had worked. In late May 2007, I placed a call to Paul, despite not having seen him in several years. Paul was as thoughtful and measured on the phone as he was in person. He listened politely as I detailed Klein's interest in his mother's book and her intention to present the feud from the perspective of the families. I explained that she was interested in visiting Pike County to meet him in person to discuss the matter. I said that I would be there as well and that I would be happy to introduce the two, although I had yet to meet Rachel in person myself. I was pleasantly surprised when Paul graciously accepted and invited us to meet him at his furniture store.

Rachel Klein was over the moon. "I think this is amazing!" she wrote in an email on June 7, 2007. Her optimism for seeing her vision of a Hatfield-McCoy project come together was unrelenting. "The contracts are at the Hatfield publishers and I might hear back from them as early as this weekend," she added.

Bobbi and I met Rachel Klein for the first time in Pikeville on Friday, June 23, 2007. In person, I discovered that Klein was as energetic and persuasive as she was by telephone and email. After a lively dinner conversation, I was certain that if there was anyone who could push a Hatfield-McCoy deal through Hollywood, it was Rachel Klein.

On Saturday morning, June 24, 2007 Paul welcomed us into his store. Although it was the first time I had seen him since M2K, Paul greeted me in the unhesitant manner that is traditional in Appalachia when it comes to receiving family. Ever the gentleman, Paul was pleasant and polite as I introduced him to Rachel, although he was decidedly unfazed by meeting an HBO producer.

As we sat around a table in the warehouse, Rachel told Paul about her sincere admiration for his mother's book and her intentions to use it as the foundation for a Hatfield-McCoy film or mini-series. Paul listened quietly but intently. Although his impassive expression was difficult to read, I believed he was as impressed with Klein's approach as I had

Paul McCoy and his wife, Janene, at the 2008 Reunion

been. Although I held no legal rights to Truda's book, since Bo and I were instrumental in having the book reprinted in 2000, Rachel included me as the "publisher" in the contract she had drafted for Paul to sign. While I had received no compensation for my involvement in brokering the deal or for the months of work leading up to it, I was honored to play a small role in what I hoped would be an unprecedented presentation of the feud story. When Rachel Klein presented the contract for Paul and me to sign, I was happy to see that Paul did so without reservation.

The contract gave Klein the option rights to use Truda's manuscript as the basis for a film or series for a period limited to eighteen months with the right to renew for four succeeding periods. Renewals would be accompanied by a nominal renewal fee paid to Paul with a more substantial payment to be made once a production deal was in place. If after six years a film was not produced, the option rights were expired. Meanwhile, Paul retained all publication rights to his mother's book, a condition on which I insisted.

Following the contract signing, Paul had a further surprise for us all. After inviting us into his home, he returned with a tattered cardboard box, yellowed from age. Paul lifted the lid of the box carefully to reveal the original 1950s era hand-typed manuscript of his mother's book. The onionskin pages were the printed text of Truda's book, complete with typos, edits and corrections, prior to the work done by Dr. Leonard Roberts for its publication in 1976.

The original manuscript included stories and notes that had not been included in the published work, information that Paul felt would be useful to Klein. Paul insisted that Klein have a copy of the unedited text to use for reference in developing a film script. Although humbled by Paul's generous offer, Rachel was reluctant to subject the delicate pages to being run through a copy machine. Paul was adamant, however, so we proceeded to a nearby office supply store where we found an available copy machine. There, we ran the 200 ancient pages through the copier, making two complete sets, one for Klein and a second for myself.

Agreement in hand, Klein returned to New York eager to continue her push for the project. She requested additional copies of Truda's book that she distributed to interested parties. One such person was Tom Fontana, an award-winning writer for HBO's series, *Oz* and *Homicide* whom Klein hoped to enlist as the writer for the series. Meanwhile, in an email dated July 11, 2007, Klein expressed frustration with the lack of help she was receiving from the Hatfield side in securing the rights to Coleman's book. "(I) haven't been getting much cooperation from the Hatfield side, so I think I am going to move forward with this based on Truda's book and then down the road, get a Hatfield consultant," she wrote. Despite the setback, her interest in the project remained high. On October 30, 2007, Klein wrote to say that the "owner of Starlight Runner (Entertainment, a Transmedia company) was so excited about this project that he stopped production at his company to tell people about it!"

By December 20, 2007, things were improving on the Hatfield front. "The Hatfields finally signed yesterday! James Cameron's people are reviewing the material right now and there is now interest from Lionsgate," she wrote, unable to conceal her excitement. Both Cameron, the Oscar-winning director of *Titanic*, and Lionsgate Entertainment, a studio well regarded for its prolific film and television output, were firmly established in the Hollywood production community. Despite an ongoing Writer's Guild of America strike, Lionsgate was hopeful about developing a feature film on the feud, an enthusiasm tampered by just one slight caveat. "There seems to be a competing script at (the) History Channel on the feud for a movie of the week in 2009. Cameron's people and the Lionsgate people are not too worried about it since we think (the) History Channel will not give it justice, especially since they never (have done) scripted (original work) before and we have you guys!" she added.

Klein continued her fight for the project through 2008. As with all major media endeavors, securing financing for the project was the principal hurdle to be overcome before the project could move forward. Studios seldom invested large amounts of their own resources, choosing instead to partner with outside sources of revenues in exchange for sharing any profits made from a project. One potential source of funding for Klein's estimated $25 million-dollar project was the owner of the investment firm, Ameritrade, who had established a fund to support the production of historically accurate films. While a two hour movie was not Klein's preferred format for telling a story as complicated as the feud, it was an option to be considered.

Meanwhile, Klein's production business began to flourish. During her tenure with *Lawman*, she continued to pitch her Hatfield-McCoy concept. The Starz Network's development team was pursuing historical projects actively and Klein met with them in July 2010. Later that same year, Klein relocated to Los Angeles to be more closely involved in the line production of *Ultimate Fighting Championship* bouts.

Despite Klein's ongoing push for her long-gestating Hatfield-McCoy project, the underpinning of the project began to unravel slowly following two untimely deaths. Dr. Coleman Hatfield passed away on

January 14, 2008, leaving the renewal rights to his book in question. Sadly, Paul McCoy followed the year after, passing away on December 17, 2009. Although the copyright ownership of Truda's book conveyed to Paul's wife, Janene, as the time came for the extension options to be renewed, they remained unexecuted, leading to increasing concern on Klein's part.

As the book options languished, the ultimate death knell for Klein's project came on May 25, 2011, when Nancy DuBuc, President of the History Channel announced that it had "green-lighted production of a new scripted mini-series, *The Hatfields and the McCoys* to premiere on History in 2012, coinciding with the 150th anniversary of America's most infamous family feud." The series was produced by Leslie Greif of Thinkfactory Media and Kevin Costner and written by Ted Mann, whose credits include HBO's *Deadwood* and ABC's *NYPD Blue*.[147] In addition to acting awards for Costner and Berenger, the series won Emmys for Makeup, Editing and Sound Mixing.[148]

With the success of the History Channel mini-series, Klein had been beaten to the punch. In her final email to me dated June 30, 2011, the indefatigable Klein, bound for a location shoot in Australia, graciously conceded defeat. "I am not sure I can do anything with the project further," she wrote "I wish you the very best and thank you from the bottom of my heart for all of your help." Klein's film based on an honest account of the feud as seen through the prism of the families involved was not to be made.

Return

"Gratitude makes sense of our past, brings peace for today, and creates a vision for tomorrow."
Melody Beattie

The path to connect with the historical past is as inimitable as the individual who dares to set out on it. What I have found to be true among those who have chosen to make the journey is the desire to share what they have learned about their heritage with others. For most, the gratitude that stems from having made the connection to their past compels them to return a portion of what they have received back into the community of their greater human family. In the case of the Hatfields and McCoys, such reciprocation usually means making recurring trips back to our Appalachian homeland to support ongoing feud preservation and tourism development efforts there.

Such was the case in 2013, when I traveled back to Pike County to support Pikeville's first annual "Hatfield McCoy Heritage Days" festival. For the inaugural event, Pike County Tourism Director Tony Tackett invited Bo, Reo and me to serve as grand marshals for a parade that concluded the event. The three-day festival, scheduled for Labor Day weekend, was reminiscent of the Reunion Festivals of years past, but was better organized, conducted and attended. Local turnout for the event was exceptional. Pikeville's Main Street, lined from end to end with craft and food vendors, was crowded with visitors. Musicians played bluegrass and gospel music from stages located at the courthouse and the park. Festival events included a classic car show, triathlon and drag race.

One memorable event scheduled for the festival was a Hatfield-McCoy paintball shootout, organized by Clifford Gene New, a descendant of both families. Although prior commitments to work the tourism booth precluded my involvement in the 2013 shootout, I assured Clifford that I would take part in the next year's event. When the 2014 festival came around, Clifford took me up on my offer of support.

For the 2014 festival, the paintball venue was set up in a parking lot behind the courthouse. Clifford and his crew had erected 30 inflatable barricades over an area of 60 x 60 feet. The Hatfield and McCoy squads of six members each, armed with chest protectors, helmets and weapons, were staged at opposite ends of the makeshift arena. "Wounded" players were instructed to remove themselves from the playing field after being hit until there was a single player left standing. A large contingent of McCoys was on hand to participate including the grandsons of Joseph McCoy, one of the men responsible for the placement of the monument at the McCoy Cemetery. When Hatfield turnout was less than expected, the younger McCoys agreed to fill out the Hatfield team, a decision those of us on the McCoy squad soon came to regret.

I had the honor of serving on the McCoy family team with my sister, Renee, on her first visit to Pike County in more than a decade. Also in attendance was my cousin Edward, whom I had not seen the 2000 reunion. Sidelined by an old sports injury, Edward wisely declined to engage in the melee.

The Hatfield team was led by William Keith ("Billy") Hatfield, pastor of Charity Baptist Church in Tulsa, Oklahoma. He was the great-grandson of "Devil Anse" by his youngest son, Tennis. Pastor Hatfield and his family had attended the reunion in 2002 and were part of the victorious Hatfield softball team. My encounter with Pikeville law enforcement in 2002 had precluded my spending much time on the ball field. For the 2014 shootout event, my interactions with Billy were limited to polite introductions and brief, passing conversations.

The attitudes of the opposing paintball teams were noticeably different. On this occasion, the McCoys were loud and rambunctious while the Hatfields were strangely quiet and focused. The McCoys should have taken notice. In the usual mix of Pike County heat and humidity, further amplified by the black asphalt parking lot, Pastor Billy and his makeshift team of "Hatfields" proved to be valiant adversaries.

From the initial order to fire until the final shot rang out, the Hatfields launched a barrage of faux bullets that made quick work of the McCoys. Those on the receiving end discovered that paintballs fired from

60 feet were remarkably potent. Renee and I sported bruises from the event for several weeks afterwards that we proudly credited to the Hatfields. After more than a century, the Hatfield and McCoy families had once again traded shots in Pike County, this time for the greater purpose of unity and friendship. I was content to have been "shot" by the Hatfields and lived to tell about it.

Nearly 16 years after my first trip to Pike County, I finally had the chance to realize a long-standing goal to visit the site of the old McCoy homestead in Hardy. Once part of the McCoy farm, it was the site of the attack on the McCoy home on New Year's Day, 1888. The assault was a horrific event that resulted in the burning of the cabin, the brutal beating of Sarah McCoy and the killing of her daughter, Alifair and son, Calvin. The raid on the McCoy home remains one of the darkest chapters of the violent feud saga. The well on the property is the last remaining vestige of the old family home place. The property on Highway 319 is adjacent to Blackberry Creek, just across the road from another former segment of the farm, the McCoy family cemetery.

For the McCoy family, the wellhead site is hallowed ground. Once the center of affairs for the McCoy clan, the homestead became a battleground, on which my ancestors had died in defense of their family. While the cemeteries in Hardy and Pikeville are lasting tributes to the memories of our ancestors, the property now owned by Hatfield descendants Bob and Rita Scott, is the actual soil on which our ancestors' blood was spilled.

Over the years, the Scotts have been accommodating hosts to thousands of visitors to the well from all over the world. Bob, a businessman actively involved in community affairs, has a heart for the preservation of feud sites and the further development of heritage tourism in Pike County. In 2013, facing strong opposition from the Eastern Kentucky Chamber of Commerce, Bob was appointed to the Pike County Tourism Commission, a rare occurrence for a resident from the eastern part of the county.[149]

In 2012, following the attention to the region prompted by the release of the History Channel mini-series, the National Geographic Channel approached the Scotts about performing an archeological dig on the property. Ironically, in the 125 years since the attack, no archaeological exploration had ever been done on the site. The Scotts consented to the dig, conducted under the watchful eye of Dr. Kim McBride, a professor from the University of Kentucky. Filmed as an episode of the network's *Diggers* series hosted by metal detector enthusiasts George Wyant and Tim Saylor, the dig was a resounding success – unearthing bullets, ceramic pieces and charred remains of the cabin, the first feud artifacts ever recovered.[150]

Failing to visit the homestead site was an oversight on my part, but never an intentional one. Over the years, I had passed the Scott's property countless times, though never at a leisurely pace. I was usually hurrying to get to a reunion event in the county or back to one in Pikeville. Visiting the well site was always at the top of my list of unfinished business. In our time spent together during the 2013 "Heritage Days" event, Bob extended an open invitation to visit his property. I finally was able to accept his kind offer during the 2014 festival.

Ron, Eddie, Robert and Renee with Bob Scott at the old well

Early on Sunday morning, Bob hosted a contingent of McCoy family members that included my cousin, Edward McCoy and his family, my sister and brother-in-law, Renee and Robert Bradshaw and their family as well as Margie and Bill Annett. Later, we were joined by local amateur historian Eric Simon and William Keith Hatfield. Bob arranged for us to enjoy an unprecedented tour of the property by way of an all-terrain vehicle excursion. The location where the cabin once stood was a flat, fertile piece of land while the remainder of the property was steep, mountainous terrain, covered by dense foliage. The guided tours along the mountain ridgeline up to the road to Mate Creek –the route taken by Hatfields on that fateful night in 1888 – represented the most extensive exploration of the property by McCoy descendants in more than a century.

Bob took us to his office to view some of the artifacts unearthed from the 2012 dig. It was a humbling and emotional experience to see and touch tangible pieces of my own family's history. For me, it was a once-in-a-lifetime experience not to be topped. Bob Scott had another idea brewing, however, one that would build upon the previous archaeological work done at the site and again make history.

Ron at the 2014 archaeological dig at the McCoy homestead

Because of the captivating findings of the initial dig on the location, Bob felt that a second and more thorough examination of the site was warranted. For the week of November 16-20, 2014, with the timely assistance of Tony Tackett and others, Bob orchestrated a return visit to the McCoy homestead site by Dr. McBride and her staff from the university and the crew from Halfyard Productions, the company behind National Geographic's *Diggers*. For this visit, Bob arranged for the crew to visit additional feud sites including the Hatfield homestead in Sarah Ann, West Virginia. Hatfield and McCoy descendants were also invited to participate in the historic archaeological excavation. It was an opportunity that those of us involved in the dig understood to be a rare and distinct privilege. We were being given the chance, quite literally, to dig into our family's history.

I was honored to be part of the contingent representing the McCoy family for the 2014 excavation along with my cousins Edward McCoy and Linda Bergmann. Sharing the experience with Edward was an exceptional honor for me. Of the many family members I have met over the years, there are few with a greater passion for our family history.

The Hatfields were represented by William Keith Hatfield and his sister, Heather Vaillancourt, great-grandchildren of "Devil Anse," and their families. Over the course of the November 2014 dig, it was a pleasure to get to know Billy and his family better. As a Pastor, Billy was consistently looking out for the welfare of others. During our time on the dig, he made certain to speak and interact with everyone onsite, be they family members, bystanders, television crew or archaeologists.

Following an initial day of taping with the television crew in Pikeville, Tuesday, November 18 offered us our first chance to take part in the historic excavation already underway at the McCoy homestead site. Dr. McBride and her hardy crew of three women from the anthropology department of the University of Kentucky had been digging at the site for nearly a week, despite adverse weather and sub-freezing temperatures. Our first day on the site was no different. With historic overnight lows of 14 degrees and projected highs of 26 degrees with light snow flurries early in the day, the weather was somehow fitting for the occasion.

Much work had been done on the site by the university crew in the week prior to our arrival. The area had been swept by sonar and mapped to denote subterranean areas of interest. Since the general footprint of the cabin had been outlined in the 2012 dig, Dr. McBride elected to focus her attention on what was presumed to be the rear corner of the structure. Her intuition proved correct. Digging in three grids near the back corner, her crew recovered many artifacts including one special item of note. Dr. McBride's crew discovered samples of partially burned industrial cotton, a rare find within the context of an 1880s era home. Examining written historical accounts of the fire led Dr. McBride to discover the significance of the find. In several court testimonies regarding the attack on the cabin, cotton was identified as the agent used to set fire to the home. I likened Dr. McBride's find to discovering a piece of the iceberg that sank the Titanic.

As the National Geographic crew scoured the hillside behind the former location of the home with metal detectors in search of bullet fragments, the university crew and an assortment of volunteers were busy digging up and sifting the soil from the area of carefully mapped out grids. Despite the overall goodwill of all involved, the gravity of the work was never far from our thoughts. As family members, we understood the opportunity we had been given to forage in the soil that once lay beneath the former home of our family, four generations prior. Under the careful guidance of the university crew, we knelt on rubber kneepads, methodically scraping away the frozen soil with masonry trowels, inch by inch. The soil we recovered was placed in buckets and carried to the sifting station where other volunteers filtered it through wire screens in search of precious clues to the events of the past. Items discovered in the screening were placed in paper bags along with other artifacts retrieved during the excavation, with the location and other details of their discovery carefully noted. As we dug methodically through the rocky soil, slicing through layers of burned wooden pieces that once had been the rear wall of the home, we could not help but to be reverential. Every bent nail, chip of porcelain or metal piece we uncovered was a reminder of the home that had stood there. Items once discarded or deemed inconsequential were now valuable proof of the story we had heard so many times. Our family had lived and died on the very land on which we knelt.

Later that morning, we were joined in the excavation by Billy Hatfield and his family, Clifford New and other volunteers. Tony Tackett and Jay Shepherd of Pike County Tourism saw to it that the entire crew was fed a steady diet of coffee, hot chocolate, snacks and pizza and kept warm by a couple of fires that provided a welcome reprieve from the cold. I joked with Tony that I was not entirely certain that it was appropriate to be building fires on the site of the McCoy cabin burning.

The following day, Wednesday, was a time of great activity on the site. Further exploration of the hillside behind the cabin site by the *Diggers* crew turned up more bullets. An exploration of the McCoy well by means of a magnet dropped down into it was less fruitful, however. While there were potential items of interest in the bottom of the well, they were sufficiently buried or entangled enough that the magnet was unable to retrieve them.

Bob invited select guests, neighbors, friends, family and dignitaries to witness the dig and the ongoing television shoot. The Hatfields were well represented. Reo Hatfield flew in for the day to take part. Jay Hatfield, a descendant of John Wallace Hatfield, a neighbor to Randolph McCoy, brought his two young daughters to participate. Cap Hatfield, a relative of Bob's, attended as well. At one point, Tony Tackett counted 120 people on site to watch the Hatfields and McCoys working side-by-side, unified by a common cause and shared history.

After nearly two weeks of digging, the collected articles were presented in a public washing of the artifacts. The event was held as a fundraiser at nearly Belfry High School. More than 500 Pike County citizens turned out for the event. Members of the community were invited to handle tangible pieces of history untouched by human hands for more than a century. For some family members, it was an especially sobering experience. Surveying the line of paper bags containing the results of the excavation, Edward noted, "It's sad that a family's possessions were reduced to a few brown paper shopping bags filled with nails and burned wood."

The experience of participating in the dig was intensely personal and, at times, surreal. I was deeply immersed in the experience and yet somehow removed from all the chaos that surrounded it. It was easy to get lost in the importance of what we were doing as we scratched the frozen soil for hours, but we cherished every scrap or remnant we recovered. The distraction of the crowd of spectators, cameras and reporters was no comparison to the honor of participating in the dig. Emotions were palpable but kept in check by the sense of responsibility that those of us digging felt. It was not until days later that I was able to appreciate the experience fully.

Leaving Pike County after any Hatfield-McCoy event is always a melancholy time. The trip home following the 2014 dig was no exception. Making the drive back to North Carolina, I could catch my breath, process the gaggle of mixed emotions and review in retrospect the events of the previous days. Somewhere between Abingdon and Marion, Virginia, the relevance of one conversation that had occurred days before struck me like the proverbial ton of bricks.

On Tuesday afternoon of the dig, William Keith Hatfield pulled up a kneeling pad and a trowel and joined me in digging in the frigid earth. Pastor Billy had made a point to be actively involved in all aspects of the dig. With the crew taking time out for lunch and a warm-up by the fire pit, he decided to spend time with me working in the ground excavation.

Pastor Billy Hatfield and Ron at the McCoy homestead site, November 2014

During our time together, Pastor Hatfield said something to me in casual conversation, the enormity of which escaped me at the time. Whether it was the cold or the physical and emotional overload of the event, I did not grasp the full implications of what he said to me at the time. Perhaps my failure to do so was just another sign of the degree of healing and unity that has developed between the families over the years. My inability to appreciate Billy's words, however, did not detract from the sincerity with which they were offered. "I'm really sorry all this happened," he said.

I remember thinking at the time that it was not entirely necessary for Billy to offer any such sentiment to me. After all, my family had done things to his that were equally egregious. The attack on the McCoy cabin, like many events in feud history, should never have occurred; but these events were important chapters in our shared history that could not be undone. The fact that Hatfields and McCoys were together working in tandem, foraging through the frozen tundra on Bob's Scott's property, searching for physical evidence of a past feud event, demonstrated that the deeds of our ancestors had been forgiven, but thankfully, not forgotten.

The importance of what Pastor Hatfield said to me did not fully strike me until the drive home several days later. The great-grandson of "Devil Anse" Hatfield had expressed his regrets to me, the great-great-great grandson of Randolph McCoy, for the actions taken by his ancestors against mine, kneeling together on the land where it had occurred. He, like the other family members gathered onsite, felt a personal connection to the events that transpired there. Each of us had walked a similar journey of self-discovery and were now reunited and reconciled with our own history.

For me, Billy's words were an acknowledgement of the common heritage that binds us together. He shared the same remorse that I did for the events of the past, yet still held pride in that very history. Without the events of the past, even tragic occurrences that we cannot change, we would not be who we are today, as families or individuals. Making the vital connection to our past helps us to realize the enormous debt we owe to generations of family before us. Reuniting with history allows us to appreciate our place in the present and acknowledge our responsibility to share the benefit of that knowledge with others. As we rediscover the merit of our own lives, we can then find value in our relationships with our greater human family and ensure a better future for generations yet to come.

Epilogue

"Forgiving what we cannot forget creates a new way to remember.
We change the memory of our past into a hope for our future."
Lewis B. Smedes

The legacy of the "Reunion of the Millennium," like the Hatfield and McCoy feud itself, endures to this day. The reconciliation of the families has added new and ongoing chapters to feud history. The story of the feud can no longer be told in its entirety without mentioning what the families achieved through the reunions. Because of their resolve, the Hatfield-McCoy feud does not end in 1890 with a hanging. It ends with the families on the Buskirk-Matewan Bridge on June 11, 2000, praying together and casting the bonds of a violent past into the waters of the Tug Fork below. It ends with the families gathered around a table in the Pikeville City Park on June 14, 2003, formally declaring a lasting peace between them, for all the world to see. It ends on November 19, 2014 with Hatfields and McCoys on their hands and knees, digging together in the soil of the old McCoy homestead to preserve their mutual history. It ends every year when descendants from across the country make the pilgrimage home to the land of their ancestors to pay their respects, explore their common history and reunite once again with the past.

Ongoing concerns threaten to overshadow the modern-day achievements of the families, however. The specter of division between the families continues to linger among those online or in the media who actively encourage and benefit from it. One writer gave this ominous prognosis in 2005: "For Hatfields and McCoys, our distinctiveness remains tied to our separateness...the clans will never really reconcile; our feud is forever etched in history."[151]

Such attrition is not limited to the families alone. In an era where the revision of uncomfortable history is common place, the preservation of feud history is impeded by those on social media who seek to undermine the integrity of the feud story or to dismiss its relevance altogether. On the ground, historic feud sites remain closed or undeveloped, in danger of being lost to the passage of time, while others remain badly in need of maintenance and upkeep. It is clear there remains work to be done.

The prognosis for the future of feud preservation remains promising, nevertheless. The Reunion Festival in Matewan is now in its 18th year as is the annual Hatfield McCoy Marathon. In 2014, the marathon boasted nearly 1,000 runners from 44 states.[152] *Blood Song,* an annual summer drama, jointly produced by the Artist's Collaborative Theater under the direction of Stephanie Richards and the Hatfield McCoy Arts Council, continues to dazzle audiences nightly at the Hatfield-McCoy outdoor theater in McCarr, Kentucky. In Pikeville, dedicated individuals like Tony Tackett, Bob Scott and others are working diligently to preserve the legacy of the Hatfields and McCoys.

In many respects, the journey for me has come full circle. After nearly twenty years, my decision to embark on a personal exploration into my family's historic past continues to reverberate through every facet of my life. While the seminal events of the past are relevant to the story of my reunion with history, they are, by no means, the defining points of the journey. Instead, they were the by-products of similar odysseys of discovery taken by me and countless others. The public events that transpired were the collective expressions of the desire of all human beings to make a vital connection with *family*.

Hatfields and McCoys are representative links in a chain of humanity that stretches across time. Exploring the story of the historic feud between the two families allows us to understand the potential for good and evil that exists in each of us. The examples set by the reconciled Hatfields and McCoys of the modern era offer an oasis of hope for the world.

It has been my distinct privilege to discover my family's rich heritage and to help introduce others to it along the way. I hope that my story will encourage others to embrace the risk and embark on a exploration into their own historic past, a heritage that is as rich and unique as the person pursuing it. The past beckons, the present day unfolds around us and the future awaits the actions we take today.

One of the great joys of the past two decades has been the time spent getting to know family. Appreciation for the brevity of life was never more apparent than it was at the annual reunions. Each reunion was a special moment in time, a rare opportunity never to be repeated in quite the same way. In the years since the 2000 reunion, family members have endured both hardships and triumphs. Some relationships have withered while new ones have blossomed to take their place. Friends and family members have passed away but the memories of our times together are unforgotten.

There are no words sufficient to describe what the heritage of the Hatfields and McCoys and the connection to my family have come to mean to me. Following the death of renowned author and poet, Maya Angelou, I heard a posthumous radio interview with the writer, recalling her own life's journey. Despite events in her past that were tragic, heinous and seemingly unforgivable, Angelou expressed no bitterness, choosing instead to consider her life as a mosaic of experiences, good and bad, that made her the person that she was. Her understated summary of her life expresses my feelings on the matter of my own reunion with the past and my greater Hatfield-McCoy family more succinctly than I ever could. "I'm just blessed beyond the telling of it."[153]

References

[1] Time.com. 'Top 10 Family Feuds - TIME'. N.p., 2015. Web. 1 Feb. 2015.

[2] Bengel, A. (2005). Not the Real McCoy. 801, (Spring 2005), pp.6-8. Columbia Graduate School of Journalism.

[3] Starr, B. 'Situation Room with Wolf Blitzer'. CNN, 2014. 26th Dec. 2014. TV program.

[4] Sun Sentinel. 'Famous Families Teach Peace'. N.p., 1998. Web. 11 Feb. 2015

[5] Rice, Otis K. *The Hatfields And The McCoys*. Lexington, Ky.: University Press of Kentucky, 1982. Print.

[6] Anderson, J. (1999). Real McCoys: Florence man helps plan national reunion. Daily News. 2000. Print.

[7] Mulvihill, G. (2000). Festivities replace feuding. *Lexington Herald-Leader*. 11 June 2000. Print.

[8] McCoy, Truda Williams (edited by Leonard Roberts). (1976) *The McCoys: Their Story*. Pikeville, Ky.: Preservation Council Press of the Preservation Council of Pike County, 1976. Print.

[9] Cdbbusinesslink.com. 'Hatfield-McCoy Feud May Predate American History…according to Carolyn Riddle'. N.p., 2015. Web. 11 Feb. 2015.

[10] Yesteryearsnews.wordpress.com. 'Notable Kentucky Feuds'. N.p., 2009. Web. 11 Feb. 2015.

[11] Hunter, R. (2012) Greenbrier family details fact/fiction in Hatfield-McCoy Feud. *501 Life Magazine*, 24 April 2012. Print.

[12] Mutzenberg, C. (1917). 'Kentucky's Famous Feuds And Tragedies: Authentic History Of the World Renowned Vendettas Of The Dark And Bloody Ground: Mutzenberg, Charles Gustavus. Internet Archive'. N.p., 2015. Web. 17 Feb. 2015.

[13] McCoy, Truda Williams (edited by Leonard Roberts). (1976) *The McCoys: Their Story*. Pikeville, Ky.: Preservation Council Press of the Preservation Council of Pike County, 1976. Print. (Page 14)

[14] Rice, Otis K. (1982) *The Hatfields and The McCoys*. Lexington, Ky.: University Press of Kentucky, 1982. Print. (Page 17)

[15] KYbar.org. The Hatfields & McCoys: From Filing Suits to Firing Shots. Freeman, L. 1st ed. Louisville, KY. (http://www.kybar.org/documents/cle/ac_material/ac2013_61.pdf) N.p., 2013. Print.

[16] None listed. (1946) United States Army, "13th Airborne Division." *World War Regimental Histories*. Book 180. Print.

[17] Burritt, C. (2000). Trying to make hay from a sad history. *Atlanta Journal-Constitution*. 10 June 2000. Print.

[18] News, ABC. 'Author A.J. Jacobs To Host Biggest Family Reunion Ever'. *ABC News*. N.p., 2014. Web. 11 Feb. 2015.

[19] Justice, B. (2000). Descendants of feuding families hold historic meet. *Appalachian News-Express*. 4 June 2000. Print.

[20] National Park Service National Register of Historic Places Inventory-Nomination Form (Pikeville, KY) 08 August 1984.

[21] TourPikeCounty.com. 'Pikeville Cut-Through Project' Tourpikecounty.Com'. N.p., 2015. Web. 5 Feb. 2015.

[22] TourPikeCounty.com,. 'Historic Dils Cemetery - Tourpikecounty.Com'. N.p., 2015. Web. 5 Feb. 2015.

[23] None listed. (1977). Legendary feuder Randall McCoy gets no rest even in the grave. *Associated Press*. 13 August 1977. Print.

[24] Purdy, C. (2013) Seeking to Lure Tourists to a Rugged Outpost Famed for a Deadly Feud. *New York Times*. 4 May 2013. Print.

[25] McCoy, Truda Williams (edited by Leonard Roberts). (1976) *The McCoys: Their Story*. Pikeville, Ky.: Preservation Council Press of the Preservation Council of Pike County, 1976. Print.

[26] None cited. (1976) Hatfield, McCoy clans gather at Cemetery Dedication to End Feud. *Associated Press*. 2 May 1976. Print.

[27] Kyenc.org. 'Pike County'. N.p., 2015. Web. 5 Feb. 2015.

[28] Coaleducation.org. 'KY Coal Facts - County Production'. N.p., 2015. Web. 5 Feb. 2015.

[29] Quickfacts.census.gov,. 'Pike County Quickfacts from the US Census Bureau'. N.p., 2015. Web. 5 Feb. 2015.

[30] Statistics, US. 'Unemployment Rate In Pike County, KY Research.stlouisfed.org. N.p., 2015. Web. 5 Feb. 2015.

[31] Burritt, C. (2000). Feud over, clans to gather in Kentucky. *Atlanta Journal-Constitution*. 8 June 2000. Print.

[32] Archive.org. 'Full Text of "Pikeville College Looks To The Hills 1889-1989"'. N.p., 2015. Web. 5 Feb. 2015.

[33] Ap.org. 'Faqs'. N.p., 2015. Web. 10 Mar. 2015.

[34] Hefling, K. (1999). Pike hopes long-dead Feud can stir Tourism. *Associated Press*.3 April 1999. Print.

[35] Roberts, M. 'Hatfields And McCoys Put Famous Feud To Rest'. WRAL (CBS), 11 July 1999. TV program.

[36] Tackett, D. (1999). McCoys and Hatfields plan Reunion for 2000. *Appalachian News-Express*. 20 June 1999. Print.

[37] Ibid.

[38] Roberts, M. 'Hatfields And McCoys Put Famous Feud To Rest'. WRAL (CBS), 11 July 1999. TV program.

[39] Ibid.
[40] Ibid.
[41] Ibid.

[42] Tackett, D. (1999). McCoys and Hatfields plan reunion for 2000. *Appalachian News-Express*. 20 June 1999. Print.

[43] Welch, S. (1999). Family Affair. *Successful Meetings*, July 1999, p.15. Print.

[44] Slater, E. (2000). Hatfields, McCoy unite at site of feud. *Los Angeles Times*. 11 June 2000. Print.

[45] Warren, J. (2010). Former tourism secretary and mayor of Prestonsburg Ann Latta dies. *Lexington Herald Leader*.29 December 2010. Print.

[46] Leslie, B. 'Record Snowfall Paralyzed Triangle 10 Years Ago: WRAL.Com'. WRAL.com. N.p., 2010. Web. 5 Feb. 2015.

[47] Clines, F. (2001) Backwoods Image Gone, Kentucky Town Revels in Hillbilly Roots. *New York Times*. 1 April 2001. Print.

[48] Ibid.

[49] None listed. (2001). Feudin' Again. *National Examiner*. 13 November 2001. Print.

[50] Hubbard, S, (2002). Howdy, Feud-y! The Hatfields and the McCoys are at it again. *National Enquirer*. 14 May 2002.

[51] McGinty, S. (2001). Feature. *The Scotsman*, pgs. 1-2. 20 Oct. 2001. Print.

[52] Onlineathens.com. 'Famous Feuding Families to Hold Reunion' | Online Athens'. N.p., 2015. Web. 18 Mar. 2015.

53 Burritt, C. (2000). Feud over, clans to gather in Kentucky. *Atlanta Journal-Constitution*. 8 June 2000. Print.

54 Hefling, K. (2000). Hatfields, McCoys plan joint reunion. *Associated Press*. 4 June 2000. Print

55 O'Brien, S. 'Morning Blend'. MS-NBC, 2000. 9 June 2000. TV program.

56 O'Brien, S. 'Today Show'. NBC, 2000. 9 June 2000. TV program.

57 Kypressonline.com. 'June, 2001: From Broadcasting to Newspapers, Backus Mad Jump And Loves It'. N.p., 2015. Web. 5 Feb. 2015.

58 Cornett, M. (2000) Pike's Tourism Director Resigns from office. *Appalachian News-Express*. 24 February 2000. Print.

59 Crawford, Theron Clark, F. Keith Davis, and Steven M Stone. An American Vendetta. West Virginia: Woodland Press, 2013. Print.

60 Rice, Otis K. (1982) *The Hatfields and The McCoys*. Lexington, Ky.: University Press of Kentucky, 1982. Print. (Page 73)

61 Hunter, R. (2012) Greenbrier family details fact/fiction in Hatfield-McCoy Feud. *501 Life Magazine*. 24 April 2012. Print.

62 Wvculture.org. 'West Virginia Memory Project - Film Transcripts'. (http://www.wvculture.org/history/wvmemory/filmtranscripts/wvwaller.html). N.p., 2015. Web. 12 Feb. 2015.

63 Wvculture.org. 'West Virginia Memory Project - Film Transcripts'. (http://www.wvculture.org/history/wvmemory/filmtranscripts/wvwaller.html). N.p., 2015. Web. 12 Feb. 2015.

64 Ibid.
65 Ibid.

66 Anderson, K. (1981). Appalachia: Hatfields and McCoys. *Time Magazine*. 14 December 1981. Print.

[67] Rice, Otis K. (1982) *The Hatfields and The McCoys*. Lexington, Ky.: University Press of Kentucky, 1982. Print. (Page 31)

[68] McCoy, Truda Williams (edited by Leonard Roberts). (1976) *The McCoys: Their Story*. Pikeville, Ky.: Preservation Council Press of the Preservation Council of Pike County, 1976. Print.

[69] Mark F. Sohn. "Leonard W. Roberts at Pikeville College: 1968-1983."Appalachian Heritage 15.2 (1987): 49-50.*Project MUSE*. Web. 25 Feb. 2014

[70] Hatfield, G. Elliott, Leonard Roberts, and Henry Preston Scalf. (2012) *The Hatfields*. Paintsville, KY: East Kentucky Press, Inc., 2012. Print.

[71] McCoy, Truda Williams (edited by Leonard Roberts). (1976) *The McCoys: Their Story*. Pikeville, Ky.: Preservation Council Press of the Preservation Council of Pike County, 1976. Print.

[72] Williams, B. (1976) Feuding McCoys tell their side. *The News and Courier Charleston Evening Post* 26 December 1976. Print.

[73] Abebooks.com. 'The Top 100 Most Searched For Out-Of-Print Books In 2013' N.p., 2015. Web. 6 Feb. 2015.

[74] Wvencyclopedia.org. 'E-WV | Williamson'. N.p., 2013. Web. 14 May 2014.

[75] Hefling, K. (2000). Hatfields, McCoys to trade guns for fun at reunion. *Associated Press*. 8 June 2000. Print

[76] Hunter, R. (2012) Greenbrier family details fact/fiction in Hatfield-McCoy Feud. *501 Life Magazine*, 24 April 2012. Print.

[77] *America's Real Family Feuders Reunite*, (2000). CBS News (WYMT), 11 June, 2000. Television broadcast.

[78] Runner's World & Running Times. 'The Hatfield & McCoy Marathon'. N.p., 2005. Web. 18 Mar. 2015

[79] Usa.com. 'Matewan, WV - USA.Com'. N.p., 2015. Web. 7 Feb. 2015.

[80] Wvculture.org. 'Matewan Massacre'. N.p., 2015. Web. 7 Feb. 2015.

[81] Burritt, C. (2000). Hatfields and McCoys gather for Reunion. *Cox News Service*. 10 June, 2000. Print.

[82] Parks, P. (2000). Families call for unity. *Williamson Daily News*. 12 June 2000. Print.

[83] Cardwell, J. (2000). Burying the hatchet. *Akron Beacon Journal*. 2 July 2000. Print

[84] Ibid.

[85] Parks, P. (2000). Families call for unity. *Williamson Daily News*. 12 June 2000. Print.

[86] Ibid.

[87] Finn, S. (2000). Hatfields, McCoys unite in Matewan. *Charleston Gazette*. 12 June 2000. Print.

[88] Ibid.

[89] May, A. (2001). New bottle unveiled for H-M Reunion. *Appalachian News-Express*. 6 June 2001. Print.

[90] May, A. (2001) Festival Fun: Rainy day does little to dampen enthusiasm. *Appalachian News-Express*. 8 June 2001. Print.

[91] Wvculture.org. 'West Virginia Memory Project - Film Transcripts'. (http://www.wvculture.org/history/wvmemory/filmtranscripts/wvwaller.html). N.p., 2015. Web. 12 Feb. 2015.

[92] Hewitt, D. (2001). Governors share same goal for unity. *Williamson Daily News* 11 June 2001. Print.

⁹³ Granta.com. 'War and Peace on the Big Sandy River' (King. D.) *Granta Magazine*, 3 September, 2011). N.p., 2015. Web. 7 Feb. 2015

⁹⁴ Reodistribution.com. 'Leadership | Full Service 3PL - Warehousing & Logistics'. N.p., 2015. Web. 8 Feb. 2015.

⁹⁵ The Daily Progress. 'Hatfield-McCoy Unity, New Book Shed Light On Famous Feud And Remarkable Ending'. (David A. Maurer) N.p., 2013. Web. 8 Feb. 2015.

⁹⁶ Matewan.com. 'Hatfield-McCoy Reunion 2000 (New page 1)'. N.p., 2015. Web. 8 Feb. 2015.

⁹⁷ Sewell, J. (2002). Hatfield Hitchin'. *Appalachian News-Express*. 9 June 2002. Print.

⁹⁸ Alford, R. (2002). Hatfields and McCoys face off in court. *Associated Press*. 28 December 2002. Print.

⁹⁹ McCoy, Truda Williams (edited by Leonard Roberts). (1976) *The McCoys: Their Story*. Pikeville, Ky.: Preservation Council Press of the Preservation Council of Pike County, 1976. Print. (Page 111)

¹⁰⁰ Commonwealth of Kentucky, Court of Appeals, No. 2005-CA-000501-MR, Action No. 02-CI-00437, rendered March 3, 2006. https://Cases.Justia.Com/Kentucky/Court-Of-Appeals/2006-03-02-2005-CA-000501. Pdf. 2015.

¹⁰¹ Loh, J. (1975). Hatfields, McCoys Bury Hatchet at Blackberry Fork. *Associated Press*. 24 November 1975. Print.

¹⁰² None cited. (1976) Hatfield, McCoy clans gather at Cemetery Dedication to End Feud. *Associated Press*. 2 May 1976. Print.

¹⁰³ Commonwealth of Kentucky, Court of Appeals, No. 2005-CA-000501-MR, Action No. 02-CI-00437, rendered March 3, 2006. https://Cases.Justia.Com/Kentucky/Court-Of-Appeals/2006-03-02-2005-CA-000501. Pdf. 2015.

[104] Alford, R. (2002). Hatfields and McCoys feuding again-in court. *Associated Press*. 3 April 2002. Print.

[105] Alford, R. (2003). Hatfields and McCoys trade shots in court. *Associated Press*. 22 January 2003. Print.

[106] Alford, R. (2002). Hatfields and McCoys face off in court. *Associated Press*. 28 December 2002. Print.

[107] Alford, R. (2002). Hatfields and McCoys feuding again-in court. *Associated Press*. 3 April 2002. Print.

[108] Commonwealth of Kentucky, Pike County Court, Division II, Action No. 02-CI-00437. Complaint. Filed March 29, 2002.

[109] Pike Circuit Court, Division No. II. Answer to Complaint. Filed May 15, 2002.

[110] Alford, R. (2003). Hatfields and McCoys trade shots in court. *Associated Press*. 22 January 2003. Print.

[111] Commonwealth of Kentucky, Court of Appeals, No. 2005-CA-000501-MR, Action No. 02-CI-00437, rendered March 3, 2006. https://Cases.Justia.Com/Kentucky/Court-Of-Appeals/2006-03-02-2005-CA-000501. Pdf. 2015.

[112] Ibid.
[113] Ibid.
[114] Ibid.

[115] Alford, R. (2003). In latest battle, the Hatfields and McCoys both find victory. *Associated Press*. 18 April 2003. Print.

[116] Commonwealth of Kentucky, Court of Appeals, No. 2005-CA-000501-MR, Action No. 02-CI-00437, rendered March 3, 2006. https://Cases.Justia.Com/Kentucky/Court-Of-Appeals/2006-03-02-2005-CA-000501. Pdf. 2015.

[117] Ibid.

[118] Incharacter.org, (2015). Ten Great Moments in Forgiveness History. In Character, A Journal of Everyday Virtues by the John Templeton Foundation. Web. 1 Feb. 2015.

[119] Granta.com. 'War And Peace On The Big Sandy River' (King. D. *Granta Magazine*, 3 September 2011). N.p., 2015. Web. 7 Feb. 2015.

[120] The Daily Progress. 'Hatfield-McCoy Unity, New Book Shed Light On Famous Feud And Remarkable Ending'. (David A. Maurer) N.p., 2013. Web. 8 Feb. 2015.

[121] The Daily Progress. 'Hatfield-McCoy Unity, New Book Shed Light On Famous Feud And Remarkable Ending'. (David A. Maurer) N.p., 2013. Web. 8 Feb. 2015.

[122] Potter, D. (2003) Feuding Hatfields, McCoys sign truce. *Appalachian News-Express*. 15 June 2003. Print.

[123] Granta.com. 'War and Peace on the Big Sandy River' (King. D. *Granta Magazine*, 3 September 2011). N.p., 2015. Web. 7 Feb. 2015

[124] Hbo.com. 'HBO: Real Sports: Jon Frankel'. N.p., 2015. Web. 12 Feb. 2015.

[125] Frankel, J. 'The Saturday Early Show'. CBS, 2003. 14 June 2003. TV program.

[126] Ibid.
[127] Ibid.
[128] Ibid.

[129] The Daily Progress. 'Hatfield-McCoy Unity, New Book Shed Light On Famous Feud And Remarkable Ending'. (David A. Maurer) N.p., 2013. Web. 8 Feb. 2015.

[130] Potter, Dena. (2003) "Editorial." *Appalachian News-Express*. 15 June 2003: 4a. Print.

[131] Author unknown. (2003) "Editorial." *Los Angeles Times*. 21 June 2003. Print.

[132] Encyclopedia Britannica. 'United States Presidential Election of 2000 | United States Government'. N.p., 2014. Web. 12 Feb. 2015.

[133] Burling, L. (2000) Make peace, say the McCoys, Hatfields. *Associated Press*. 12 December 2000. Print.

[134] Medicalleader.org. 'Hatfield-McCoy Reunion Festival Coming Soon'. N.p., 2015. Web. 8 Feb. 2015.

[135] Marchione, M. (2007). Disease Underlies Hatfield-McCoy Feud. *Associated Press*. 5 April 2007. Print.

[136] Ibid.

[137] Alford, R. (2003) They're Still At It Folks: McCoy Kin Abandon Plans to Erect Statue. *Associated Press*. 23 April 2003. Print.

[138] Wvgazette.com. '| Statehouse Beat: The Case of the Missing Shotgun'. N.p., 2015. Web. 8 Feb. 2015.

[139] IMDb. N.p., 2015. Web. 8 Feb. 2015.

[140] NPR.org. 'Robert Duvall, Still Living in the Potential'. N.p., 2010. Web. 8 Feb. 2015.

[141] Hollywoodreporter.com. 'History's 'Hatfields & McCoys' Beats Own Record With 14.3 Million Viewers'. N.p. 2012. Web. 8 Feb. 2015.

[142] McNamara, M. (2012) Review: 'Hatfields & McCoys' has vivid detail, fine acting. *Los Angeles Times*. 28 May 31, 2012. Print.

[143] Television Academy. 'Hatfields & McCoys'. N.p., 2015. Web. 8 Feb. 2015.

[144] Fleming, Michael. 'Feud For Thought'. Variety. N.p., 2003. Web. 8 Feb. 2015

145 Sneider, Jeff. 'Duvall: Pitt Eyeing 'Hatfields And McCoys' Movie'. The Wrap. N.p., 2010. Web. 8 Feb. 2015.

146 Klein, Rachel. 'Rachel Klein'. IMDb. (http://www.imdb.com/name/nm1114417/#producer) N.p., 1980. Web. 12 Feb. 2015.

147 Bettinger, Brendan. 'History Announces 'The Hatfields and the McCoys' Mini-series And 'The Bible' Docudrama'. Collider. N.p., 2011. Web. 12 Feb. 2015.

148 Emmys.com. (Television Academy). 'Hatfields & McCoys'. N.p., 2015. Web. 12 Feb. 2015.

149 News, Williamson, and Williamson News. 'Pike Tourism Board Appointment Over Objections - Williamson Daily News'. *Williamson Daily News*. N.p., 2013. Web. 12 Feb. 2015.

150 Kentucky.com. 'Hatfield-McCoy Battle Artifacts Highlighted In National Geographic Show | Travel | Kentucky.Com'. N.p., 2015. Web. 8 Feb. 2015.

151 Bengel, A. (2005). Not the Real McCoy. 801, (Spring 2005), pp.6-8. Columbia Graduate School of Journalism. Print.

152 Marathonguide.com. 'News'. N.p., 2015. Web. 16 Mar. 2015.

153 *Mom and Me and Mom*, (2013). 'Diane Rehm Show'. NPR. 8 May 2013. Broadcast.

Photo Credits

Pages 17-19 Public domain
Pages 34 -73 Personal
Pages 76 -100 Jerry D. Hatfield
Page 106 Betty Howard
Pages 116 -125 Personal
Pages 127 -142 Jerry D. Hatfield
Page 144 Matewan.com
Page 149 Pike Co. Judge-Executive's Office
Page 158 Personal
Page 164 Public domain
Pages 166 -198 Jerry D. Hatfield
Page 208 Personal
Page 214 Jerry D. Hatfield
Page 224 Personal
Page 231 Renee Bradshaw
Page 232 Clifford Gene New
Page 236 William Keith Hatfield

Additional Information

Pike County Tourism	www.tourpikecounty.com
Pikeville City Tourism	www.visitpikeville.com
City of Williamson	www.cityofwilliamson.org
Town of Matewan	www.matewan.com
Hatfield McCoy Marathon	www.hatfieldmccoymarathon.net
Hatfield McCoy Arts Council	www.hatfieldmccoyarts.com

www.ingramcontent.com/pod-product-compliance
Lightning Source LLC
Chambersburg PA
CBHW071902290426
44110CB00013B/1249